LANCASTER DOWN!

The extraordinary tale of seven
young airmen at war

STEPHEN DARLOW

BBounty
Books

First published 2000
under the title *Lancaster Down*
by Grub Street Publishing
Copyright © 2000 Grub Street Publishing, London
Text copyright © 2000 Stephen Darlow

This edition published 2007 by Bounty Books,
a division of Octopus Publishing Group Ltd
2–4 Heron Quays, London E14 4JP

ISBN-13: 978-0-753715-27-7
ISBN-10: 0-753715-27-9

A CIP catalogue record for this book is available
from the British Library

Printed and bound in Spain

CONTENTS

ACKNOWLEDGEMENTS

England, Canada and Australia

My thanks extend to the surviving crewmember of my grandfather's crew, namely, Alex Nethery. His willingness to assist in the telling of the story is much appreciated. The two sources of Alex Nethery's quotes were either personal interview or published accounts, which are mentioned in the footnotes. My thanks to Bernie Wyatt for granting permission to use Alex Nethery's previously published quotes. Trevor Utton and Allan Burrell also assisted in putting this story together. Unfortunately, Allan and Trevor recently passed away. My thanks also to the families of other members of the crew: Derek Lorimer, Bronwyn Lorimer, Peter Richards and his wife Lesley, Julia Barnes (née Richards) and Dave Richards. For help with research, I thank Mr W.R. Chorley, Peter Hinchliffe, Martin Middlebrook, Martin Bowman, The Public Record Office, Albert Chivers, Michael Mortimer, Richard Payne, and the people of Great Gransden, in particular Mr Marr and Mrs Blott. For their anecdotes, I am indebted to Minnie Jenkins (Arthur's cousin), Derrick Bell, Gordon Puttick, Douglas Hutchinson and Mrs Lorna Hayes (including a guided tour of Gransden Lodge airfield), and for their assistance in translation, Marie Jeanne Cole and Kathy Hewson. My gratitude extends to the many establishments that helped make the research process so enjoyable: the staff of Stotfold Library, 427 Squadron Association, 405 Squadron Association, RCAF Association, RAF Association, The Belgian Embassy, Malaysian Embassy, Malaysian Ministry of Defence, Air Historical Branch, Bursledon District Council, Wendy Lyne, Steve Fraser, RAF Personnel Management, Canadian National Search Unit, The Caterpillar Club, The RAF Escape and Evasion Society.

Belgium

I am also grateful for invaluable assistance to: Amicale des Resistants de Péruwelz, and L'Amicale des Associations Patriotiques de Péruwelz, and in particular Mr Jacques Nachez, whose tireless research efforts in Belgium and hours of translating were invaluable in enabling the completion of the whole story. I will forever remain grateful and cherish the friendship that we have. The people of Bon-Secours and Péruwelz, Jean and Madeleine Henrard (and their grandsons), Albert Bargibant (Secretary of Amicale des

Resistants de Péruwelz), Claire Praet, Pierre Fastrez, Raymonde Rock, Yvonne Delmée, Marcel Delangre, Le Centre de Documentation Historique des Forces Armées and Mr Bernard Delcourt, Cynrik De Decker, Dominique Van Den Broucke, Wim Govaerts, Georges Place and Pierre Bachy.

I am also indebted to: Martin Drewes (Brazil), Walter Telsnig (Austria), Theo Boiten and E. Ragas (Holland).

Every effort has been made to identify the copyright holders of the material quoted in the book. I would like to thank all those who gave permission to use the extracts. Please also note that all diary extracts are quoted *verbatim*.

PREFACE

The years 1942-44 were grim times for the crews of Bomber Command. Losses were very high, with the number of missing airmen reaching almost 600 on some nights. We were soon aware that our chances of survival were one in seventeen. Prior to arriving at an operational squadron, there were personnel losses at the training units. On our last unit, before operations, we lost 29 men in 30 days! On our last squadron, No. 405 Pathfinder Squadron, 801 airmen lost their lives during about four years of combat. With 14-15 Lancasters and approximately 100 airmen, our squadron was wiped out eight times.

Training hazards were many: getting lost, fire, crashing, engine failure, collisions and would your parachute work? The parachute section told everyone the same thing; 'If it doesn't work – bring it back!' Add to this, the dangers of operational flying and it was not a morale building situation. A very few young men could not stand the strain and had to be sent home or assigned non-flying duties. Adding to our problems were blackouts, poor food, enemy bombing, very little heat during the winter months, etc. The only food not rationed was peanut butter!

Our English crew members were fighting to keep the enemy off British soil, but at least they could visit their families and friends every few months. As Canadians, young and far from home, our common lot was loneliness and homesickness. This was in spite of the gallant effort by the British people to keep our spirits up.

It is my hope that this preface will, in some measure, prepare you to read between the lines of this story about the lives of one World War II Bomber Command crew.

Flying Officer L. Alex Nethery (ret'd)
Ex. Royal Canadian Air Force, Radar Navigator and Bomb Aimer

INTRODUCTION

I was born the year we defeated Germany. It had been an immense struggle, both forces giving all toward their ultimate goal. The whole world had taken part, its people watching the move of every nation. In fact the game had gone into extra time before the 1966 Football World Cup Final was finally settled by two Geoff Hurst goals. We had won 4-2 and the nation celebrated. Since then the only adversity I have really come up against has been in the field of sport, but, recently I became conscious of something that had happened many years before I arrived. Something that had enabled me to live in this society of level playing fields. In 1939 the world had gone to war as tyranny threatened to create the rules. I knew my ancestors had done their bit; for I was the grandson of an RAF pilot and a soldier in the Middlesex regiment. What exactly they had done, however, had been of only passing interest. To me the Second World War consisted of *The Desert Rats*, *The Longest Day* and *A Bridge Too Far*, or television documentaries with seemingly endless black and white reels of screaming Stukas and ransacking tanks.

Although I knew my father's father had flown Lancasters and been shot down, to me there was nothing out of the ordinary in being a bomber pilot. I had seen The Dam Busters, but even that did not have the glamour of a Spitfire chasing down a German bomber as it prepared to release its load over London.

In May 1996, however, my father passed on to me a black and white photograph of a field, in which a number of people, some in uniform, were looking over the wreckage of an aircraft. On the back of the photograph was a message from a certain Alex Nethery giving brief details of the location of the crashed aircraft. My father told me it was that of the Lancaster bomber in which my grandfather was pilot, which made me a little curious. Who exactly was this man?

I began to look into our family archives, paid a visit to the library and borrowed a few books on Bomber Command. The more I researched, the more intrigued I became. There was one particular statistic that amazed me: over 55,000 men from Bomber Command lost their lives during the war. In one raid alone, to Nuremberg in March 1944, more airmen lost their lives than were lost in the Battle of Britain. The extraordinary odds the men of Bomber Command were up against soon became apparent to me and I needed to know more about what my grandfather, Arthur Darlow, had done.

I became aware of the extensive Bomber Command records held at the Public Record Office at Kew. I also paid a visit to the former Second World War airfield at Gransden Lodge, Cambridgeshire where my grandfather had been based, and saw the perimeter track, various disused buildings, a hangar converted into a barn and the old control tower, now a gun club's store. My father had maintained contact with Trevor Utton, one of my grandfather's crew, and through Trevor I was able to get in touch with two other crew members. A letter to the Belgian Embassy resulted in contact with the Belgian Resistance members who had assisted some of my grandfather's crew, and in the summer of 1997 I made contact with the families of two more members of the crew who were able to help complete the story.

I came to feel a deep respect for the courage of not only this group of men but for all the men of Bomber Command. Although many of the veterans will say they were only doing a job, they nevertheless encountered and dealt with adversity time and time again. Any man who climbed into a bomb-laden aircraft in the middle of the night, to fly for hours on end, over very hostile territory with a relatively brief period of utter turmoil over a burning city, deserves respect.

There have been numerous published accounts of Bomber Command and the men that flew the bombers, of accounts of Allied POWs and their experiences whilst in captivity, and of the heroic tales of Resistance members who assisted fallen airmen to evade capture. All these stories are fascinating in their own right. I felt there was another story to tell: the fate of a complete bomber crew, who faced death over and over again, and all of whom were at an age when I was worried about passing an exam, getting on with my girlfriend or winning the next game.

In the following account, I have tried to place the crew's actions within the context of the overall war situation, in particular the struggle in Western Europe. The account is in two parts. The first part deals with the crew's operational life and I have taken nine operations in particular and expanded upon them, detailing some of the planning that went into a raid. The second part deals with events surrounding the crew members after their aircraft had been shot down. Most of the story is drawn upon first-hand accounts. In a few places I have drawn on already published material to put the story into context; in particular *The Bomber Command War Diaries* by Martin Middlebrook and Chris Everitt gives an excellent background to raids, and the *RAF Bomber Command Losses* series by W. R. Chorley provide details of crews lost on raids.

I have tried not to romanticise the account. The ordinary men of Bomber Command did not and do not receive the recognition they deserve, and this story is the straightforward recounting of what some of those 'ordinary' men went through.

Steve Darlow

PART 1

CHAPTER ONE

BOMBER COMMAND AND A NEW RECRUIT

Poland had fallen. In April and May 1940 the German war machine swept through Norway expelling the Anglo-French Expeditionary Force. Belgium, Holland and France were next to succumb to the Wehrmacht's *Blitzkrieg* and once more the Allies initiated a mass evacuation of troops, this time at Dunkirk. In the summer the Luftwaffe engaged the RAF in the skies over England in preparation for invasion, and British cities began to feel the full weight of the night bombing campaign. The Allied fighters, providing some comfort to the beleaguered British population, managed to stall German invasion plans. In the summer of 1941 Hitler turned his attention to Russia, but the English Channel was still all that remained between England and the seemingly invincible might of the German army. The German navy, and in particular the U-boats, were scoring numerous successes as they seriously disrupted British supply lines across the Atlantic. Rommel launched his North African offensive driving the British forces eastwards. The Allies were on the back foot. How could the morale of the British people be maintained? What could Britain do in Europe to show to the enemy that it could still offer resistance? One answer lay with Bomber Command.

Bomber Command had been ready to operate as soon as war was declared, initially receiving orders that to ensure there were no civilian casualties in attacks on military targets, there would be no bombing operations over Germany itself. Operations consisted of attacks on naval targets or propaganda leaflet drops. Its role in the defence of Norway was to attempt to slow the German advance but its effectiveness was severely limited by the long distances involved in reaching targets and the lack of fighter support.

Following the *Blitzkrieg* through the Low Countries and the German bombing of Rotterdam on 14 May 1940, Bomber Command effected a turn around in policy. From that point Bomber Command penetrated into Germany, putting into place plans formulated before the war. German industry was to be a priority, in particular oil, but there were to be various other requirements for the bomber forces, as the situation in Europe developed. During the Battle of Britain, Bomber Command, in the main, provided a supporting role to the fighter defence over England, attacking Luftwaffe airfields and the channel ports where the Germans were assembling their invasion barges. On the night of the 25/26 August 1940 Bomber Command sent a force on a retaliatory raid to Berlin following German raids the night before on London and other British cities.

Early in 1941 as the threat of invasion diminished, Bomber Command's energies could once more be directed toward an offensive strategy. The German oil industry would still remain a priority, but the Bomber force was to be redirected once more. The situation on the Atlantic supply routes became critical and Bomber Command targeted the threat to Allied shipping from the U-boats and the German long range aircraft. In July 1941 Bomber Command, again, looked to German industry, receiving new directives with express orders to attempt to destroy the morale of the German civilian population and in particular that of the industrial workers, together with destruction of the German transportation system. Specific strategic targets were listed and intensive operations were made to inland German targets.

One problem for the Air Ministry lay in the recruiting and training of the young airmen who could take the offensive to the enemy. The Empire Air Training scheme met that need as young recruits were taken to the far reaches of the British Empire, away from the theatres of war such as Europe, to train for operational duties.

Arthur Darlow was born on 6 September 1921. He grew up as one of four children brought up by First World War Royal Marine Major William Darlow MSM and his wife Emma. From 1936 to 1939 he took a commercial course at Portsmouth Municipal College and then began working as sub postmaster at Wrotham, Kent. Whilst there, he met and married Anne Pickles, daughter of Royal Marine Harry Pickles and his Greek wife Calliope. It was not long before Arthur followed the family tradition of military involvement. Arthur was not, however, to follow his father's example. Instead of the sea he chose the sky where he could be a part of the latest and most exciting and romantic way of conducting a war. In the air the war was a little more sanitised, take off, combat and home for tea, unlike the trench warfare of World War I in which three of his uncles had been killed. On 4th August 1941 Arthur began his RAF career as a raw recruit, 19 years of age, already married and a father within a day of joining up. He was one of many who had idealistic visions of becoming fighter pilots to defend their country and take the fight to the opposition.

Arthur began his RAF career with a month at Air Crew Reception Centre, Regent's Park, London, then transferring to No. 7 Initial Training Wing (ITW) Newquay, Cornwall. Six months here without contact with an aircraft proved frustrating for this aspiring airman, but eventually he was transferred to 29 Elementary Flying Training School (EFTS).

From Arthur's diary

Jan 25 Sunday: Entrained from Newquay for Clyffe Pypard, 29 EFTS am travelling overnight, stopping 6 hours at Bristol. Cheerio Newquay & drill.
Jan 26 Monday: Arrived Clyffe Pypard, what a dismal, lonely place. Met P/O Smith and looked over D.H. 82. Reached a plane at last.
Jan 27 Tuesday: Went up this morning. Flying's grand sport; took over controls, did turns etc. Off to bed early ready for more flying tomorrow.

On 4 March 1942 Arthur arrived at Heaton Park, Manchester to await a posting overseas, but plans were put on hold as he went down with mumps spending three weeks in confinement. Following his recovery and a farewell visit to Anne and baby Eric, Arthur became part of the Empire Air Training Scheme and found himself on a ship bound for Canada.

Early in the war it became obvious that preliminary flying training would have to be isolated from Britain, because of enemy action and lack of airspace. In the first few weeks of the war Canada, Australia and New Zealand sided with Britain and began to develop large air forces of their own to serve with the RAF. However there remained a need for space to train the RAF men, and initially Southern Rhodesia and South Africa took some responsibility for this. As the war progressed the Dominions took on increasing responsibility for training. On 17 December 1939 the UK, Canada, Australia and New Zealand signed an agreement initiating a massive joint programme of air training. The UK undertook to supply all the aircraft and a nucleus of skilled men. The programme in Canada consisted of the elementary flying training schools, service flying training schools, air observer schools, bombing and gunnery schools and air navigation schools. Courses opened in Canada, Australia and New Zealand on 29 April 1940 and by mid 1942 the organisation reached its full size and was capable of producing no less than 11,000 pilots and 17,000 other aircrew each year.[1]

From Arthur's diary

May 18 [1942] Monday: First day on board, waiting to leave port for Canada. Have been loading up provisions all day. Set sail 2030 hrs. Lovely scenery on both sides of river. Cheerio England.
May 19, Tuesday: Second day out & seasick already – eating

---

[1] From *Royal Air Force 1939-1945 Volume 1: The Fight at Odds*, Denis Richards HMSO 1953 pp.73-74.

too much chocolate etc. Sea is rather swelly. Shall be glad when trip is over. Started letter to Anne, she's a great woman.

May 20, Wednesday: Three days out & running into mucky weather. Nearly reached ½ way mark. Hurt top of leg & groin, shall have to rest up a bit. Rather bored, would rather be at home.

May 21, Thursday: Sea quite rough & strong wind blowing. Am now immune from seasickness. Ship is very unstable & the wind too strong for a stroll. Slept this afternoon as leg still hurts.

May 22, Friday: Nice weather this morning, fog later. Speed reduced to 12 kts. Sea is much calmer, thank goodness I didn't join the Navy. In bed early, nothing else to do.

May 25, Monday: Sighted land (Canada) about 1430 hrs. Docked 1800 hrs & entrained Moncton. Greeted by RAF band & free oranges. Wish Anne was here with me. Sent wire home.

Arthur entrained almost immediately, and four more days travelling, including a stop at Montreal, brought him to Elementary Flying Training School, Assiniboia, Saskatchewan, starting his training with two weeks of lectures owing to an unusable runway. After three month's training on Tiger Moths and below average results Arthur was posted to No. 33 Service Flying Training School, Carberry, Manitoba on 14 August 1942, disappointingly to fly 'twins'. As his heart was set on single-engined aircraft, his fighter pilot dream was dashed. After a further four months training, flying the Anson I and II with average results, all was ready for Wings Day on 3 December. The day before Arthur took a routine training flight.

From Arthur's diary

December 2nd, Wednesday: Catastrophe! Undercarriage on Anson II collapsed on S/E [single-engine] landing. Have put report in & been colaborated (*sic*) by ACP Petrel. May be washed out & lose wings. Just my luck at this stage – Keeping fingers X'd.

Fortunately the episode only resulted in his logbook being endorsed. He now looked forward to the prospect of receiving his wings and a posting back to England, home and a young family.

Early in the RAF's bombing campaign, missions took place under the cover of darkness, mainly because of high daylight loss rates. Navigation to and from bombing targets proved extremely difficult, most target bombing executed via dead reckoning, and considerable errors were frequent. The bombers were comforted by the fact that although losses were inflicted, German night fighter strength was equally ineffective.

On 18 August 1941 the Butt Report, an investigation into the efficiency and effects of the RAF's bombing campaign, was completed. The report concluded that bombing up to this point had been extremely inaccurate. Of those raids studied, only one in ten bomb loads landed within five miles of the target, one in fifteen if there was bad weather. These statistics, taking into account the rising casualties in bomber crews, initiated a relaxation of operations while the future of Bomber Command was debated.

Through the winter of 1941/1942 a new plan surfaced for the Bomber Force. Certain German targets would be subjected to continuous air attack, with the intention of a general destruction of cities. The Air Ministry believed a concentrated bombing effort on the heart of Germany would foreshorten the war considerably. Effectively this sanctioned the introduction of 'area bombing', large forces of bombers swamping enemy defences with resultant bomb damage over large areas of the targeted city.

On 22 February 1942 Bomber Command received a new leader, who would stay with it for the rest of the war. Air Chief Marshal Sir Arthur Harris's first major task was to implement the new directives. The most famous of them was the one sent to Bomber Command on 14 February 1942, requiring its operational focus to be on the morale of the enemy civil population, and in particular of the industrial workers.

When Harris took over, Bomber Command had 378 aircraft serviceable with crews, of which only 69 were heavy bombers[2]. With the bomber force restricted to night raids, this compounded the problem of target finding without radar navigational aids. Harris was aware of the lack of trained crews. Harris was realistic, but he recognised the importance of the bomber force.

> This then was the force with which I had to begin an immediate offensive against Germany; it was also the only force in the West which then could take any offensive action at all against Germany, our only means of getting at the enemy in a way that would hurt at all . . .
>
> The importance of beginning the offensive as soon as possible could hardly be overestimated. The bomber offensive, or rather what could be made of it, was the only means we had of actively helping the Russians, who, though the German offensive in Russia had halted, had every appearance of being *in extremis*. Even if this could not be done directly, by destroying the enemy's war industries and communications, at least it could be done indirectly, and to a

---

[2] *Bomber Offensive* by Sir Arthur Harris, Greenhill Books, 1990 p73.

very material extent, by forcing the enemy to keep his fighters in Germany. In the same way, if not directly, then indirectly by containing the enemy's air force and compelling it to be used for the defence of Germany, the bomber offensive was at that time the only means we had of doing anything to give measurable help to our armies engaged in a desperate struggle in the Middle East; a bomber offensive would also have the effect of making the enemy keep his anti-aircraft guns at home, and every German anti-aircraft gun was a dual purpose weapon, convertible at will into an anti tank gun.

By the bomber offensive, and only by this means, could we force the Germans to keep any large proportion of their manpower for defence; a serious bomber offensive would compel the enemy to keep many hundreds of thousands of men on active and passive defence, in the night fighter force, in the anti-aircraft batteries, in the fire-fighting services, demolition squads, and so on. In the same way Bomber Command, by getting on with its minelaying campaign, could put a large part of the German navy on to the work of minesweeping, and many workers on to the repair of ships.[3]

Indeed Albert Speer, Hitler's armaments minister, wrote of the need to use vast resources to defend the Reich against bombing attacks:

Our heaviest expense was in fact the elaborate defensive measures. In the Reich and in the western theaters of war the barrels of ten thousand anti-aircraft guns were pointed toward the sky. The same guns could have well been employed in Russia against tanks and other ground targets. Had it not been for this new front, the air front over Germany, our defensive strength against tanks would have been about doubled, as far as equipment was concerned. Moreover, the anti-aircraft force tied down hundreds of thousands of young soldiers. A third of the optical industry was busy producing gunsights for the flak batteries. About half of the electronics industry was engaged in producing radar and communications networks for defence against bombing. Simply because of this, in spite of the high level of the German electronics and optical industries, the supply of our frontline troops with modern equipment remained far behind that of the Western armies.[4]

The Air Ministry concluded that the only way of attacking German cities

---

[3] *Bomber Offensive, op.cit.*, p73-74.
[4] Albert Speer, *Inside the Third Reich*, Phoenix, 1995, p381-382.

by night was by area bombing. Much has been written in the years following the war, arguing the case for and against the area bombing policy, but it is the purpose of this account only to give the background to the decisions that affected Arthur Darlow and his crew's operations.

Arthur Harris was certainly a believer in area bombing, but as the war progressed took exception to the Air Ministry's avoidance of the morality of the issue. Harris believed in his Command's ability to be the decisive factor for victory in the Western theatre of war, and below is a quotation from correspondence between Harris and the Air Ministry which sums up his views. On 2 March 1944, the Air Ministry sent Harris a letter acknowledging the fact that Bomber Command attacks were aimed deliberately at the destruction of vast acreages of German industrial cities, to which he responded on 7 March.

> I also note that the destruction of any German city which contains any military installation or any war production or organisation potential is agreed to fall within the terms of my directive. This being the case, it is clear that the elimination of every German city and town included in the Bomber's Baedeker issued by the Ministry of Economic Warfare is recognised as the aim of the Bomber Command Offensive and it is unnecessary to enter into purely verbal discussions as to what constitutes a town or city as such. It is equally clear that any civilian who produces more than enough to maintain himself is making a positive contribution to the German war effort and is therefore a proper though not necessarily a worthwhile object of attack. Here too the question of attacking civilians as such, i.e. because they are civilians and for no other reason, seems to me merely academic.
>
> Now that the aim of the Bomber Offensive has at length been clearly formulated, I trust that it will be given due prominence in Air Ministry publicity. I regret, however, that it is still considered inexpedient to recognise fully the strategic importance of results achieved and to be expected from the offensive. Such recognition would, no doubt, be embarrassing to those who have already decided that the war can be won only by more hazardous and costly methods, but this hardly seems an adequate reason for withholding it.[5]

Soon after Harris's appointment and with him no doubt wishing to make a statement, he stepped up the bombing raids on Germany, in particular the Thousand Bomber raids initiated with an attack on Cologne on 30 May 1942. Bomber Command dispatched 1,047 aircraft to the city, drawing on

---

[5] Public Record Office AIR 24 269.

operational training units to back up the front line strength. The raid devastated 600 acres at a cost of 41 aircraft. It initially sent shock waves through the Nazi hierarchy and Reichsmarschall Hermann Goering, Commander in Chief of the Luftwaffe, refused to accept the reports from the beleaguered city. On 1/2 June 956 aircraft attacked Essen and on 25/26 June 960 aircraft attacked Bremen. These new operations gave plenty of propaganda opportunities for both sides, and with regard to Bomber Command's tactical decision making, the scale of the attacks and the concentration of the bomber force began to expose weaknesses in the German night fighter defence system.

Whilst strategy for the bombing offensive developed, considerable technical advances were made improving the night bombing techniques. One major development was the introduction of the navigational aid, Gee, by which a navigator could fix his aircraft's position. Two stations, one called the master, the other the slave, sent out a radar signal simultaneously. On board the aircraft the Gee apparatus measured the time difference between the two signals, which enabled the navigator to place his aircraft on a certain line. Then a second slave station transmitted a signal at the same time as the master station. Again the navigator could place his aircraft, now on a second line. He could then locate his aircraft at the position where the two lines crossed.

Gee had certain limitations. Once a few Gee sets had fallen into enemy hands they were able to jam signals over enemy territory. It was limited in its range, for example it could pinpoint an aircraft at 20,000 feet only up to a range of 400 miles from the English coast, but nevertheless it proved invaluable for returning bombers trying to locate their airfield in bad weather conditions. There was hope that it could be used as a blind bombing device, but after analysis of the results of some raids using Gee these hopes were dashed. Visual identification of the target, at this stage of the bombing campaign, remained the key to a successful operation in terms of damage caused.

Most of the early Bomber Command raids involved aircraft finding their own ways to targets and circling until they definitely identified the target. With the change to area bombing, Harris believed that a concentration of the bomber force, into a bomber stream, would result in a number of advantages: the German night fighters would have less time and therefore opportunity to engage many bombers; the searchlights and flak at the target would be saturated; and on the ground the burning city's firecrews would be overwhelmed. Gee certainly helped concentrate bomber forces on the routes to the targets before the signals were jammed.

During this time Pathfinder forces were introduced, involving bombers sent out with the purpose of locating, identifying and marking targets, which considerably eased the task of the main forces. Although Harris opposed the introduction of these Pathfinder bombers, which were to be manned by selected crews, on 11 August 1942 definite instructions were received from the Air Ministry.

On 20 December 1942 the first 'Oboe' Mosquitos were ready, to act as Pathfinders. Oboe was a blind bombing device, with aircraft receiving signals from England and transmitting back. These signals informed the Oboe-equipped aircraft exactly when to release the bombload. One ground station signalled a system of dots and dashes to the Oboe aircraft whenever it deviated from a given course. This course was the circumference of a circle, which passed over the target. A second ground station received signals from the aircraft, which were used to determine its position along the arc. It was then possible to calculate, at the ground station, the exact moment the bombs should be released, at which point another signal was sent to the aircraft. Oboe Pathfinder marker aircraft (Mosquitos at first) would initially identify the target on a major raid with other non-Oboe Pathfinder aircraft backing up.

The systematic bombing error of these new Oboe-assisted aircraft was less than 300 yards but the device's range was limited by the curvature of the earth and the operational height of the Oboe-equipped aircraft. Also the number of aircraft that could use Oboe was small owing to the limitations of the signalling stations. Further details on Pathfinder operations will be covered later in this book.

Subsequent to this, the ability of aircraft to locate targets improved when a ground scanning radar set became available called H2S. Surface features such as woods, rivers, coastlines and built up areas could be distinguished by aircraft that had the device, thus assisting navigation and bomb aiming. It was not as accurate as Oboe however. One spin off from H2S was 'Fishpond', a piece of equipment using H2S transmissions to display echoes of other nearby aircraft on a screen. The wireless operator would see not only the echoes from hostile aircraft, but also those from friendly aircraft and he determined the displayed aircraft's intentions by its course. Other on board defensive equipment included 'Monica', whereby radio pulses were transmitted and reflected from nearby aircraft, resulting in audible clicks in the wireless operator's headphones. The shorter the gap between clicks the nearer the other aircraft and the rate of change of clicking could indicate the other aircraft's intentions. There was also 'Boozer', a set of red and yellow lights, which would light up if the aircraft was being tracked by German ground or airborne radar. The problem, however, was that the lights were constantly coming on and off when the aircraft was over German territory, owing to the massive amount of defensive radar activity. There was also 'Mandrel', ground-based equipment, introduced to jam German ground radar stations alongside 'Tinsel', a small microphone attached to one of the bomber's engines tuned by the wireless operator into the conversation going on between a German night fighter pilot and his ground controller, disrupting their ability to share information. Both Mandrel and Tinsel were minor but irritating disruptions for the German defences.

With the American entry into the war in December 1941, the strategic air offensive became a joint concern. The American bomber forces engaged in relatively small raids during 1942, but the RAF and USAAF soon embarked upon a combined bombing offensive. On 21 January 1943 at the Casablanca Conference, President Roosevelt and Prime Minister Churchill put their signatures to a document drawn up by their Combined Chiefs of Staff.

> *Directive to the appropriate British and United States Air Force Commanders to govern the operation of the British and United States Bomber Commands in the United Kingdom.*

Your primary objective will be the progressive destruction and dislocation of the German military, industrial and economic system, and the undermining of the morale of the German people to a point where their capacity for armed resistance is fatally weakened.

Within that general concept, your primary objectives, subject to the exigencies of weather and of tactical feasibility, will for the present be in the following order of priority.

a)   German Submarine Construction Yards
b)   The German Aircraft Industry
c)   Transportation
d)   Oil Plants
e)   Other Targets in the Enemy War Industry.[6]

The directive went on to mention other objectives, including 'Berlin, which should be attacked when conditions are suitable for the attainment of specially valuable results unfavourable to the morale of the enemy or favourable to that of Russia.'

The directive was issued to Bomber Command and the United States Eighth Air Force on 4 February 1943. Major-General Ira Eaker, commander of the US Eighth Army Air Force directed his American bombers to use daylight precision bombing, believing in the defensive capabilities of a well armed bomber formation. Bomber Command still favoured night bombing methods. Whilst listing the types of targets, the directive still allowed scope for a continuation of the Bomber Command policy of area bombing, something Harris exploited.

In the spring of 1943 Harris began the Battle of the Ruhr, targeting the German industrial heartland. The target area lay within the range of Oboe and could be reached within the short nights of spring and summer. Bomber Command's offensive would be greatly enhanced by the accuracy of the

---

[6] Webster, Sir Charles, and Frankland, Noble, *The Strategic Air Offensive Against Germany 1939-1945*, HMSO 1961. Crown copyright is reproduced with the permission of the Controller of her Majesty's Stationery Office.

Oboe-assisted Pathfinder Mosquitos, but the bombers had to contend with the flak and searchlight defences around the Ruhr, which were the most effective in Germany and the fact that routes in and out of the target areas were patrolled by experienced and well equipped Luftwaffe night fighters. Beyond the Ruhr and the range of Oboe successful operations were small.

During the same period the American bomber forces began to suffer greatly at the hands of the Luftwaffe on their daylight raids. Eaker realised that to attain air superiority, the German air forces must be directly attacked. The Combined Chiefs of Staff accepted a requirement for a change of priorities and on 10 June 1943 the 'Pointblank' directive was issued amending the Casablanca decision by placing considerable emphasis on destroying the Luftwaffe and German aircraft industry. However Harris still found scope within this amendment to pursue his campaign of area bombing.

CHAPTER 2

NEW CREW, TRAINING AND FRUSTRATION

On 5 January 1943 the liner *Queen Elizabeth* departed from New York for England, with Arthur Darlow on board accompanied by about another 11,000 troops. The journey across the Atlantic took seven days during which two American soldiers favoured their chances with the ocean rather than a war-torn Europe. Arthur disembarked from the *Queen Elizabeth* at 1315 hours on Tuesday 12 January and went straight onto a troop train bound for Harrogate, which arrived at 2340 hours that night.

From Arthur's diary

January 18th 1943, Monday: On parade early at 0810 hrs & had security lecture. Later on in afternoon went before Air Crew Selection Board, & was told I was down for Twin Night Fighters, failing that Medium bombers. My report said 'above average' for Night Flying. Had some gen. given out about leave & am going on 14 days tomorrow, should be home about 7 pm. I'm so happy to be nearing home again.
January 19th, Tuesday: Second turn for train left Harrogate about 11.40 & arrived Gillingham 1930 hrs. Had rather rotten journey, but didn't mind as train was going in right direction. Had lovely evening with Anne, she's still as beautiful & wonderful as ever. Eric has grown tremendously, he didn't recognise me at first.
January 20th, Wednesday: Didn't get up till about 11 am & had lovely dinner about 1400. Anne's cooking has certainly improved a great deal, & what's more she still loves me – goodness knows why. She's so sweet. Played with Eric, did bit of shopping. Went to cinema together, but had to leave owing to air raid.

The next few months for the keen young pilot were spent between laborious training units and dashes home when gaps in the schedule allowed. His personal diary recorded his increasing impatience. '*February 12th, 1943:*

A.O.C. turned up this morning, had inspection and then gave us a pep talk, crowd not very appreciative of his efforts, as it's past the funny stage hearing such excuses for delay.'

As the weeks went by and Arthur still did not receive the posting he was looking for, he killed time watching films, getting fit and writing plenty of letters.

From Arthur's diary

March 8th, Monday: Had posting parade this morning, no luck for me again, shall be here for duration at this rate. Saw S/Ldr Hoftman about rejoining P.T. squad & start this afternoon. Played in inter-squad football match as goalkeeper & game was drawn 4-4. Did quite well considering I'm no goalkeeper, boys were pleased anyhow. Had bath & went to see All through the Night a 5th column film.

March 11th, Thursday: Still not posted & on usual routine of P.T. & cross country. Had tea at Crag Hotel half way. In the afternoon played goalie & played very poor, our team lost 4-0. Feel stiff & sore at present. In evening went to cinema with Don Bruce & saw Adventures of Martin Eden, not a bad film. Received letter written by Mum on Dec 29th.

March 12th, Friday: Should be plenty of postings this weekend, umpteen rumours going round. Did usual P.T. & football both morning & afternoon, & made up for yesterdays bad goalkeeping. Stayed in in evening, after playing billiards & wrote to Anne in answer to short letter received.

On 15 March Arthur received news of a posting to Perton Satellite, an auxiliary aerodrome for RAF Codsall, near Wolverhampton. The next month involved flying Oxfords, navigation, dual flying, solo flying, bumps and circuits, nipping home at any opportunity. On 14 April Arthur was posted to Wheaton Ashton for night flying and day night flying, beam cross country (a navigational exercise) and lectures.

Finally on 17 May Arthur received his long awaited posting, and on 19 May a young, keen and fresh 21-year-old pilot arrived at 24 Operational Training Unit, Honeybourne, Worcestershire. His task that day was to begin picking up his crew.

Now there was an opportunity to start some serious flying, albeit in an operational training unit. At the OTU airmen from all the different training units came together to sort themselves into operational crews. There was no official forming of crews, instead it was each to his own, good luck and see what you can get.

From Arthur's diary:

May 19th, Wednesday: We pick our crews up here, & have my eye on navigator (Bob Clark) already. Hope to have an all London crew, but cannot get bombardier or rear & mid gunners for fortnight's time ...

May 20th, Thursday: Reported CGI's block and collected white pollaneck sweater, flying underclothing & electric waistcoat. Posted letter to Anne. Started lectures in afternoon, & have fixed up Bob Clark as my navigator. He seems a good lad, & keen on astro. Think I've spotted my w/op (wireless operator) too.

May 21st, Friday: Had fuselage drill & an hours link this morning. Weather very hot, could do with coats off. Have [Allan] 'Bert' Burrell (Half pint or Tich for short) as w/operator. He's also from London, & has several months ground experience, nice chap & should be pretty good with radio.

The all London ideal was soon to be displaced with the addition of Alex Nethery, a 22 year-old Canadian, to act as bomb aimer in the crew.

Alex Nethery: I was not aware, as a young man, of 'propaganda'. The news movies, in the theatres, Hitler's declaration of world conquest plus the invasions of all the countries in Europe, were enough to convince me that my family and Canada was in great danger.

In 1939 the Air Force were only accepting university graduates. I wanted to fly, like most of the young men I knew! So I waited a year or so until the demand for airmen and my education were compatible. I was accepted and trained for almost a year, graduating from Air Observers' School at London, Ontario, Canada, as an observer. There was no such thing as an observer in Bomber Command and I was reclassified as Air Bomber.

They were subsequently joined by 18-year-old Englishman Trevor Utton as air gunner, mid upper. (Trevor's older brother, Peter, in the RAFVR [Royal Air Force Volunteer Reserve], was with 264 Squadron acting as a navigator/radio operator in night flying Mosquitos). Also 20-year-old Englishman Philip 'Pip' Richards joined the crew as flight engineer, his main reason for joining the RAF, like Trevor, being that flying would be preferable to being in the Navy or Army. The position of rear gunner was filled by Canadian Don 'Pop' Copeland, the most senior member of the crew in age, as he edged toward his thirties.

Alex Nethery: When Arthur approached me and asked if I would like to join his crew, I had an instant impression of a man of solid, responsible character. I quickly said yes. Don Copeland was almost a twin of Arthur. Coming from 'small town Ontario' he was very quiet and unassuming, and we were quite comfortable having him in the rear turret. Trevor Utton was brash, lively and gung-ho. To me he was keen and alert and with Don's maturity they made a good gunners team. Allan Burrell was very self-assured, knew his job to perfection, was inclined to rebel against authority, but knew when to stop. I don't think Philip Richards cared one damn bit about any part of the war. Perhaps his marriage caused him to worry more than the single men.

Overall we had a crew of two cultures, English and Canadian with a mixture of age and youth. Added to this was a blend of maturity and youthful enthusiasm. We were all united in our desire to get the damn job done and get home safely.

Training for the fresh crew continued but mainly on the ground. Fuselage and airmanship, navigation, lectures, pigeon handling, dinghy lectures, signals and airmanship again, dinghy drill, 'passing out' parade, more dinghy drill, more lectures, yet more dinghy drill. Frustration set in and extracts from Arthur's diary record:

June 3rd, Thursday: Had 'passing out' parade & march past, with band this morning. Collected parachute & locker key in afternoon. Packed up at 4 pm. Had tea & 2 games pool. Shaved & cut off moustache. Wrote to Anne.
June 4th, Friday: Reported to flights at 0815 & did 15 mins PT then wasted morning hanging around. Did some dinghy drill with crew in afternoon. Stayed in mess all evening.
June 5th, Saturday: CO's parade this morning at 0715 hrs, therefore up at 6 am, bags of bull. Am getting browned off with this dump. Lectures morning & afternoon. Went to Evesham with lads in evening.
June 6th, Sunday: Flying programme today, but went out to five kites – all u/s. Just waited around did 1hrs Link, whilst crew did Anson trip. Wrote to Anne in evening, & stayed in mess.
June 7th, Monday: Same again today, shall never get in an aircraft at this rate, & there's no chance of 48 hrs either – absolute waste of time & bad organizing. Dinghy drill. Mess all evening.
June 8th, Tuesday: Am I cheesed, still messing around & on lectures today. No mail from Anne or anyone, wish this bloody

war was over and I was in civvies again. Wrote to Anne after
RCAF consent.
June 9th, Wednesday: No flying again, only promises, that's all
I get.

On 10 June the crew flew for the first time, circuits and bumps, in an
Armstrong Whitworth Whitley V. At last some flying although initially
most of it was dual with an instructor as first pilot. A little taste of things to
come occurred on 16th June when a cross country run took the plane into
bad weather; they were struck by lightning and the charge crackled down
the aerial setting off two smoke bombs. On returning to land, the
undercarriage had to be pumped down by lifting up the floorboards. Allan
'Bert' Burrell recalled one other unusual occasion whilst training. The
flight went pretty much unsupervised despite the presence of the instructor.
He lay on the floor of the aircraft for the whole trip, completely drunk.

One circuits and bumps routine enabled Alex to plan a most important
operation. As Arthur circled the aircraft, fairly low, back to base, they
passed over a large house. In the gardens a number of girls in gym kit
waved to the aircraft. Alex, convinced that some of them were not waving
but actually beckoning, made a quick request to Arthur who radioed back
to the airfield that they required more time to try something or other out.
Their request was granted and Alex went to work, memorising the road
system from the airfield to the large house.

At the next available opportunity Alex tested his map making and honed his
navigational skills. He came across a pub very close to the large house and
upon entering found himself considerably outnumbered by the young girls
also enjoying the surroundings of an English pub. The name and whereabouts
of this pub? Possibly one of the best kept secrets of the entire war.

Whilst training the crew began to experience and understand the
perils of their war contribution. Even at the OTUs the mortality of aircrews
became apparent. The daily record kept at OTU 24 Honeybourne records
the following.

> *10th June 1943:* Nickel [leaflet] raid. 5 aircraft took off to
> Nantes. 3 completed the raid, 1 returned early due to W/T
> trouble. The other aircraft failed to return. [Information
> regarding the fate of the missing crew would have not reached
> Honeybourne for some time. In fact from the crew of six only
> one member survived becoming a POW. The aircraft was
> presumed to have crashed in the target area.]
> *20th June:* A Whitley on circuits and landings at the satellite
> (Long Marston) crashed just off the airfield. The aircraft was
> burnt out and one of the crew seriously injured.
> *28th June:* A Wellington from Gaydon made a forced landing
> at Long Marston on one engine. The aircraft hit two Whitleys

in a dispersal, and all 3 aircraft were burnt out. Four members of the Wellington crew were killed.

16th July: A Hudson from Defford crashed at Ashton-under-Hill. The aircraft was burnt out and there were no survivors.

20th July: An Anson crashed on the airfield. The aircraft was badly damaged and one of the crew slightly injured.

23rd July: A Whitley crashed after High Level Bombing at Ildlicote. The aircraft was burnt out and the crew of five killed.[7]

Many inexperienced crews' first taste of operations came with leaflet drops (Nickel raids) over enemy territory. These were often considered inconsequential, but there is evidence that some did have an effect. Most raids involved the dropping of propaganda leaflets, but there were drops of items such as false ration books, a constant nuisance for the German administration. Our crew's first operational flight, a Nickel raid, took place on 23 July 1943. Seven aircraft at Honeybourne were detailed for the operation, four to drop leaflets on Paris, three on Melun, Montereau and Fontainebleau. Arthur took his Whitley V BD238 to Paris, released the load and returned safely to base, a round trip of 5 hours 15 minutes. All the other aircraft returned after successful missions, two with slight damage due to flak.

On 27 July the crew flew their last trip at the OTU, a four-hour cross-country. Arthur graduated from the course after 92 hours 50 minutes of flying, with an assessment mark of average (consisting of 16 hours 25 minutes of day flying and 38 hours 10 minutes of night flying when accompanied by an instructor pilot, 12 hours 40 minutes of day flying and 25 hours 35 minutes of night flying as the sole pilot). Just before they left Honeybourne the crew lost Sergeant Clark who, they were told, had an eyesight problem. They offered to wait but were paraded in front of the Commanding Officer and basically told 'No way'. A replacement was provided and the crew was pleased to note that he was actually a navigational instructor. The crew were posted to 1659 Conversion Unit Topcliffe.

Arthur and his six fresh crew members arrived at Topcliffe on 6 August 1943. The conversion units provided crews with training on the four-engined heavy bombers, which was a different proposition to twin-engined Whitleys. On 20 August 1943 the crew had their first flight on a Halifax Mark II. The course was intense, consisting of familiarisation flights, considerable cross-country runs, circuits and landings, fighter affiliations and flying on three or two engines. On 3 September 1943 the crew graduated from the unit and Arthur received an above average grade for his 44 hours 45 minutes of flying. Of these, only 7 hours 50 minutes were as sole pilot flying at night. The crew received news of their posting to an operational unit, Royal Canadian Air Force 427 Squadron.

---

[7] Public Record Office AIR 29 668.

CHAPTER 3

NEW SQUADRON, JOINING THE AIR BATTLE

On 24 July 1943, Bomber Command began its offensive against Hamburg. During this operation, Bomber Command first used 'Window', which was strips of coarse black paper with aluminium foil stuck to one side and released in large quantities during operations. Window resulted in the German defensive radar being swamped by false echoes, thus countering radar controlled Luftwaffe night fighters and flak which were rendered virtually useless. The effects of Window had been known for some time, but with Britain on the defensive, its use would give the Germans the opportunity of developing something similar to use against the British defences. In fact the Germans had also known for some time about the effects of metallised paper on radar, but they too had feared it would be used against their own defences. In August 1942 Bomber Command's Operational Research Section provided evidence of increasing numbers of losses due to enemy radar-assisted defences, but although Arthur Harris pressed the Air Ministry for the introduction of Window, his appeals were ignored. Over the next months, Harris repeatedly requested introduction of the metallised strips of paper and finally in July 1943 the Air Ministry relented.

Bomber Command sent four major forces to Hamburg in the space of ten nights, backed up by two USAAF raids. The target provided a good H2S image owing to the docks, the River Elbe and the recognisable coastline on the bombers' approach run. Hamburg received extensive damage and the civilian population suffered greatly, in particular from the infamous firestorms created by concentrated bombing. Approximately 40,000 people were killed, and the destruction of Hamburg sent shudders through the German hierarchy. Goebbels, the German Reich's propaganda minister, recorded in his diary:

> *July 29, 1943:* During the night we had the heaviest raid yet made on Hamburg. The English appeared over the city with 800 to 1000 bombers. Our anti-aircraft succeeded in shooting down only very few, so that one cannot claim any serious losses.

Kaufmann [the local Gauleiter], in a first report, spoke of a catastrophe the extent of which simply staggers the imagination. A city of a million inhabitants has been destroyed in a manner unparalleled in history. We are faced with problems that are almost impossible of solution. Food must be found for this population of a million. Shelter must be secured. The people must be evacuated as far as possible. They must be given clothing. In short, we are facing problems there of which we had no conception even a few weeks ago. Kaufmann believes the entire city must be evacuated except for small patches. He spoke of about 800,000 homeless people wandering up and down the streets not knowing what to do.[8]

Not surprisingly considerably more resources would in future be applied to the defence of the skies over the Reich.

After the Battle of Hamburg, Bomber Command's attention briefly diverted to operations against Italian cities to hasten Italy's capitulation from the war. At the end of August 1943 Harris returned to his main offensive, launching the Battle of Berlin for he believed that the war could be considerably foreshortened by a continued attack upon the German capital. Towards the end of August and beginning of September Harris sent three large forces to the city, but these initial attacks were not anything like as successful as the raids to Hamburg. Poor bombing concentration and heavy losses persuaded Harris to draw back a while concentrating on targets less fiercely defended.

The use of 'Window' rendered the radar-controlled German night fighter box defence system ineffective and the German night fighters adapted, becoming more mobile in their efforts to defend their country against the bomber streams. Bomber Command therefore ran 'spoof' diversionary operations, involving small numbers of ordinary bombers or Mosquitos attacking targets on the same nights as the main bomber force in an attempt to deceive German night fighter controllers as they directed the movements of their fighters.

And so, as the battle over the night skies of Germany grew in intensity, our fresh crew started their operational tour.

On 2 September 1943, Arthur Darlow and crew arrived at Leeming near Harrogate in Yorkshire, home of Royal Canadian Air Force 427 Squadron. Nicknamed 'The Lion' Squadron after having been adopted by the film company Metro-Goldwyn-Mayer. The squadron formed at Croft, County Durham on 7 November 1942 as part of No. 4 Group before being assigned to No. 6 RCAF Group on 1 January 1943. The first operational mission was by one Wellington, minelaying in the Frisian Islands on 14 December 1942; two other Wellingtons had aborted. The first bombing operation was by six

---

[8] *The Goebbels Diaries*, translated by Louis P.Lochner, Hamish Hamilton, London 1948.

Wellingtons to Lorient. Early in May 1943 the squadron moved to Leeming where the Wellingtons began to be replaced by Halifax Vs. The Leeming airfield consisted of three runways and when our crew arrived it was also playing host to 429 Squadron. The personnel strength of 427 Squadron at the end of September 1943 consisted of:

	Aircrew	**Groundcrew**	**Total**
RCAF Officers	39	3	42
RCAF Airmen	93	342	435
RAF Officers	30	1	31
RAF Airmen	81	71	152
Totals	**243**	**417**	**660**

From Arthur's Diary

September 2nd, Tuesday: Arrived on operational squadron at Leeming; now in 'A' Flight 427 Sqdn. . . . Know several of the lads, Fletcher & Perry-Knox-Gore. Spent rest of day getting arrival form signed.

The next day our crew attended a number of genning up talks, but there was no flying, and neither was there any the following day owing to bad weather. On 5 September twelve 427 Squadron aircraft were detailed for operations. Often new pilots gained experience as a second dickey (second pilot), individually accompanying an experienced crew on an operation. Arthur celebrated his 22nd birthday with a first taste of raids over Germany.

From Arthur's diary

September 5th, Friday: On tonight, target 'MANNHEIM' with P/O Rodwell & crew. 8½ hr trip. Op. successful, fires well concentrated. Fine start to a birthday.
September 6th, Saturday: On operations again tonight, this time 'MUNICH'. Pretty hot target, bags of fighters & flares. Went with F/Lt Arnot & crew. Diverted RAF Manston on return of 8.40 hrs trip, touch down about 2.30 am. Twice over Germany on one birthday, some going!

The trip to Mannheim turned out to be a successful raid for Bomber Command, causing severe destruction, but 34 aircraft out of the 605 that took part were lost, one of them from 427 Squadron. The Munich raid was less effective, poor marking and cloud cover led to scattered bombing, with 16 aircraft out of the 404 that took part lost. In this operation 427 Squadron lost two of their ten detailed aircraft and squadron morale suffered. The two men mentioned in Arthur's diary entry of 2 September were both lost,

Flight Sergeant Fletcher on the Mannheim raid and Pilot Officer Perry-Knox-Gore on the Munich raid. Pilot Officer Biggs and crew also failed to return from Munich. The exact fate of missing crews would not be known at the squadron for some time, if at all. In fact Fletcher, Perry-Knox-Gore and their crews were all killed. Biggs' aircraft, which on that night had a crew of eight, was hit by German night fighter fire and crashed near Starnberg. Biggs and four members of his crew were killed, and the other three became POWs.

On 7 September Arthur returned from Manston and slept most of the day. On the next two nights our crew were briefed for raids to Berlin, but operations were scrubbed on both occasions. The crew missed out on a debut raid to one of the most heavily defended targets in the whole of Germany and the cancellation of the raid on 8 September was more than welcome, as the squadron personnel were able to celebrate Italy's capitulation from the war.

For the next five nights the squadron remained non-operational. Bad weather and the moon period putting a stop to any bombing raids. But on 15 September 13 aircraft were detailed for operations and our crew began preparing for their first bombing raid together.

> *Alex Nethery:* There wasn't too much you could do by way of preparation prior to finding out where the target was. Obviously, you got your equipment ready – your flying helmet, parachute, warm clothes, the lucky scarf, your supply of cigarettes, as well as your emergency rations, which included oranges, chocolate bars and a survival kit containing foreign money (German marks, Dutch guilders, French francs), a compass, food tablets and so forth.
>
> Once you knew you were going on an op, that was sweating time. We'd just sit and talk quietly. You couldn't go off the station, of course, for a beer or anything like that. Sometimes we'd try and sleep, but it was no use. It was the waiting that got to you.

Along with the other crews detailed for the night's operation all would eventually assemble in the briefing room to learn of their mission.

> *Alex Nethery:* Final briefing, generally, took place four or five hours before take off and in my opinion was more propaganda than anything else. Your training and skills as an individual and as a flying crew were ten times more important than any information you were going to get during the briefing.
>
> *Trevor Utton:* After you entered the briefing room you sat down with your crew at tables. There was the map on the wall,

at that moment covered. When everybody was all in, the doors
were shut and security in place, the Wingco would come up,
the curtains drawn and there was the route.

Alex Nethery: The navigation officer would point out a few
hazards by way of navigation. The Intelligence officer would
tell you how many gun placements and fighter stations were
around the target. The met man would forecast the weather
and wind strength and direction, which was the most vital
information for us. This was extremely important for DR
(dead reckoning) navigation. It certainly was not significant if
there was 1,000 or 2,000 anti-aircraft guns around the target.
What could you do about it in any event?

  Briefing ended up something like a pep rally for a football
game; a little bit of a team ritual. Rah, rah, rah and away we
went. You would come to attention when the CO arrived and
again when he left but, other than that, briefing was quite
informal. You could ask questions and take notes if you so
wished.[9]

On the afternoon of 15 September the crews at 427 Squadron looked up at
the large map in front of them and followed the ribbons representing their
intended route. This time they were to go to Montluçon in France and
attack the Dunlop rubber factories situated there. After the main briefing
certain crew members dispersed to their own relevant sections for
additional information.

  Prior and during all this groundcrews would prepare the aircraft, load
bombs, fuel up. The load of fuel and bombs would give the crews a clue as
to the target for that night. The more fuel the longer the trip.

  Following a quiet bacon, eggs and toast in the mess the airmen met again
in the crew room where flight clothing would be adorned and survival and
escape equipment collected. Once ready the crew transferred to the
airfield's dispersal, to board their aircraft. At this stage of the war the main
aircraft used to deliver bombs to a target were the Halifax and Lancaster.
The Stirling (or 'Flying Coffin' as it was to be nicknamed) participated in
lessening numbers, as did the Wellington to an even smaller degree.

  In September 1943 427 Squadron had 20 Halifax Vs with which to carry
out orders, but in the new year they began to receive the superior Halifax
IIIs which had marked improvements in operating height, time to height
and range. Neither could compare with the Lancaster, however, something
crews quickly discovered once they had flown in the 'Lanc'. Both aircraft
required the same crew of seven, with virtually the same responsibilities.
All the crew entered by the rear door. For take-off and landing the gunners

---

[9] Quoted in *Maximum Effort* by Bernie Wyatt, The Boston Mills Press, 1986 p43.

remained in the fuselage. Once airborne the rear gunner climbed into the most exposed, isolated and dangerous position in the aircraft to take his place in his cold, cramped revolving turret where he acted as the first line of defence for the bomber. He scanned the night sky, searching out any stalking night fighters, telling the pilot should the enemy be sighted and firing his four Browning .303 machine guns should the enemy attack. Again once airborne the mid upper gunner climbed up into his cramped turret where the lack of space meant he could not wear his parachute which was stowed away beneath him. Once behind his four Browning .303 machine guns (two in the Lancaster) he was there for the duration of the trip, unless ordered otherwise by the captain. He needed to concentrate, sometimes for hours on end, peering through the mid upper blister; if he saw the night fighter before they were seen, their chances of evading combat were greatly enhanced.

The remainder of the crew went down the fuselage over the main spar to reach their positions. Just in front of the main spar sat the wireless operator, before his high frequency radio. Next to him were the hot air outlet pipes of the aircraft, the only position in the aircraft to have any such luxury, although the wireless operator suffered the heat as his shivering crew mates requested the levels be turned up.

Behind the pilot sat the navigator, maps and briefing papers spread across his table. The flight engineer stood close by the pilot, with his control panel on the starboard side of the cockpit, which displayed engine oil levels, temperatures, coolant temperature, fuel levels. The flight engineer was responsible for the fuel management of the aircraft, pumping fuel between the tanks held in the wings as and when necessary. The pilot was strapped into his chair on the port side of the cockpit. In front of him was his blind flying control panel, to his right the boost gauges and rev counters for the four engines, manual flying controls, and to the side the throttle mixture and propeller controls.

At the front of the aircraft the bomb aimer, doubling up as the front gunner, took up his position in the nose blister. On the approach to the target area he would be peering out searching for the marker flares, taking aim through the stabilised bombsight.

Once aboard the aircraft, each crew member carried out a number of routine checks before the pilot set the aircraft in motion, taxiing along the perimeter track, using rudder, bursts of power and careful application of the breaks, in single file with the other aircraft, to the end of the runway. The engines then revved to 3/4 power with brakes on, until he received a green light from the flying control caravan. Then brakes were released, flaps partly down, full power applied.

Alex Nethery: Most of the time I sat or stood with Arthur on take offs & landings. Both of us held the throttles at full power on take off. If an emergency occurred i.e. not enough power for take off, we would ram all four levers through the gate (restraining wires) to emergency pressure. Also if for any reason Arthur had to move his hand off the throttles I was to maintain maximum pressure.

Eventually the accelerating bomb laden aircraft, engines roaring, lifted off the runway. As one aircraft climbed, the next in line got the green light. Each aircraft circled the airfield, navigation lights on, and upon reaching an altitude specified at briefing the navigator gave the pilot his course for the first leg of the flight plan and it became part of the bomber stream.

15/16 September 1943,
Operation to Montluçon Dunlop Rubber Factory, France

Crew:		
	Captain	Sgt Darlow, A.E.
	Navigator	Pilot Officer W*
	Bomb aimer	Sgt Nethery, A.
	Wireless operator	Sgt Burrell, A.W.
	Rear gunner	Sgt Renaud, J.C.H.
	Mid upper gunner	Sgt Utton, T.E.
	Flight engineer	Sgt Richards, P.W.

Aircraft Type and Number:		Halifax V	LK644

Time up:	20:42	*Time down*:	01:07
Flying Time:	4 hours 25 minutes		
Bomb Load:	1 x 2000lb. HC (High Capacity) Nose Inst.		
	48 x 30lb Inc. (Incendiary)		
	600 x 4lb Inc.		
	30 x 4lb 'X' type Inc.		
	(Explosive incendiaries intended to hinder smothering.)		
Total:	**5960lb**		

Arthur's crew had the addition of a Canadian, Sergeant Renaud for his only mission with them, standing in for Don Copeland. The Operations Record Book for 427 Squadron recorded Halifax LK644's trip as follows:

> Halifax was caught in flak at 2154 hours over enemy territory, which delayed them to the extent that the target could not be reached in time. As a result pilot decided to abandon task and returned early after jettisoning load at 2337 hours from 8,000 feet.[10]

In fact the official record of the crew's flight bears little resemblance to what actually happened on this particular operation.

---

[10] Public Record Office AIR 27 1945.
* Name witheld (see also pp26 and 44).

The normal approach to a target involved 'circling' it in dog-legs, bombing it, then straightening out the other side and off home. However on this occasion the crews were to fly straight down and then straight back, a decision that would have a bearing upon later decisions. The navigational instructions were to fly south to the coast of England, aiming for Southampton, and then cut across the Bay of Biscay, down into France, bomb the target, and straight back.

Well just over an hour after leaving Leeming our crew found themselves over London, under intensive anti-aircraft fire and receiving the attention of the searchlights. The navigator had wandered off the intended track and brought the aircraft right over London, as it was being attacked by German aircraft. Arthur turned the plane back west, and tried again to find the right flight path. Unfortunately they returned to the skies above London, once more running the danger of encountering friendly fire. Arthur turned again, taking the plane further west, to get on track for the scheduled turning point, but by now they had not even started for Southampton, and were running twenty minutes behind their scheduled time. As such, on arrival at the target they would have been the only ones there. Discussions started, and amidst choice remarks coming from the rear gunner, Sergeant Renaud, directed toward the navigator, they debated whether or not to carry on to Montluçon or jettison the bombs and return to base. It was pointed out to Arthur that if the plane arrived twenty minutes late they would be in danger of running into the aircraft that were on the return journey. Arthur decided to jettison the bombs over the sea and return to Leeming.

Back at base the crew's reception obviously excluded congratulations upon completion of their first raid and no doubt the crew's lack of moral fibre was questioned. With little surprise the crew found themselves detailed for another operation the next night. As seen above, the official squadron report for their first raid was worded somewhat in the favour of the crew.

Of the 13 aircraft detailed for the operation at 427 Squadron, three returned early owing to various troubles and the other ten successfully bombed the target. Tragically Sergeant Chibanhoff's aircraft crashed at West Drayton on the way home and all the crew were killed. The remaining aircraft landed safely.

Following the previous night's misadventures the crew were given the opportunity to redeem themselves. A major raid to Modane, in south-east France, was planned. The target consisted of three distinct parts: the international rail station, the marshalling yards and the entrance to the Mont Cenis Tunnel, all located in a steep sided valley. Modane was the location for the point of change of the French rail system to the Italian system, and thus an important supply and communication line between the two countries. The French and Italian customs houses were located there, and the yards contained sidings and a relatively long and narrow locomotive

shed lying between a river and the high mountains. Just beyond Modane the
railway line looped back upon itself as it climbed towards the entrance of
the 8¹/₂ mile long Mont Cenis Tunnel, linking France with northern Italy.[11]

Halifax LK644 was prepared along with eight other Halifaxes from 427
Squadron. The only change to the crew was that rear gunner Sergeant
Squair replaced Sergeant Renaud. Don Copeland was still unavailable.

Crew:	Captain	Sgt Darlow, A.E.
	Navigator	Pilot Officer W
	Bomb aimer	Sgt Nethery, A.
	Wireless operator	Sgt Burrell, A.W.
	Rear gunner	Sgt Squair, G.B.
	Mid upper gunner	Sgt Utton, T.E.
	Flight engineer	Sgt Richards, P.W.

Aircraft Type and Number:	Halifax V	LK644

Bomb Load:	1 x 1000 lb MC (Medium Capacity) TD 0.025
	4 x 1000 lb GP (General Purpose) TD 0.025
Total:	**5000lb**

Zero hour for the raid was scheduled for one minute past midnight.

Navigation: The outward route for the 427 Squadron aircraft, took them
first to Peterborough, then via Reading to Selsey Bill. (Arthur's crew was
careful, of course, to avoid the defences of London.) From Selsey Bill it
took them across the Channel to Cabourg, then on the long trek across
France to Grenoble to locate some route markers. Red spot fires, to guide
the main force aircraft, were to be placed at position 4511N 0545E by all
the Pathfinder visual markers, using an H2S fix on Grenoble.

Below are the details of the bombing schedule for the raid, which quite
clearly demonstrate the complexity of bombing operations in the autumn of
1943. Even more elaborate bombing and marking schemes were to
develop. Mentioned below are Target Indicators or TI. These were the
standard marker dropped by the Pathfinders on a raid, and were 250lb
packs of candles which would be released by a barometric fuse to cascade
in reds or yellows or greens to the target below and nicknamed by the
Germans 'Christmas Trees'.

Pathfinders

Time over target	Aircraft type	Marking Method
z – 4	10 Visual Markers	The Visual Markers would make a timed run from the

---

(i.e. zero hour – 4 mins)

z	4 Backers-up	
z + 1	2 Backers-up	
z + 2 to z + 24	23 Backers-up (1 p/min)	

route markers and attempt to identify the aiming point visually. Marking of the aiming point then achieved by dropping red TI (Target Indicator). Backers-up had the responsibility of keeping the target marked throughout the attack, for the benefit of the main force. On this raid early Backers-up would aim their green TI at the red TI dropped by the Visual Markers, the main force then aiming at the centre of the green TI. Subsequent Backers-up detailed to maintain the marking with their green TI.

NB: See pages 70-71 for explanation of colours.

Main Force

Time over target	Aircraft numbers	Bombing Method
z + 2 to z + 7	26 Stirlings and 35 Halifaxes	Instructions to the main force bombers involved aiming at the centre of all the green TI seen.
z + 7 to z + 12	26 Stirlings and 35 Halifaxes	
z + 12 to z + 17	25 Stirlings and 35 Halifaxes	
z + 17 to z + 22	26 Stirlings and 36 Halifaxes	
z + 22 to z + 27	25 Stirlings and 36 Halifaxes	

Arthur and crew took off from Leeming at 1759 hours, amidst continuous rain. The aircraft carried one 1000lb MC (medium capacity) bomb and four 1000lb GP (general purpose) bombs. The medium capacity bombs had the higher charge to weight ratio than the general purpose bombs and as such enabled greater blast damage, but with less penetrative capabilities. The obvious mission for the crew, and indeed the whole bomber force was to blast the railway yards apart to cut the enemy's communications.

After a reasonably quiet outward flight with only a little light flak encountered, LK644 approached the target area. It was a clear moonlit night with no cloud and Alex, preparing for the bomb run, prone on the

floor and peering through the blister on the nose of the Halifax, pinpointed
the primary target easily. The bomb run was one of the most tense times for
crews. Arthur attempted to keep the aircraft level and on a straight course,
amidst upward streaming, curving tracer and black clouds and shock waves
of the bursting flak. Alex relayed to Arthur the occasional 'left a bit' or
'right a bit' or 'steady' as he tried to keep the aiming point within his
bombsight awaiting the release point. The rest of the crew gazed into the
night sky searching out any stalking night fighters, occasionally witnessing
the downing of another aircraft and tensely awaiting the 'bombs gone' from
Alex and the upward lurch as the aircraft parted company with a few tons
of blast, fire, death and destruction.

The crew received a reasonably warm welcome from the enemy for their
first bombing appearance over a target area. The blister in the nose of the
aircraft was penetrated by flak, but the damage was inconsequential and no
one was injured. There was no contact with any night fighters.

Much of the main force above Modane were behind the bombing
schedule, including LK644, indeed Alex gave the 'bombs gone' at 0047
hours, from 15,000 feet, 19 minutes after the planned close of the raid. Alex
followed instructions to the letter, releasing the bomb load on the centre of
the green TI ground markers. He observed and later recorded seeing large
fires and minor explosions just to the west of the green markers. Arthur
maintained course for another anxious few seconds until their photoflash
fell and lit up the night sky, providing the aiming point picture from which
Bomber Command Operational Research could make an initial assessment
on the success of the raid.

Once the bombload was released with the subsequent photoflash, Arthur
turned the aircraft for the journey home, crossing the moonlit snow-capped
peaks of the Alps, taking care not to cross into neutral Swiss airspace. As
they approached England, Allan received and relayed to the crew the news
that there was bad weather at Leeming, which resulted in a diversion to
Bassingbourne, Cambridgeshire, where they landed at 0420 hours. Spirits
were high as the crew, believing they had completed their first successful
mission, returned to Leeming and went to debriefing a little more
confident, to relate their flight details.

> *Alex Nethery:* The debriefing officers were really profes-
> sionals. They had to have a great deal of patience with
> aircrews who were tired, sleepy, cold, damp and generally
> cheesed off. A tremendous reaction sets in after successfully
> coming back from a raid and finally getting on the ground.
> However the debriefing officers had questions they had to ask.
> Even though some of the questions might've been absurd,
> they were really just doing their job, and that job was to
> extract every bit of information from us that they could
> possibly get.

> We used to get a shot of rum after every operation and occasionally, if you were in with the padre, you'd get a double. I certainly enjoyed my shot, but some of the crew who were not too active in the debriefing used to fall asleep after their sip and we'd have to wake them up. We were just anxious to get to the mess, have our bacon and eggs, then get to bed.
>
> We never did get any feedback about information we gave them, so we never knew if any of the information was helpful to the war effort or not.[12]

After Bomber Command collated all the intelligence from the operation, it became clear that the raid, as a whole, had not gone according to plan. The aiming point was at the eastern end of the marshalling yards, approximately half a mile from the international station. Unfortunately the first visual marker, approaching from the west, having possibly mistaken the target, dropped their red TI on the station. Subsequent visual markers dropped their TI on the station or further east. The backers-up managed to drop their green TI among the reds but of course their centre of concentration ended up about 1 to 1½ miles north-east of the aiming point.

Further errors in marking occurred when red TI dropped from the last visual marker at $z + 9$, did not fall immediately, overshooting the main concentration by about three quarters of a mile. Subsequent backers-up only saw these reds and further bombing, by about 75% of the main force, concentrated around them. It would appear Alex had done his job well, placing his bombload in the centre of the green TI, but unfortunately these were away from the aiming point. The results demonstrated the need for accurate Pathfinder marking, as a few misplaced TI seriously jeopardised the whole success of a raid.

Bomber Command Night Raid Report, Modane, 16/17 September 1943: Day Reconnaissance

> The marshalling yard, the International Station, the entrance to the Mont Cenis tunnel and a large area to the east, including the loop formed by the railway doubling back to the Mont Cenis tunnel, were covered on photographs taken a few days after the attack. A great concentration of craters was seen, running from the east end of the station, completely filling the loop in the railway. About 6 hits on embankments partly cut the tracks, and debris, fallen from the side of the cuttings, through which the loop runs, could be seen on the railway lines. Many houses were destroyed or damaged, and the

---

[12] Quoted in *Maximum Effort, op.cit.*

western end of a large industrial plant east of the loop was also
damaged.[13]

The Bomber Command, Operational Research Section plotted the night
photographs taken by the bomber crews of the Modane raid, which clearly
showed the spread of bombing to the east.

Of the nine aircraft detailed for operation at 427 Squadron, eight
completed the mission and one returned early. Bomber Command suffered
three losses to the enemy out of the 340 that actually took part in the raid,
two aircraft to flak, and one believed lost to fighter activity. However there
were other risks to bomber crews besides the enemy. Further casualties
included two aircraft destroyed when they crashed on return to England,
another aircraft was hit by incendiaries dropped by a bomber above them,
and another aircraft was hit by friendly fire from a Stirling.

After analysis, Bomber Command was detailed to follow up this
unsuccessful raid. A force of 313 Lancasters was sent to the rail yards on
the night of the 10/11 November 1943. The bombing was more
concentrated on this occasion, owing to better Pathfinder marking resulting
in considerable damage to the target.

---

[13] Public Record Office AIR 24 259.

CHAPTER 4

OPERATIONAL SQUADRON

After September's Modane operation 427 Squadron avoided enemy action for five days. Of those aircraft that had been diverted to Bassingbourne and the one that had been diverted to Cowingsbay because of the adverse weather on the return from Modane, all returned to base, some rather reluctantly. As Alex Nethery said, 'We hated to leave Bassingbourne. An American Station, food, drinks, hospitality!' Arthur 'expressed' his crew's gratitude on departure, 'shooting' up the airfield's tower with the Halifax.

On the 21st of the month the squadron transferred temporarily to Skipton whilst runway repairs were carried out at Leeming. Arthur and crew did not become active again until the 29th, but the squadron remained operational. On 22 September the squadron sent 15 aircraft on a raid to Hanover. Four returned early due to technical defects and the remaining aircraft took part in a relatively unsuccessful attack, returning to base safely. The next day 11 aircraft were detailed for a raid to Mannheim, but with one non-starter through a technical defect. The remaining aircraft bombed the target and the whole raid proved to be successful causing considerable and significant damage. All of the ten aircraft that bombed returned safely to base. Hanover was revisited by the squadron again on 27 September, with 14 aircraft detailed for the raid. Three returned early owing to technical trouble, and the remaining aircraft took part in an unsuccessful attack resulting from poor Pathfinder marking. Upon return to England the aircraft were diverted to other stations due to adverse weather.

On the same night as Bomber Command's raid to Hanover on the 27th, the intruder Mosquitos of 264 Squadron were operational. Three Mosquitos from the squadron were detailed for intruder patrols attacking airfields and communication lines on the other side of the channel. One of these was Mosquito 852 piloted by Flying Officer Est with his crewmate Flight Sergeant Utton, Trevor's brother. They took off at 1940 hours but failed to return from the operation and were posted as missing. In fact no trace has ever been found of the aircraft or crew, and both men are now named on the Runnymede Memorial.

On 29 September 13 aircraft at 427 Squadron were detailed for operations, five to take part in minelaying, which was scrubbed early evening, the other eight to raid Bochum. Arthur's crew was one of those to

31

take part on the Bochum raid. They received two different operational crew members for the mission. Sergeant Boustead took over as navigator for the only operation he was to fly with them. Sergeant Donald Copeland took up his rear gunner position and remained operational with the crew for the rest of their missions.

They took off, in Halifax DK182, at 1813 hours laden with one 2,000lb HC bomb and 3,840lb of incendiaries. After experiencing moderate heavy flak on route and over the target, Alex released the bombload on some red TI markers dropped by the Pathfinders. This was most of the crew's first visit to a target in Germany.

> *Trevor Utton:* Going over the continent you would see the beacons [for the night fighters] and if late coming back you could see the glow [of the burning target] in the sky. When over the town it was terrific, lights, fires, different colour flares . . . you could have read a newspaper in your turret. You could see all the streets and housing through the fires, it was amazing . . . Once Alex said bombs gone that was when we felt most vulnerable . . . with the bomb doors wide open.

> *Alex Nethery:* The view of the sky, on approaching the target area, was made up of black flak bursts, glaring searchlights, anti-aircraft streams of tracer bullets and almost daylight conditions. There were also white flares [dropped by the German night fighters], helping them see us and partly destroying our night vision. On the ground there were big and small fires, green and/or red ground markers, smoke, haze and plenty of dust. The Germans put coloured ground marker decoys in outlying areas, but they never had the brightness of ours and with experience you were not fooled.

Returning home, the crew reported being able to see the glow of fires in Bochum some 150 miles from the target. Arthur landed the weary crew at 23.45 hours. The operation proved successful for Bomber Command, as of the 352 aircraft that left England only nine were lost and the Oboe-assisted Pathfinders marked the target accurately, resulting in concentrated and effective bombing. Josef Goebbels, the next day, commented in his diaries:

> During the night several hundred aeroplanes again flew over the Reich. This time the Ruhr was on the programme. Bochum especially was heavily attacked. Damage there was pretty substantial. Unfortunately the weather was such that our defence could not do much.[14]

---

[14] *The Goebbels Diaries, op.cit.,* p397.

No. 427 Squadron suffered no losses; seven of those aircraft detailed had bombed the target, and one returned early owing to a technical defect.

The squadron was not operational again until 3 October when 15 aircraft and crews, including Arthur's, were detailed for a raid against Kassel. Our crew once more received a change in personnel, once more at the navigator position. Flying Officer Constable stepped in to direct the aircraft across the enemy territory, an experienced crew member near completion of his tour. F/O Constable demonstrated his ability to the crew on the outward journey when he said over the intercom to the crew, 'A route marker should be being dropped to our side just about now.' Sure enough there it was. A reassuring sign for the crew for they had a man who knew what he was doing. The Form 541 report (a squadron's record of details of sorties or flights) given by the crew after the raid notes ' . . . considered to be good trip from a navigational standpoint'.

Halifax EB241 took off at 1827 hours with its bomb weight the same as the previous operation. This was our crew's third different aircraft in four operations. Fresh crews flew in what they were given, as they did not have enough experience to influence the allocation of aircraft. The target area was found to be cloudless and visibility good, which certainly helped Alex as the bombsight had become unserviceable. He had to rely on experience in making an educated guess for a release point, so that the bombload would come down on the centre of the red markers seen. The crew experienced their first close call with a flak shell exploding near to the aircraft. One splinter penetrated the mid upper blister, shot just past Trevor's shoulder and fell into the aircraft. Allan Burrell on the wireless operator's seat, was even more fortunate. The seat rested on a metal support consisting of two crossing metal bars and when a flak splinter penetrated the fuselage, it hit the metal support just where the metal bars crossed, thus saving Allan from a very uncomfortable experience. Whilst over the target one of the engines also became unserviceable, perhaps owing to the flak and Arthur had to bring the Halifax back on just the three engines. Halifax EB241 touched down at Leeming at 0121 hours.

This was a round trip of just under seven hours. These long flights tested the concentration of crews, in particular the gunners as they scanned the blackness for any hostile aircraft, throughout the flight. Boredom and lack of concentration no doubt cost many a crew their lives as a German night fighter crept up on them. Once back over British soil our crew would occasionally relax and Arthur sometimes allowed Allan to tune the radio to a civilian channel, dance music battling against the roar of the engines. Fortunately the Luftwaffe, at this stage of the war, had all but given up intruder operations in which they patrolled over airfields along the east of England, awaiting the unsuspecting bomber.

The aiming point at Kassel had not been marked accurately and most of the bombs fell on suburbs and outlying towns and villages. However fires were started at the Henschel and Fieseler aircraft factories and an ammunition dump at Ihringhausen was hit by chance attracting further bombs. Bomber Command sustained 24 losses on the night out of the 547 aircraft that took part in the raid.

One of the 427 Squadron Halifaxes piloted by Flight Lieutenant Laird, engaged an enemy aircraft at 20.10 hours as it crossed the enemy coast on the outward journey. The rear gunner, Pilot Officer Findlay and wireless operator Pilot Officer Rogerson were killed by the enemy cannon fire and the flight engineer, Sergeant Cardy critically wounded. As such, the aircraft was forced to return to base at which point the undercarriage was found to be locked up. The captain was instructed to abandon ship by radio transmission from base. However the pilot Flight Lieutenant Laird feared for the wounded Sergeant Cardy and did not believe his crew member would be able to survive a parachute jump. He argued the case with base and eventually persuaded them to let him make a landing attempt. Following successful attempts by the semi conscious Sergeant Cardy to get the undercarriage down the aircraft was successfully landed. The situation had been even more dangerous in view of the fact most of the bombs were still aboard. Flight Lieutenant Laird subsequently received the DFC and Sergeant Cardy received news of his CGM whilst still on the critically injured list. The navigator of this crew, Sergeant George Lorimer, survived physically unscathed, although emotionally he may have suffered, as he had been holding one of his fatally injured crewmates when he died from his wounds. We will be seeing more of George later.

All the other 427 Halifaxes managed to bomb the target and bar one injury to a navigator from flak all returned safely.

Twelve 427 Squadron aircraft were detailed for a raid to Frankfurt the next night, and the groundcrews were highly commended by the wing commander for their efforts in getting the bombers ready. Arthur and crew took off at 1728 hours in Halifax LK627, yet another change of aircraft, and after just over four hours' flying during which they encountered moderately heavy flak, they released their load of one 2,000lb HC bomb and 3,960lb of incendiaries. On the return flight the starboard engines became unserviceable and Arthur was forced to land the Halifax at Bruntingthorpe, Leicestershire.

The raid to Frankfurt proved to be the first serious blow to the city in the war with considerable damage to the eastern half of the city and the inland docks on the River Main. Bomber Command lost ten aircraft out of the 406 that took part in the raid, one of which was 427 Squadron's LK920 'J Johnny' piloted by Warrant Officer Champion, which crashed at 2230 hours at Haut-Fays in Luxembourg. All the crew were killed. All other 427 Squadron aircraft returned to England safely.

The next day Arthur and crew flew their Halifax from Bruntingthorpe back to Leeming and the crew did not become operational again until 22nd October.

Bomber Command was currently introducing another technical measure, 'Airborne Cigar (ABC)', in an attempt to try and outwit the German night fighter defences. Airborne Cigar aircraft were Lancasters carrying an extra German-speaking crew member whose responsibility it was to tune into enemy broadcasts. He could then jam these transmissions by broadcasting a disruptive signal on the same frequency. No. 101 Squadron was given the task of carrying the ABC equipment.

One of the pilots with 101 Squadron was Derrick Bell, who had joined up in August 1941 and done most of his training overseas in California, (we will be meeting him again later in this story.) On his return to England he eventually arrived at Ludford Magna, Lincolnshire, to fly on seven operations with this special squadron:

> We had the seven normal crew members and one more associated with the Airborne Cigar. We had a different person each time. The normal crew would go down to dispersal and it was here that the other crew member joined you, during the hour waiting before take-off. Immediately you landed he was taken away. At the time we never knew what he was doing.

Whilst Arthur's crew enjoyed time away from the rigours of operations other members of the squadron still performed operational duties. On 5 and 6 October 427 Squadron aircraft were detailed for operations, only for the raids to be scrubbed owing to the weather. On the 7th the squadron was on stand-down, but on the 8th ops were on. Eleven aircraft took off for a raid to Hanover, of which two returned early, and the aircraft of Sergeant Kelly was lost. He and his crew were all killed. The other eight aircraft bombed on the target in what was probably the most successful raid on the city in the war, but were forced to land at diversion bases in the south of England upon their return. The whole squadron then enjoyed a non-operational period, although there were other activities.

Our crew took part in a number of training duties including two air to sea firing runs (a gunner's exercise). During these quieter periods some crew members could broaden their flying training.

> *Alex Nethery:* While at Leeming I took about 30 hours flying training on the Link Trainer. Thus I could possibly steer fly our plane to England where we could all bale out. This was in the event of Arthur suffering injury or sickness. During practice time in England, Arthur let me do some flying. Once he had to go to the Elsan [Chemical toilet] at the rear of the aircraft. The rest of the crew did not care for this! I loved every minute I was at the controls, but the crew didn't think much of their second pilot.

Losses of crews were certainly prone to affect morale within squadrons, but when crews were not preparing for operations, many was the time that most would let their hair down and try to forget it all. The drinking exploits of Bomber Command crews has become legendary.

> *Alex Nethery:* There were a few airmen that went right around the bend and had to stop flying, while others were loners. But our crew did things together. We'd relieve the tension by going to the pubs and singing those dumb songs and drinking beer, and then we'd go staggering back to base on our bicycles. We had a lot of laughs.[15]

Certainly at 427 Squadron such behaviour was not frowned upon, and many liquid adventures receive mention in its official Operations Record Book. Indeed it contains many jocular entries, all mixed in with the more serious stories of operations, enemy air combats and missing crews, an obvious reflection of the 'take it as it comes, live life while you can' nature of operational life. Between 9 and 21 October the squadron did not take part in any operations and personnel at the base found alternative ways to occupy themselves.

> *11.10.43:* Ideal flying weather prevailed throughout the day but no kites were scheduled for operations. Personnel, removed to Skipton for the past few weeks while the runway was being repaired at Leeming, took advantage of the lull, to return to base. Notwithstanding, aircrews journeyed to nearby targets and proceeded to thoroughly drench themselves in fragrant English brews, leaving a wide area of devastation at all objectives that were pranged.
> *12.10.43:* The 'old sol' favoured the environs of Leeming with all its splendour, a further day of standown was declared. Personnel both aircrew and groundcrew alike found it difficult to concentrate at their respective duties as serenity reigned throughout the entire squadron and it was reported that it was actually possible to be heard once again . . .
> F/L Don Morrison, one of the veterans of the squadron and bomb leader since the formation, was toasted [at] a farewell party by his mess-mates [and] much to the displeasure of all who know him, he has been posted to Con. [Conversion] Unit at Dalton. The highlight of the brawl occurred when Knobby Clark was able to part S/L Earthrowl with a few of his 'shekels' towards the purchase of a 'down-the-hatch'. Knobby reports that when Earthrowl pulled out his bulging wallet in payment of this crowning achievement, last year's 'cobwebs' were still to be found amidst the masses of notes.

---

[15] Quoted in *Maximum Effort, op.cit.,* 1986, p23.

17.10.43: The periodic 'Flarepath', an occasion when all squadron tenderfeet officers are initiated, came off last night. During the course of the festivities, more uniforms were saturated with the brew, than was actually consumed. In the forefront came 'Chas the adj.', who in his own inimitable style showed the sprogs how simple it was to balance a mug of beer on the noggin while at the same time co-ordinating with mind, body, and battling against inebriation to proceed through a flarepath of beer glasses. What a man our adj.

20.10.43: A soccer match between the officers and NCOs aircrew took the limelight this afternoon during the operational lull. The NCOs overwhelmed the disorganised officers team to the tune of 10-2. The biggest laugh of the whole tussle occurred when OC [Officer Commanding] 'B' Flight, S/Ldr Ganderton, appearing in neatly pressed and pleated battledress, began voicing his qualifications and skill, at the game. Soon after the soliloquy a few short moments after the kick-off whistle had blown, he tripped and found himself neatly in the centre of a well formed oasis with the aforementioned dress covered from head to foot in mud and gleaming redness peering through his virtually black countenance.[16]

Sometimes, however, the alcoholic activities resulted in unfortunate incidents. The 427 Squadron Operations Records Book:

25.10.43: One of our Canadian armourers met with a rather unfortunate end after an escapade to the town local this evening . . . AC1 Olson, H.O., was picked up on the Great North Road just beyond the Willow Tree (the local), at Leeming, by the Morris Ambulance Crew of this station at 23.20 hours and brought to SSQ, [Station Sick Quarters] where he was examined immediately by the senior medical officer. Examination at the time of admission revealed a stuporous irrational individual. No signs of violence were apparent, and no skull fracture was found. The patient was placed in the crash ward under the supervision of the nursing orderly, and after oxygen was administered for a period of ten minutes, the patient was breathing normally. 03.00 hours the report from the nursing orderly would indicate that the patient was resting quietly and breathing in a sonorous manner. At 06.00 hours the duty nursing orderly found the patient dead. The cause of death is unknown; but it is supposed that there must have been a basalar fracture of the skull.[17]

Amidst all these episodes crews continued to apply themselves to the task of taking the war to Germany.

[16/17] No. 427 Squadron Operations Record Book, Public Record Office AIR 27 1845.

CHAPTER 5

'CORKSCREW PORT – NOW!'

On 22 October 1943 sixteen aircraft from 427 Squadron were detailed for operations against Kassel. Our crew left Leeming at 1725 hours in Halifax LK633, arriving over the target and dropping their one 2,000lb high capacity bomb and 4,080lb of incendiaries on a group of red TI at 2101 hours. The aircraft arrived back at Leeming at 0015 hours.

The squadron suffered this night. Six aircraft returned early: Halifax 'R' had an oxygen failure in the mid upper turret, resulting in the mid upper gunner passing out; Halifax 'V' abandoned the operation after three generators in the engines became unserviceable; Halifax 'Y's' port outer constant speed unit became unserviceable, the pilot abandoning the operation; Halifax 'K' crossed the enemy coast off track and came across accurate and intense heavy flak. The aircraft was holed 14 times, before the pilot threw the Halifax into evasive manoeuvres and managed to shake off the attention of the defences. The navigator was then unable to establish their position and after jettisoning their bombs somewhere over the Ruhr they returned to base. Halifax 'F' encountered intense heavy flak after crossing the enemy coast which vibrated the aircraft into a spiral dive. After losing 7,000 feet the pilot managed to get the aircraft under control at 12,000 feet. About 30 minutes had been lost and since they would not have arrived at the target with the rest of the main force, the pilot brought the aircraft straight home. Halifax 'E' DK182, piloted by Warrant Officer Welch, attempted to return to base early for some unknown reason, but it crashed near Marston Moor in Yorkshire and all the crew were instantly killed. A week previously the pilot had become a bridegroom. Our crew had flown this aircraft on the Bochum raid three weeks earlier.

Three crew failed to return: Flight Lieutenant Weston's crew in LK959, whose navigator Flying Officer Oakley had also married two weeks earlier, crashed at Ostiven, a hamlet near Achtmaal, Holland, and all the crew were killed. Pilot Officer Harrison's Halifax crashed at Harzberg. The pilot and two of his crew were killed, the other four men becoming POWs. The third was Flight Sergeant Minter's Halifax, DK234, which crashed near Düsseldorf; none of the crew survived.

There is an anomaly concerning the records of the above aircraft numbers. In the squadron Operations Records Book, Arthur and crew are down as flying in Halifax LK633 on this raid. However, W R Chorley in *RAF Bomber Command Losses* 1943 lists the Halifax of Pilot Officer Harrison as LK633. It is more than likely that Mr Chorley's sources are accurate as clerks in charge of Operation Records Books (ORBs) were not infallible. Indeed all the 427 Squadron operations in the ORBs in which our crew were involved name Trevor as the rear gunner and the other gunner as mid upper gunner. We know this was not the case. For the rest of this story I have had to take the ORBs as the source for the aircraft numbers that our crew flew in. They may well be correct but should not be relied upon. For losses on raids I have used W.R. Chorley's more reliable *RAF Bomber Command Losses* series.

On the same night as the Kassel raid Squadron Leader Earthrowl, the 'A' Flight Commander, completed his 20th trip and second tour of operations (a first tour consisted of 30 operations). The screening from operations of this well respected leader along with the casualties mentioned cast an air of gloom over the squadron.

In total Bomber Command lost 43 aircraft out of the 569 sent on the Kassel raid. However the operation proved successful with accurate Pathfinder marking. A firestorm resulted and areas of the city were devastated, including serious damage to the Henschel aircraft factories which were involved in the production of V-1 flying bombs at the time. Goebbels commented on the raid in his diaries:

> *November 2, 1943:* A report from Kassel describes conditions in that city as pretty desolate. Weinrich [Gauleiter of Hessen] has in no way proved equal to the demands made on him by the recent air raid. The number of people killed is at present estimated at 5,000; it may even increase to 6,000.
> *November 6, 1943:* I arrived at Kassel early in the morning . . . Prince Waldeck [SS Obergruppenführer (General) in charge of Fulda-Werra sector of the Kassel area] accompanied me during my trip through the damaged areas of Kassel.
> The impression is devastating. The entire centre of the city and most of the outlying sections have been destroyed. It is a gruesome picture. Destruction here can be compared only with that in Hamburg. A catastrophic fire of vast extent ran its course unhindered.[18]

The day after this raid 427 Squadron was on stand-down, allowing it the opportunity to recuperate from the previous night's losses. News reached the squadron that Flight Lieutenant Laird was to receive his DFC and his flight engineer Sergeant Cardy his CGM from their exploits on the raid of 3 October. The squadron celebrated:

---

[18] *The Goebbels Diaries, op.cit.,* p400,403.

In one of the rowdiest mess whirls that has ever been experienced by an officer, either living or dead, members of the mess met last night to celebrate F/L Laird's award which also coincided with S/L Earthrowl's screening. During the course of the drenching, our Wingco was instituted in the Royal Order of Leos as the 'Grand Lion', and was duly initiated under the revised policy in said Order, whereby all potential Lions are required to (in official terms) osculate the rectum of Leo, the M.G.M. presentation. F/L Reilly, the station adjutant was permitted into the sacred order after going through the usual channels and has now become an Hon. member.[19]

It was not until 3 November that the squadron returned to ops, with thirteen aircraft detailed to take part in a raid to Düsseldorf, Arthur and crew were not one of them. All bombed the target in a relatively successful raid. Eighteen aircraft were lost out of the 589 on a raid that inflicted considerable damage to housing and industrial premises. Three of the 427 Squadron crews enjoyed the companionship of an enemy fighter for a brief period, but none of them sustained any damage. All bar one returned to a fog-shrouded base safely; the exception being aircraft 'Q' landing at Church Fenton owing to unserviceability of the constant speed unit.

On this day our crew had been on a rather different official ceremony. A few weeks earlier the squadron received a letter signed by Winston Churchill, in response to their request to adopt one of the Prime Minister's lions at Regent Zoo.

I was very pleased to hear on my return to this country that the Lion Squadron of the Royal Canadian Air Force had made the suggestion that the squadron should adopt 'Mareth' one of the lion cubs at the zoo.
With every good wish for the success of your squadron
Yours very faithfully,
(Sgd) Winston Churchill[20]

On 3 November squadron personnel who were on leave in London were present at the adoption ceremony in London Zoo. Adjutant Flight Lieutenant Chasanoff and Wing Commander Turnbull made speeches to the gathered civilians and servicemen, and the Wingco went even further.

Allan Burrell: All the crew went to London Zoo and gathered around the cage. The Wing Commander got in the cage with the senior keeper. The Lion cub attacked the Wing

---

[19/20] No. 427 Squadron Operations Record Book, Public Record Office AIR 27 1845.

Commander and he bolted out of the cage, much to the hilarity
of those watching.

The squadron then again enjoyed a non-operational period but on 11
November five aircraft were detailed for a specialist raid, in the full moon,
to the furthest target the squadron had yet undertaken, the marshalling
yards at Cannes in southern France. The squadron called upon its most
experienced crews for the raid. All the crews returned safely after bombing
the target and their reports suggested a very successful raid. However, the
railway yards were not in fact hit and the railway workshops suffered only
blast damage. Most of the bombing actually fell in the working class suburb
of La Bocca and there were civilian casualties, something German
propagandists used to their advantage. Four aircraft were lost on the raid
out of the 134 that took part.

For the next week the squadron avoided operational duties but on 18
November 1943 ops were back on.

Early in the war, German defensive techniques involved the use of anti-
aircraft guns and searchlights over specific areas, with night fighters flying
to operational areas and attempting to locate and engage the bombers
visually. In most cases, without the help of radar, night fighter contact with
the enemy bomber was a case of luck. So the obvious conclusion was
made, if the night fighters were unable to find the bomber due to the
darkness, they had to be illuminated.

Major-General Josef Kammhuber, 'General of the Night-Fighters'
established a long line of searchlights and sound detectors, exclusive of flak
defences, behind the North Sea coastline from Norway down to France.
Individual night fighters were allocated a sector within the searchlight line,
enabling them to engage the bombers without anti-aircraft interference.
However this method of interception was far from ideal as many bombers
were able to penetrate and exit the searchlight screen, before the fighters
could react.

Kammhuber further enhanced the defences by establishing an integrated
chain of radar boxes, 'Himmelbett' zones, in which the night fighters would
patrol and their movements aided by ground stations. 'Funkhorchdienst'
enabled German operators to listen in on Allied bombers' R/T
communication whilst still on the ground in England and hence warn of an
impending bomber force attack. Then each box had 'Freya' radar supplying
early warning of the bombers as it detected the general direction of the
attack, therefore alerting searchlight and flak operators and scrambling
fighters. Subsequently 'Würzburg' radar, a more local detection device,
plotted the direction, range and altitude of the bomber, with another
'Würzburg' plotting the night fighter. The information from the radar was
plotted on a 'Seeburg' evaluation table, on which green and red dots
appeared representing the bomber and the night fighter and their relative

positions. The controller on the ground was able to direct the night fighter by radio-telephone to the proximity of the bomber, where it was hoped supporting searchlights would illuminate it. As the bomber left one defended zone it would enter another, but if a fighter had not picked up a bomber visually by the time it reached the end of its box, the pursuit had to break off.

On 9 August 1941 the capabilities of the fighters were further enhanced with the introduction of airborne radar, 'Lichtenstein'; the aircraft was still guided by the ground radar until the night fighter had picked up the bomber on its own radar. If the fighter made radar contact with the bomber before it reached the boundary of its zone it could now continue the pursuit.

The main German night fighter used in the defence of the Reich during this period was the twin-engined Messerschmitt Bf 110. It had the ability to close on an RAF bomber and was relatively well armed: the Bf 110G had two 30 mm cannon, two 20 mm cannon at the front and twin 7.9 mm machine guns at the rear of the cockpit. With the technological war expanding during the night bombing campaign, it had enough space to take on board any new equipment. The aircraft initially had a crew of two, the pilot and a gunner, doubling as a radio operator and providing help with the difficulties of night navigation. When the first variant of the aircraft was produced, specifically for night fighting, space was made for a third crew member to operate the on board radar.

In addition, the twin-engined Junkers Ju 88 was adapted from being a high speed bomber to fulfil night duties. The Ju 88C's armament consisted of three 20 mm cannon, three 7.9 mm machine guns at the front and one 13 mm machine gun at the rear of the cockpit. There were also the twin-engined Dornier variants, in particular the Do 217J, but owing to poor performance it was phased out in 1943.

In the autumn of 1943 an extremely deadly addition was installed on the German night fighters. 'Schrage Musik' (or jazz music) was a pair of upward-firing cannon, placed just behind the pilot's canopy. The night fighter pilot used this weapon by bringing his aircraft beneath the bomber using the darkness of the ground to hide his position from a searching gunner's eyes. With the bomber silhouetted against the brighter night sky, the cannon were fired without tracer, in order not to give their position away. Aiming at the main fuel tanks in the wings was the preferred target, which would inflict a mortal wound on the bomber, as opposed to firing into a fuselage that might contain bombs and bring down the night fighter with the subsequent explosion and scattering of debris. These attacks were deadly. Bomber crews were usually completely unaware they were under attack before their aircraft were fatally struck. Indeed it was not until after the war that the RAF became aware of the 'Schrage Musik'.

As a result of German defensive enhancements the rate of bomber losses increased and Bomber Command began to question its operational flight patterns. What if the bombers stopped entering the defensive system individually and started coming in formations that only crossed a few of the Himmelbett zones? When Arthur Harris began his mass bombing campaigns these limitations were exposed; the zones manned by single fighters were now penetrated by waves of bombers. The Germans attempted to counter this by extending the belt of zones and new ground control methods were developed, enabling two and then three fighters to patrol simultaneously. But events, once more, were to overtake the programme of changes.

As stated previously, the Bomber Command attacks on Hamburg on 24 July 1943 and the use of Window rendered the radar-controlled box system virtually useless. Window resulted in false echoes displayed on German Freya, Würzburg and airborne radar. As such it was impossible for any ground control of fighters' movements. German defences, for a time, became totally ineffective relying once more on visual contact. But despite the initial shock of the loss of radar, the German defences were able to respond quickly.

Just prior to the events over Hamburg a new defence tactic was being developed. 'Wilde Sau' (Wild Boar) involved single-engined fighters, with no radar ground control support. They would assemble at radio beacons located all over Germany and once the target for the bombers had been identified they would engage the bombers over or near targets. Flares, searchlights, and the glow of the fires below, would provide the fighters with their means of locating the bombers. Searchlights would even be used should the target be cloud-covered, with the lightened cloud base providing a backdrop to silhouette bombers to higher flying fighters. The Wild Boar fighters, flying in single-engined Messerschmitt Bf 109s and Focke-Wulf 190As, would operate above flak defences, and it became a test of courage for a fighter pilot to follow a bomber once it entered the flak area. Once the Hamburg raids begun with Window used, Wild Boar was seen to be the best means of defending targets. Twin-engined fighters were also directed to become involved in Wild Boar operations.

This new development involved considerable changes for crews of the German night fighters. What had previously been engagements close to their airfield controlled from the ground, now involved considerable flying distances to locate the bombers, and then visual combat over a burning city, sometimes with flak and ground commentaries that were often confused or jammed. Until an effective counter to Window was found, Wild Boar would be severely tested in the months following the Hamburg raids. Some of the more experienced night fighter crews decided to avoid the battles over cities and elected to seek out bombers on their route to and from the target. This was the forerunner to a new tactic 'Zahme Sau' (Tame Boar).

The position and direction of the bomber stream was still monitored by radar and also 'Korfu' receivers were introduced which picked up the radar transmissions of Bomber Command. The radar controllers adapted, no longer looking just for the aircraft but for the Window image as well, and hence the direction of the bomber stream. Also, some Junkers 88s were used for reconnaissance, locating and flying alongside the bomber stream, and relaying positional information back to a ground controller. Other Junkers 88s, which had located the bomber stream, were used to illuminate the night sky around the bombers, dropping flares, attracting comrades. The ground controller could use all this information and, via a running radio commentary, direct his Tame Boar night fighters into the predicted bomber route. The Lichtenstein radar was modified owing to the interference of Window; Lichtenstein SN-2, an interference-secure airborne interception radar, was first fitted to a Bf 110 and tested in September 1943. Over the next months it was slowly introduced to the aircraft of the night fighter force.

In February 1943 the Germans got hold of a slightly damaged H2S set. Soon they had developed 'Naxos', a device that could pick up and home in on H2S transmissions, which came into use in early 1944. A device by the name of 'Flensburg' was developed which operated by homing in on a bomber's Monica transmissions. There was also 'Freya Halbe', enabling the operator to home in on an aircraft using Mandrel. All these homing aids proved invaluable to Tame Boar operations.

There were, however, problems from the longer flights including navigational problems and the need to land sometimes at unfamiliar bases. Bomber Command, as it recognised the German change in defensive strategy, attempted to confound the German controllers' task by further changing its tactics. Diversionary 'spoof' raids were carried out, there were various course changes on route to the target and attempts made at the radio jamming of the running commentary. In the autumn of 1943 the air offensive against Germany, and the electronic counter-measures involved, entered its tactically most interesting period, as each air force vied for that crucial advantage.

On 18 November 1943 14 aircraft from 427 Squadron were detailed for a major raid on the Farben Chemical works at Mannheim. Bomber Command had visited the city the previous night with a force of 83 aircraft, and was now to send another 395 aircraft. At the same time Bomber Command sent a force of Lancasters and Mosquitos to Berlin, Mosquitos to Essen, Frankfurt and Aachen, Wellingtons minelaying off the Dutch coast and the French Atlantic ports respectively, and Wellingtons with a small force of US Fortresses dispersed leaflets over northern France.

Crew:	Captain	Sgt Darlow, A.E.
	Navigator	Flying Officer W
	Bomb aimer	Sgt Nethery, A.
	Wireless operator	Sgt Burrell, A.W.
	Rear gunner	Sgt Copeland, D.
	Mid upper gunner	Sgt Utton, T.E.
	Flight engineer	Sgt Richards, P.W.

| *Aircraft Type and Number:* | | Halifax V   LK972 |

Bomb Load:	1 x 2000lb H.C.N.I.
	750 x 4lb Inc.
	32 x 30lb Inc.
	60 x 4lb 'X' type Inc.
Total:	**6,200lb**

Zero hour for the raid was 2030 hours.

Navigation: The outward route for the 427 Squadron aircraft took them from base to Beachy Head and across to Cayeux, then across the north of France into Germany before turning at a point marked by yellow TI of the Pathfinders toward Mannheim. After bombing the city the aircraft were then to return across the north of France, looking out for some Pathfinder red spot fires near Saarbrucken, then eventually back to Beachy Head and subsequently base.

Window was to be dropped at the rate of one bundle every two minutes to a point 20 miles from the target; one bundle every half-minute within 20 miles of the target in both directions; and one bundle every minute for the rest of the homeward route.

Pathfinders

Time over target	*Aircraft type*	*Marking Method*
z – 6	18 Blind Markers	The Blind Markers flares to use their H2S and drop yellow TI on the aiming point, each at the same time releasing a string of flares: the first bundle 20 seconds before the TI, and the rest at 10 second intervals.
z – 6	25 Supporters	Supporters to bomb on H2S if possible, otherwise at centre of yellows or at visually identified ground detail.
z – 4	6 Visual Markers	The Visual Markers, guided by the yellows, to mark the exact aiming point with reds, provided they were certain of their position, dropping white flares if necessary. If unable to identify the aiming point visually, to retain their reds and aim greens at the centre of all visible yellows, with a 1 second overshoot.

z – 1 to z	4 Backers-up (2 p/min)	Backers-up to aim greens at
z + 1 to z + 4	4 Backers-up (1 p/min)	reds early in the attack; later,
z + 5	2 Backers-up	at the centre of greens with a
z + 6 to z + 10	5 Backers-up (1 p/min)	one second overshoot (If no
		reds were visible in the early
		stages, to aim at the centre of
		yellows with a 1 second
		overshoot).

Main Force

Time over target	*Aircraft numbers*	*Bombing Method*
z to z + 4	126 Stirlings	Instructions to the main force
z + 4 to z + 8	105 Halifaxes and	bombers involved aiming at
	7 Lancasters	reds or the centre of the
z + 8 to z + 12	105 Halifaxes and	greens.
	6 Lancasters	

Halifax LK972 piloted by Arthur Darlow, took off from Leeming at 1630 hours. The crew's original navigator, the instructor, returned to the crew. For the initial phases of the operation Gee fixes were taken, but eventually, because of jamming, navigation relied upon dead reckoning. There should have been little problem getting to Mannheim owing to the size of the target and the activity of the anti-aircraft guns and searchlights.

Just before bombing time, Arthur called Alex over the intercom: 'Get ready to drop the bombs because you only have a few minutes to go.' Alex went to the nose of the Halifax, got the bombsight going and checked everything over. With one minute to go Arthur, expecting to be in the bomber stream and over the target, opened the bomb doors.

> The attack opened on time with 5 salvoes of yellows dropped by the blind-markers; these fell 2 to 4 miles N-NE of the aiming point, apart from one 3½ miles S-SE. They were backed-up by a solitary green salvo dropped approximately 2½ miles NE which was bombed by some 50 of the 81 main force aircraft attacking during the first 10 minutes. A compact area of fires resulted, measuring 2 x 2½ square miles and centred 3 miles E-NE of the aiming point; this was mostly wasted in open country, but covered the NE corner of the built up area. After zero +5, 8 further salvoes of green were dropped, 6 of which seem to have fallen in the main area. The other 2 landed in woods 4 miles N of this concentration, but attracted very little bombing. The attack remained fairly well concentrated, although tending to drift away to the E-NE where decoys N of the Wallstadt fire site deceived a number of crews who claimed to have bombed on reds.[21]

---

[21] Bomber Command Narrative of Attack, Public Record Office AIR 24 261.

This narrative quite clearly describes area bombing. Despite use of words such as 'compact area' and 'concentrated', the measure used is always in miles or half miles. Not exactly precision bombing but nevertheless accurate considering the equipment and circumstances of the raid.

However our crew missed the spectacle of the colourful TI; Alex peering through the nose blister of the Halifax couldn't see anything below. Nothing. No searchlights, ground markers, flak, fire or anything. Just darkness. Alex looked ahead and then back underneath the plane to see if they had overshot the target, but nothing.

Arthur picked up the intercom, 'Does anybody know where we are?' There had been no navigational problems reported. 'We're completely lost.'

Don from the rear turret picked out in the distance some flares, searchlights and fires and called out over the intercom, 'Skipper I think I see the target. It's behind us and off about twenty-five degrees. It's about a hundred miles behind us.'

The fact that they had returned from their first mission without dropping their bombs was at the forefront of the debate that followed. They decided to proceed and drop the bombs on the target this time. Arthur said to the navigator 'Don't bother giving me a course, I'll just head straight for the fires. Get ready to give me a course to get home.'

> *Alex Nethery:* Very foolish of us to carry on with that raid because nobody in their right senses, in one four engined bomber, would attack a heavily armed city. We did it anyway.

The aircraft arrived at the target a good twenty minutes late to find itself the only bomber in the sky; everyone else had already dropped their bombs and gone home. It was a clear night but smoke haze affected visibility.

Alex yelled to Arthur, 'I can't see anything but fires and smoke! What should I do?'

'Well what do you think?' Arthur replied.

'I guess I'll just aim for the biggest concentration of fires and let the bombs go.'

At 2058 hours the bombs were released but no sooner had the bomb doors closed than the Halifax was caught by searchlights. Out of the bomber stream, the protective Window screen and safety in numbers, Halifax LK972 could best be described as the proverbial sitting duck. Pretty soon they were coned by what seemed like every searchlight over the city. Once the master blue searchlight (generally radar-guided) picked up the aircraft, others soon swung round intensifying the cone. The Halifax was isolated in the night sky, a visible target to receive the full attention of the city's flak batteries and any night fighters still prowling in the area. Inside the Halifax, anyone peering out quickly shielded their night-accustomed eyes against the intensity of the searchlight cone. Artificial light streamed through gaps in the fuselage illuminating the inside of the aircraft as if it were day. Then came the chaos of the anti-aircraft guns firing up the searchlight beams. Each shell exploding near the aircraft resulted in rocking and shaking. Was the next one going to be a direct hit and oblivion?

The solitary illuminated Halifax also became visible to others in the night sky. The German night fighters seized their opportunity. The Bomber Command combat report read:

> While on the outward journey from the target of Mannheim (Ludwigshaven) on the night of November 18th, 1943, Halifax 'F', Serial No. LK 972 of 427 Squadron was attacked by two enemy fighters at a position 4920 N – 0825E, at 2100 hours, flying at 240 m.p.h. TAS, on a course 225 degrees M. at 18,000 feet altitude.[22]

Trevor, from the mid upper turret, sighted a stream of tracer coming from the port bow above the aircraft. Subsequently a Messerschmitt 109, no doubt Wilde Sau, came down on the bomber silhouetted against the burning city, at 400 yards' range, and Trevor immediately opened fire, shouting into the intercom 'corkscrew port – *now*'.

Arthur took the aircraft into its combat manoeuvre with a diving turn to port and threw the aircraft in stomach-churning twists and turns around the sky, steeply banking, dropping for a thousand feet then steeply climbing before repeating the move. The Me 109 broke off the attack on the starboard beam down and the enemy was lost to view. Trevor had seen his tracer tear into the fighter. Arthur had just resumed course when Don, from the rear turret, sighted a Dornier 217, again probably Wilde Sau, attacking from the port quarter up, at a range of 400 yards. 'Corkscrew port – now' resounded in Arthur's ears, and again the churning combat manoeuvre was adopted. Don and Trevor, along with the night fighter pilot, opened fire simultaneously from 350 yards' range. The Dornier broke off the attack on the starboard quarter at 100 yards. Both Don and Trevor saw their tracer strike the fighter. Arthur checked with his crewmates for any injuries or damage to the aircraft, but so far they had survived unscathed.

> *Alex Nethery:* After the fighter attack we were still coned by searchlights and Arthur was twisting and turning the aircraft in a vain attempt to escape from them. We finally realised our only hope was to dive and get out of range, which he promptly did. We went screaming down, at least 300 mph, for low level, and we got out of range, finally, of the searchlights. Now we were alone on the way home to England at quite a low level. There was a little discussion, not much, about climbing back

---

[22] Public Record Office AIR 50 256.

up for safety and to go home in a normal manner. However we obviously were somewhat low on gasoline because we were already 20 minutes late to the target to start with. Also it was evident that the fuel consumption was much better at lower flying levels because of the oxygen situation and the cost in gas to climb back up. The final factor was German radar. If you stayed down below the German radar, at 500 feet, it was not possible for them to pick you up.

So the remainder of our crew's flight was at low level, on their own, over 200 miles of enemy territory. Tension must have been high. The gunners still high on adrenaline, on high alert, searching the darkness outside for any movement.

> *Alex Nethery:* I think that secretly Arthur was more than pleased, because it gave him a chance to do some low level flying. It was exhilarating and dangerous and I pretty well knew Arthur was loving it. Occasionally a lonely gun or two would fire at us as we went over a town or city, but Arthur had given Don, the rear gunner, permission to fire back which he did with great enthusiasm and duly shut down any ground fire that was coming at us.

Eventually the aircraft crossed over the Channel and the crew could relax a little. They finally landed safely at Leeming at 0050 hours where the crew left the plane by wading through the empty .303 casings. The official combat report stated that in the few minutes of combat Trevor and Don had fired off about 1000 rounds.

Two aircraft from the squadron had returned early, both with engine trouble. Pilot Officer Kennedy's Halifax LK976 failed to return. None of the crew survived and the aircraft was believed to have crashed in the English Channel. The body of only one member of the crew was found.

Bomber Command lost 23 aircraft out of the 395 sent on the raid and attributed most of the losses to fighter activity. Three bombers were seen to go down in combat over the target, six on the way out and one on the way home. Three were destroyed by the target guns, two more at Chalons-sur-Marne and north-west of Trier. Reports were received that two aircraft may have collided over the target. The cause of the other six losses could not be determined by Bomber Command.

In total, 36 night fighter interceptions were reported on the Mannheim raid, against only 16 on the Berlin raid of the same night. The weather hampered the night fighter activity on the Berlin raid, many being ordered to land before the attack because of fog. Only nine Lancasters were lost out of the 440 Lancasters and 4 Mosquitos that took part in the Berlin raid. However the German running commentators, controlling the night fighters, had identified both main targets well before the attacks commenced, resulting in considerable losses to the Mannheim bomber force.

Photographs taken on 29 November by Bomber Command reconnaissance revealed scattered damage caused by the two consecutive raids to Mannheim. Most occurred in the north of the city, but there was considerable destruction to some industrial buildings. Bomber Command recorded new damage in I.G. Farbenindustrie, severe damage at the Daimler Benz engineering works, damage to the priority F.A. Neidig Sohne Industrie Hafen. Heinrich Lanz AG (AFVs and tank components), Boehringer GmbH (quinine refineries) and eight industrial and five commercial premises were also affected.

All our crew, who were sergeants, bar the navigator, a flying officer, got together on the day after the raid, and decided that they would refuse to fly with the navigator any more because, as Alex Nethery states, 'we were beginning to think we weren't going to last much longer if he stayed.' This was only their seventh operational flight together and twice they had gone off track, twice putting them in real danger. Arthur approached the CO asking him directly, to change their navigator. The CO refused what was undoubtedly an unprecedented request, so Arthur asked if all the other crew members could be brought into the room. The CO allowed them in and they all stood in front of him pointing out their solidarity. The CO had no real choice and an investigation was called, resulting in their receiving a new navigator. It was not an easy thing for the crew to do. They all felt the navigator was a nice enough fellow, but his navigating skills left a little to be desired. However our crew now became one of the least popular crews with squadron authority, which may have had a bearing on later events.

During the investigation, our crew was one of twelve detailed for a raid that night to Leverkusen. There had been no time to make any immediate crew changes and so all seven remained together. Halifax DK186, our crews' eighth different aircraft, took off from Leeming at 16.25 hours, with a bombload of one 2,000lb HCNI and 4,200lb of various types of incendiaries. After an uneventful outward flight the crew arrived at a completely cloud covered target. Owing to an equipment failure preventing Pathfinder Oboe marking, Alex found the expected green flares scattered over a large area and he had to bomb on ETA at 1922 hours from 20,000 feet. The crew experienced intense flak over the target and the Halifax was hit by splinters in a number of places. None of the damage proved critical and Arthur brought the crew home, landing at base at 23.25 hours. Two of the 427 Squadron Halifaxes had returned early or 'boomeranged' as the squadron records book put it, one owing to the unserviceability of the rear guns and starboard inner engine failure, and the other to failure of all electrically controlled instruments and the cutting out of the port inner engine. All other aircraft from the squadron bombed the target and returned to base, many of them flak ridden.

The damage caused to the target was very poor indeed. The Oboe-marking failure compounded by the bad weather resulted in scattered bombing, and only one high explosive bomb is recorded as having fallen in the town itself. Only four out of 266 Bomber Command aircraft were lost on the raid, a result of the poor weather hindering the night fighter operations. But Bomber Command aircraft suffered at the hands of the weather on the return to England and three aircraft crashed. On this night four Halifaxes from 35 Squadron made the first use of FIDO, fog dispersal equipment, when landing at Graveley airfield. This involved oil burners placed at the sides of the runway, and following on from its initial success its use became widespread at other airfields in the following months.

On the next two nights 427 Squadron enjoyed a rest from operations, but on 22 November our crew were one of those detailed to attack Berlin.

CHAPTER 6

THE BIG CITY

On the night of 24/25 August 1940, German bombers on raids in England had, whilst returning home, jettisoned their load over London. On the following night of 25/26 August, Bomber Command sent a retaliatory 103 aircraft on the first raid of the war to Berlin. The raid proved ineffectual with regard to damage, but the point was made: bombers had been in the sky over the German capital. In the following months Berlin continued to be regularly targeted, but it soon became obvious that very little damage if any was being inflicted upon the heart of Germany.

At the end of 1940 the Secretary of State for Air, Sir Archibald Sinclair, received information regarding the bombing of Berlin from Captain Schrader, the US naval attaché in the German capital. Schrader commented on the lack of success, saying that there had been no damage of the slightest importance until the raid on 15/16 December when Tauenzien Strasse was badly damaged. He did point out, however, that the raid shook the morale of the population.

On 17/18 April 1941 Bomber Command sent 118 aircraft to the German capital (eight aircraft lost). Bombing was not concentrated but a report eventually reached the Air Ministry concerning the impact of the raid on the civilian population of the city. The wife of the consul of the American Embassy in Stockholm was staying at the Hotel Adlon in Berlin at the time and she had 'never seen such panic as existed among the civil population. There was complete chaos and disorganisation and a repetition of panic conditions as then existed seemed to her to lead to the most serious influence on morale. More attacks of this nature would help materially in shortening the war.'

In mid to late 1941 as Bomber Command began to concentrate its attack on the morale of the civilian population in Germany, Berlin was overlooked in favour of nearer and hence easier targets, although no targets were easy. A few raids on the capital did take place with limited success. On the night of 7/8 November 1941 Bomber Command dispatched 169 aircraft on the perilous long journey above occupied Europe to Berlin, of which only 73 reached the city. The bombing was scattered with very little damage and 21 aircraft were lost, an unacceptable 12.4 per cent. Bomber Command, at that time, did not have the means or weaponry to penetrate and inflict a serious blow deep into Germany. This proved to be the last major raid to the city for some time.

On 17 August 1942 the Air Ministry received a cypher telegram from Winston Churchill who was meeting Stalin in the Kremlin, Moscow. 'Stalin attaches special importance to bombing Berlin and is going to start himself soon. Should be glad if we also struck hard as soon as darkness permits.' Stalin's obvious motive was to draw German resources from the Russian front to the defence of the German capital.

The next day the Air Ministry, Chief of the Air Staff Sir Charles Portal, and Arthur Harris, responded saying that in the next moon period they could only send 250 aircraft and might have to draw on the operational training units; in view of the strength of the enemy defences there might be heavy casualties in the most experienced crews. They considered that 500 would need to be the minimum number of aircraft they could send, to be effective, and to have acceptable casualties. They proposed a delay until a larger force became available.

Churchill found this unacceptable and the next day he sent a further cypher arguing that 250 aircraft far exceeded the weight and number of any previous attacks. He did appear to agree that there might be unacceptable losses, and asked whether 500 might be available by September.

Deputy Chief of the Air Staff Sir Norman Bottomley pursued the matter further with Harris, and they concluded that only 300 serviceable aircraft could be ready by then. They would not use the OTUs but could draw on the conversion units increasing the number to 350. They also concluded that they could not say when 500 might be available. Harris warned that on an operation of this nature they might lose between 50 and 100 aircraft, an amount Bomber Command could ill afford.

The issues were put to Churchill, and a recommendation made that they should wait until a larger force became available. Despite Churchill's keenness to attack Berlin he accepted the need for a 300-400 aircraft operation, which could not be achieved until the end of 1942 or early 1943.

On the nights of 16/17 and 17/18 January 1943 the city was once more targeted by major forces of 201 and 187 Bomber Command aircraft respectively. These aircraft numbers were well below the numbers previously talked about, because the vast majority of aircraft used on these raids were Lancasters, which had the capability of delivering a more substantial bombload than the Halifaxes, Wellingtons and Stirlings. Both raids proved unsuccessful in terms of bomb damage at a total cost of 23 aircraft and crews.

By the end of January 1943 the war situation for the German forces in Russia became critical. At Stalingrad the German Sixth Army suffered enormous losses and was forced to surrender. The effect on the German Army and Luftwaffe was immense, the myth of invincibility shattered. On 16 February Bomber Command received a prompting from the Air Ministry for a further attack to capitalise on the situation in the theatre of war as a whole.

> Recent events on the Russian Front have made it most
> desirable in the opinion of the cabinet that we should rub in
> the Russian victory by further attacks on Berlin as soon as
> conditions are favourable. The CAS wishes you to act
> accordingly.

On the night of 1/2 March 302 aircraft, over half of which were Lancasters,
were dispatched to Berlin in a raid that caused more damage to the city than
any other previous raid in the war, mainly due to the number of aircraft
taking part and the greater bombload. Bomber Command suffered 17 losses
that night. Churchill sent a telegram to Stalin that 700 tons had been
dropped on the city. Stalin replied:

> I welcome the British Air Force, which yesterday bombed so
> successfully Berlin. I regret that the Soviet Air Force absorbed
> in the struggle against the Germans at the front is not yet in a
> position to take part in the bombing of Berlin.

Following two unsuccessful raids at the end of March by 396 (9 losses) and
329 (21 losses) aircraft respectively, Berlin received a respite from attack
whilst Bomber Command turned its attention to the Battle of the Ruhr and
the Battle of Hamburg.

On 19 August 1943 Portal sent a cypher telegram from the 'Quadrant'
conference in Quebec to the Vice Chief of the Air Staff, Air Vice Marshal
Sir Douglas Evill asking when attacks on Berlin could resume, prompted
no doubt by the success of the Hamburg raids. On 21 August he received a
reply, Harris would start the attacks when the present moon period waned
and a total of 40,000 tons would be required if the Hamburg scale of attack
was to be applied. The operations would require a prolonged period since
it would be necessary to shift attacks intermittently to other targets,
preventing the undue concentration of enemy defences at the German
capital.[23] Harris's 'Battle of Berlin' was to begin and he had a stirring
message for his Commands' aircrews. 'Tonight you go to the big city. You
have the opportunity to light a fire in the belly of the enemy and burn his
black heart out.'

Harris opened with a series of three raids between 23 August and 4
September, involving a total of 1669 aircraft. These proved unsuccessful
with poor concentration of bombing and losses totalling 125 aircraft, an
unacceptable loss rate of 7.5 per cent. In the next two months Bomber
Command attacked targets less well defended, but on the night of 18/19

---

[23] Major source on the development of attacking Berlin comes from the Public Record
Office file AIR 8/435.

November 1943 the battle began in earnest when 440 Lancasters and four Mosquitos ventured out to a Berlin covered by cloud. Bomber Command were unable to get information on the effectiveness of the raid, but they were encouraged by the low loss rate of nine Lancasters, only 2 per cent. A few days later Harris prepared what was to be the largest raid to Berlin to date.

On 22 November orders were received at Leeming for 427 Squadron to prepare for a raid to Berlin. Fourteen aircraft and crews were detailed, including LK644 piloted by Arthur Darlow. This was to be the crew's first trip to the 'Big City'.

> *Alex Nethery:* If there was one dreaded target that we hated to hear as our objective, it was Berlin! Goering once said that no Allied bomber would ever reach Berlin, and he pulled a lot of fighter squadrons and guns from other parts of Germany to defend the German capital. In addition to the heavy defenses, this was a long trip – seven or eight hours – and practically every fighter station in Germany got a whack at you going over as well as coming back.[24]

Crew:	Captain	Sgt Darlow, A.E.
	Navigator	F/O Constable, F.S.
	Bomb aimer	Sgt Nethery, A.
	Wireless operator	Sgt Burrell, A.W.
	Rear gunner	Sgt Copeland, D.
	Mid upper gunner	Sgt Utton, T.E.
	Flight engineer	Sgt Richards, P.W.

Aircraft Type and Number: Halifax V   LK644

Time up: 1700 hours   *Time down:*   0010 hours
Bomb load: 1 x 2000lb HCNI
               840 x 4lb Inc.
               24 x 30lb Inc.
               60 x 4lb 'X' type Inc.
               Nickels
Total: **6,320lb**

Zero hour for the raid was 2000 hours.

Navigation: Bad weather was anticipated over enemy territory and it was expected that the Germans would keep most of their night fighters on the ground. As such, a scheduled route for the bomber stream was devised, almost directly to the target. Route marking using green TIs would take place on the way out, 35 miles at 326 degrees from Brunswick and on the

---

[24] Quoted in *Maximum Effort, op.cit.,* p43.

way home, 9 miles at 211 degrees from Brandenburg and 30 miles at 320 degrees from Brunswick.

Window was to be dropped at the rate of one bundle per minute to a point 30 miles from the target, two bundles within 30 miles of the target in both directions and one bundle per minute for the rest of the journey home.

Pathfinders

Time over target	Aircraft type	Marking Method
z – 2	19 Opening Blind Markers	The Opening Blind Markers flares to mark the aiming point with red TI and to drop a bundle of red with green stars release point flares.
z – 2	1 Special Blind Marker	Using a new improved H2S Mark III the Special Blind
z + 1 to z + 3	3 Special Blind Markers	Markers to mark the exact aiming point with reds and yellows in salvo, and 4 bundles of release point flares.
z + 1 to z + 19	18 Later Blind Markers	To mark the aiming point with greens on H2S and drop a bundle of release point flares.
z and z + 1 to z + 19	23 Backers-up (4 at z)	Early Backers-up to aim greens at salvoes of red and yellows if visible (dropped by Special Blind Markers) otherwise estimated centre of reds (dropped by Opening Blind Markers) with a 3 second overshoot. Later Backers-up to aim greens at centre of earlier greens with a 3 second overshoot. If cloud obscured the TI the backers up to retain their greens, bombing on release point flares along with the supporters. The latter to bomb on these flares only if their H2S was unserviceable.
z – 2	32 Supporters	Supporters to bomb on release point flares only if their H2S was unserviceable.
z + 2	6 Supporters	

Main Force

Time over target	Aircraft numbers	Bombing Method
z to z + 4	121 aircraft	The main force to bomb the
z + 4 to z + 8	120 aircraft	centre of all visible greens
z + 8 to z + 12	120 aircraft	with a 3 second overshoot, or
z + 12 to z + 16	121 aircraft	if cloud obscured the TIs then
z + 16 to z + 20	121 aircraft	to aim at the release point
		flares.

The density of aircraft over the target would be 34 per minute, the more experienced crews at the front, newer crews to follow. 'Creepback', often accredited to inexperienced crews, had become a problem for Bomber Command. Some crews dropped bombloads as soon as possible on the first TI, flare or even fires on the ground and hence the pattern of bombing throughout a raid often spread back along the incoming aircraft's flight path. By placing more experienced crews at the front of the raid, Bomber Command hoped to concentrate the bombing.

In addition to the Berlin raid 12 Mosquitos attacked chemical works in Leverkusen, 14 Wellingtons laid mines off the Frisians and the Dutch coast, and 11 Whitleys and Wellingtons dispersed leaflets over northern France. Crews on the trip to Berlin were warned that spoof fighter flares, bright white in colour, were to be dropped north of the target. This involved six Mosquitos of 139 Squadron, which were attempting to confuse German night fighters into believing the flares had been dropped by their own illuminators and thus draw them away from the true return route of the bomber stream.

Halifax 'C' LK644 took off from Leeming at 1700 hours, with Arthur piloting this aircraft operationally for the third time. Flying Officer Constable had returned to duties with the crew, stepping into the vacant navigator's position.

On the outward route to the target the only trouble they experienced was a slight amount of icing. Upon approaching the target area there was virtually complete cloud cover and as such there was no chance of seeing any of the Pathfinder ground markers. The defensive searchlights had been rendered useless by the cloud cover, but the heavy guns remained active, putting up a barrage around the Pathfinder marker flares between 17,000 and 23,000 feet. Halifax LK644 was hit by the flak, but with no serious damage caused. Alex was unable to see any of the green TI dropped by the blind markers and he released the bombload at 2012 hours from 20,000 feet on the centre of the red with green stars release point flares. The crew witnessed various fires reflecting on the clouds and recorded, at 2022 hours, a large explosion lasting about 5 to 10 seconds.

Albert Speer, the Nazi Armaments Minister, was in Berlin on the night of the raid:

I was having a conference in my private office on November 22, 1943, when the air-raid alarm sounded. It was about 7:30 p.m. A large fleet of bombers was reported heading toward Berlin. When the bombers reached Potsdam, I called off the meeting to drive to a nearby flak tower, intending to watch the attack from its platform, as was my wont. But I scarcely reached the top of the tower, when I had to take shelter inside it; in spite of the tower's stout concrete walls, heavy hits nearby were shaking it: Injured anti aircraft gunners crowded down the stairs behind me; the air pressure from the exploding bombs had hurled them into the walls. For twenty minutes explosion followed explosion. From above I looked down into the well of the tower, where a closely packed crowd stood in the thickening haze formed by cement dust falling from the walls. When the rain of bombs ceased, I ventured out on the platform again. My nearby Ministry was one gigantic conflagration. I drove over there at once. A few secretaries, looking like Amazons in their steel helmets, were trying to save files even while isolated time bombs went off in the vicinity. In place of my private office I found nothing but a huge bomb crater.[25]

All 14 aircraft from 427 Squadron returned to Leeming. Arthur landed Halifax LK644 at 0010 hours following an uneventful return journey. The only incident of note for the squadron was that Flight Sergeant McQuade landed his Halifax on only two engines and his rear gunner had sustained a slight flak injury.

Examination of night photographs and subsequent day reconnaissance were unable to determine the full extent of damage to the target and Bomber Command had to surmise the results of the raid from the returning crews' evidence.

Bomber Command Narrative of Attack:
The attack opened with red TI and skymarker flares, which were maintained without a break until the close of the planned period. 6 blind markers had marked the target area and release point by zero-hour. The markers and flares were concentrated, although the absence of any photographic evidence makes it impossible to assess their accuracy. Crews' reports suggested a highly successful attack, and this opinion was confirmed by the enemy's complaint of a 'heavy terror raid'. A Mosquito over the target at zero + 7 reported that 2 main fire concentrations 7-10 miles apart were reflected on the clouds. This reflection could be seen for 80 miles on the way home.[26]

---

[25] Albert Speer, *op.cit.*, p393-394.
[26] Public Record Office AIR 24 261.

Joseph Goebbels recorded in his diary:

> *November 24, 1943:* Trouble began early this morning. First,
> Schach [Gauleiter of Berlin, Goebbels' chief assistant] gave
> me a general picture of the situation in Berlin, which is a sad
> one indeed. I just can't understand how the English are able to
> do so much damage to the Reich's capital during one air raid.
>   The picture that greeted my eye in the Wilhelmplatz was
> one of utter desolation. Blazing fires everywhere . . . Transport
> conditions are still quite hopeless but I trust we shall soon
> master our difficulties sufficiently at least to start an
> emergency service to all sections of the city . . . In our home
> in Hermann Goering Street things are pretty desperate. The
> top floor is burnt out completely. The whole house is filled
> with water. It is practically impossible to live there; there is no
> heat, no water, and all rooms are filled with pungent smoke
> . . . The poor people, who are the victims of these low-down
> methods of English warfare, are really to be pitied.[27]

It was not until 20 December 1943 that a photograph of the city was
obtained revealing damage caused by six major raids of which the operation
of 22 November was the second. In fact the raid was extremely successful
for Bomber Command, subsequently believed to be the most effective raid
on Berlin throughout the whole war. Several firestorms were reported,
approximately 2000 people killed (500 in a shelter which received a direct
hit and 105 crushed in a panicked rush at a shelter next to the Neukoln
gasworks, where the large explosion witnessed by our crew took place) and
175,000 bombed out. Importantly for the war effort the city had to draw in
more than 50,000 soldiers to help in the following days.

   Only 26 aircraft were lost out of the 764 that eventually took part in the
raid, an acceptably low 3.4 per cent of the force. The result was due mainly
to weather conditions having seriously hampered the ability and desire of
the German night fighters to get airborne. Landing in such conditions was
extremely hazardous due to poor visibility, probable low fuel and possible
damage. Improvements in British jamming of German navigation signals,
along with the probability of intruder Mosquitos patrolling near to
Luftwaffe airfields added to a night fighter crew's reluctance to get
airborne. Goebbels expressed his dismay at the RAF losses:

> *November 24, 1943* . . . Ley [Dr Robert Ley, head of German
> Labour Front and Reichsleiter of the political division of the
> Nazi party] has returned meanwhile. He had carried out a
> number of assignments I gave him . . . He was furious

[27] *The Goebbels Diaries, op.cit.,* p425-426.

because the fighter planes did not take to the air during the
unfortunate night. What if the weather was bad! After all the
English fly in bad weather from their southern English
airports all the way to Berlin; but the German fighters can't
rise from the ground in Berlin because the weather is
unfavourable! You can't simply surrender the capital of the
Reich to the terror of the enemy. If we conduct war on such
squeamish principles we won't get very far.[28]

Bomber Command could only account for ten losses, five to flak in the
target area, two to controlled fighters in the Deelen area on the way home
and three lost to controlled fighters around Berlin.

---

[28] *The Goebbels Diaries, op. cit.*, p426.

CHAPTER 7

DEEP INTO THE REICH

Following the crew's first visit to the capital of the Reich they were no doubt pleased to find no operations scheduled the next day. Their officer commanding, Wing Commander Turnbull, congratulated his crews with the following written Order of the Day, detailed in 427 Squadron's ORB.

> Last night we sent 14 aircraft from our squadron to bomb Berlin. 14 aircraft successfully took off, bombed Berlin, and returned safely to this country. My congratulations to all ranks under my command whose combined efforts made this outstanding success possible.[29]

On the night of 23/24 November Bomber Command sent a force of 383 aircraft to Berlin but 427 Squadron were not called upon. Many crews bombed on fires still burning from the previous raid, and further destruction resulted. Bomber Command lost 20 Lancasters from the attacking force.

Personnel at 427 Squadron recognised that the long awaited Battle of Berlin had begun and on 24 November ground crews at Leeming responded by working throughout the night to make all available aircraft serviceable. On 25 November 17 aircraft from 427 Squadron were detailed for a raid on Frankfurt, with 16 actually taking off. Halifax 'G for George' had a taxying accident with aircraft 'G' of 429 Squadron. The squadron's ORB recorded the incident as 'the Battle of the G's in which the aircraft of our friendly rivals came out second best.' Despite this jovial comment, the possible consequence of two aircraft colliding whilst taxying, both full of fuel and with a maximum bomb load, would not have been overlooked.

Arthur and crew took off from Leeming, in Halifax LK974, at 23.50 hours arriving over the target early at 0248 hours and releasing their load of one 2,000lb high capacity bomb along with 4,320lb of incendiaries on the centre of three red Pathfinder flares. The target was cloud-covered and they could still see the fires reflecting off the cloud base some 60 miles from the target area. Arthur's logbook records being attacked by a Junkers 88 but after evasive manoeuvres the assailant was lost with no damage

---

[29] Public Record Office AIR 27 1845.

sustained. They landed back at base at 0720 hours, one of 14 aircraft that had bombed the target and returned; the other two aircraft had returned early. The whole attack suffered because of the weather, with most of the bombing scattered, at a cost of 11 Halifaxes and 1 Lancaster from the 262 aircraft Bomber Command sent on the raid.

> *Josef Goebbels:* November 27, 1943: Last night it was Frankfurt's turn to suffer fairly heavy attacks. The damage is not too bad, except for cultural monuments. Thus, for instance, the Goethe House has been hit. One's feelings are already so blunted by air raids that this hardly seems like sacrilege. There's nothing one can do about it anyway! Air raids hang over us like fate.[30]

The next night, ops continued, this time to Stuttgart. Eight out of the ten aircraft detailed for operations at 427 Squadron found the target; one failed to take off, the other returned early because of faulty controls. Arthur and crew were not one of the operational crew, which took part in this unsuccessful raid, with six Halifaxes lost out of the 157 Halifaxes and 21 Lancasters.

On the same night Bomber Command sent 443 Lancasters and 7 Mosquitos to Berlin. The two forces initially took the same flight path, heading directly for Frankfurt in an attempt to fool the German controllers. Just before reaching Frankfurt they separated. The diversionary tactics may have had some effect in limiting the night fighters' effectiveness on the outward flights, but the Berlin bomber force suffered many losses on the return journey, with 28 Lancasters lost. Also 14 Lancasters crashed on returning to England. The raid was fairly successful as regard bomb damage to the city and no doubt added to the confusion resulting from the raids a few days earlier.

The crews of 427 Squadron enjoyed the next six nights away from operations. Although crews were detailed on a couple of occasions, unfavourable weather stepped in to relieve them of their duties. On the night of 2/3 December, however, Bomber Command did despatch 458 aircraft back to Berlin to continue the assault, although 427 Squadron was not called upon. The route for the raid was very direct and unfortunately for the bomber crews the Germans identified the target early and the night fighters notched up a successful night's work. 40 bombers were lost on a raid of scattered bombing, but some of which damaged important war industry.

The next night 427 Squadron became operational once more. Halifax LK974, piloted by the newly promoted Flight Sergeant Darlow, was one of 14 aircraft receiving a considerable quantity of fuel to take them far into the

---

[30] *The Goebbels Diaries, op.cit.,* 1948, p434-435.

Reich for a raid on Leipzig, along with a bombload of one 2,000lb high capacity bomb and 3,240lb of various incendiaries. This was the lowest weight of bombs the crew had taken so far, a result of the necessary increase in the quantity of fuel required owing to the considerable flight time. Halifax 'J' took off at 2340 hours and after four hours began to close on the cloud-covered target area. Despite the aircraft being hit by flak just prior to the target Alex released the bombload at 0400 hours, zero hour for the raid, on the centre of some Pathfinder red flares and green stars. Unfortunately not all the bombs released: the ninety 4lb 'X' type incendiaries were hung up and brought back.

On the return flight, at 0500 hours, the aircraft was approached from astern by a Junkers 88. Both Trevor and Don held their fire lest they gave their position away. Instead, before the Ju 88 could get in range, the message was passed onto Arthur 'corkscrew port-now'. He threw the Halifax into the undulating evasive corkscrew and the enemy aircraft was lost to view and did not return. The rest of the flight proved uneventful and they landed back at Leeming at 0800 hours, after the longest operational flying time the crew had so far experienced, of 8 hours 20 minutes. Arthur recorded in his logbook a successful operation, and in particular his delight with 'Navigation Exceptional'.

Of the fourteen 427 Squadron aircraft detailed, the aircraft of Flying Officer Cozens returned early due to increasing engine trouble. Just after reaching the English coast the pilot decided to abandon the aircraft, but after opening the throttle he restored some power then attempted and safely carried out a crash landing at Woodbridge. The only injury was a broken ankle for one of the crew who had parachuted prior to the crash landing. The other 13 aircraft reached the target and bombed on the Pathfinder marking. Crews reported columns of black smoke issuing from the conflagration below, with the glow of fires on the clouds visible for a distance of approximately 150 miles from the target.

The raid was a fairly successful one with accurate marking by the Pathfinders resulting in effective bombing. Martin Middlebrook and Chris Everitt in *The Bomber Command War Diaries* claim this as the most successful raid on Leipzig during the war, with a large area of housing and numerous industrial premises severely damaged. Again we refer to Josef Goebbels, who records the day following the attack:

> *December 5, 1943:* Unfortunately the air raid on Leipzig last night was exceedingly severe and fateful. The city was not prepared for such a massive attempt at terrorization. The fire department was not adequate. As a result whole rows of houses went up in smoke. The centre of the city was especially hard hit. Almost all public buildings, theatres, the university, the Supreme Court, exhibition halls, etcetera, have either been completely destroyed or seriously

damaged. About 150,000 to 200,000 people are without shelter.[31]

Bomber Command lost 24 aircraft on the raid, many of them on the return flight when they strayed into the defended area of Frankfurt.

As those crews who had been to Leipzig returned only in time for breakfast the next day, it was deemed impossible to detail them for operations. The only activity for the squadron involved intensive ground training for those crews who had not been operational the night before. Indeed this proved to be the start of a quiet period for the 427 Squadron personnel as inclement weather combined with the advent of the moon period to curtail any possibility of operations. As well as ground training, some air training was possible, but on 14 December even the air training had to be cut as the station became engulfed in a 'pea souper' fog. Again on the next day fog descended leading to the Wing Commander making, some would consider, a rash decision. The squadron operations book records:

> *15.12.43:* With operations not scheduled, and local flying at a standstill due to the fog, the Wing Commander personally led the aircrew personnel of the squadron, on a route march around the perimeter track, in an effort to keep them in condition physically as well as mentally. Those who had been out the previous evening were easily pin-pointed from the others, after the distance of three miles had been covered. Good idea![32]

Allan Burrell was one of those who could not really see the point. A short while after the march had begun Allan, along with a group of others, started to lag behind. The climatic conditions then acted in their favour, shielding them from the view of those eager marchers accompanying the Wingco at the front of the column. This opportunity was seized upon and they slunk back to the more hospitable environs of the station huts leaving their red-cheeked comrades to the delights of a Yorkshire winter.

The fog persisted for another four days at Leeming, keeping 427 Squadron free from operational duty. The Battle of Berlin continued, however, as 483 Lancasters and 10 Mosquitos carried out a reasonably accurate raid on the night of 16/17 December. Bomber Command lost 25 Lancasters on the raid and there were further losses when the returning crews encountered low cloud over their bases. In fact 29 Lancasters were involved in crashes or were abandoned by crews parachuting out. *The Bomber Command War Diaries* states that a probable 148 men were killed in the crashes, 39 injured and 6 presumed lost at sea.

---

[31] *The Goebbels Diaries, op cit.*, 1948, p445.
[32] Public Record Office AIR 27 1845.

By 20 December the visibility at Leeming had improved and the squadron became operational. The target once more was Frankfurt, and 427 Squadron detailed 16 aircraft for the operation. Arthur lifted Halifax LK975 from the Leeming runway at 1620 hours laden with two 1,000lb medium capacity bombs and 4,320lb of various incendiaries. After an uneventful outward flight they reached a fairly clear target, bombing at 1935 hours on the centre of some green target indicators. After a similarly quiet return flight they touched down at Leeming at 2305 hours. The crew's raid report commented on the scattering of Pathfinder markers and fires seen over the target area. However the raid was reasonably successful in terms of bomb damage. Unfortunately night fighters were able to penetrate the bomber stream on the outward flight and a total of 41 aircraft were lost from the 650 that took part in the raid. No. 427 Squadron suffered its losses as well, as the aircraft LK627 of Flying Officer Lacerte and LK644 of Flying Officer Grieve failed to return. Our crew had flown operationally in both aircraft, three times in LK644 and once in LK627. All the members of Lacerte's crew became POWs. Grieve and his whole crew were killed.

Arthur lost navigator Pilot Officer Constable from the crew at this point, as he completed his operational tour and was subsequently posted to an operational training unit. There was no doubt the crew were sorry to see him go. Arthur continually made comments about the excellent navigation in his flight records and after their earlier navigational problems the crew were anxious for a competent replacement.

For the next eight nights 427 Squadron avoided any operational duties, which enabled the personnel to enjoy Christmas to the full, and the traditional Christmas dinner was served to the airmen by the officers. Other Lancaster squadrons in Bomber Command were not so lucky. On 23/24 December a force of 364 Lancasters, eight Mosquitos and seven Halifaxes were despatched to bomb the capital of the Reich. Sixteen Lancasters did not return from what was an unsuccessful attack.

On 29 December 427 Squadron, including Arthur's crew, became operational again, with 16 aircraft taking off destined once more for Berlin. The vacant navigator position was filled by 26-year-old Canadian Flight Sergeant George Lorimer. This was to be the last personnel change in the crew for the rest of its wartime flying days.

> *Alex Nethery:* George was a quiet person, perhaps with good reason. His former crew and their aircraft had gone through hell, including some deaths. His navigating experience was a great asset to the crew. [Later on] we worked side by side and never had a cross word.

George Lorimer had been part of Flight Lieutenant Laird's crew, joining them at 23 OTU satellite, Stratford on Avon. The crew then passed through 1659 Conversion Unit at Topcliffe before joining 427 Squadron. George's

first operational flight coincided with Arthur's first bombing raid to
Mannheim on 5 September 1943, and as readers may recall, George's crew
suffered casualties on 3 October during the Kassel raid. George's next three
operations were with the promoted and decorated Squadron Leader Laird
DFC but he was soon to leave them. Rather than have new recruits fill the
vacant places in Laird's crew, gaps in other crews were filled and George
was directed to fill the vacant position in Arthur's crew. On 22 December,
George successfully directed his new crew on a Bullseye run to London.
The Berlin raid and the long trip involved, on 29 December, would give
Arthur the opportunity to see his new navigator's skills put to the test
during the intensity of an operation, or so he thought.

Part way across the North Sea Arthur found his Halifax V unable to gain
height, owing to an inversion in temperature in the engines which led to
overheating. Arthur asked the crew whether or not they should return to base,
receiving a unanimous 'yes'. Allan signalled back to base their predicament
and was somewhat perturbed to receive orders to land back at base with their
6,320lb bombload. The bombload would normally be jettisoned into the sea
since keeping the bombs on the aircraft made landing that much more
difficult through weight and the obvious danger of explosion should anything
go wrong. Again Arthur consulted the crew, asking their opinion on
jettisoning the bombload and Philip Richards and Alex Nethery recall that the
bombs were then released over the sea, but the official squadron record states
that the aircraft was landed with all the bombs on board. As Alex was the
bomb aimer, we can assume the bombs were jettisoned. Arthur managed to
land the Halifax without any problems, but the CO had all the station fire
engines and ambulances waiting by the runway when they came down. Our
crew was summoned to appear in front of him and he launched into a tirade
accusing the crew of being 'yellow', and then dismissed them. Arthur told
them to remain where they were, however and informed the CO that they
would not leave the room until they received an apology for being called
cowards. Eventually some kind of compromise was reached and the crew left
the room, but there had been further damage to their relationship with the
higher echelons of the squadron.

Three other 427 Squadron aircraft returned early from the operation.
Halifax 'F' had a failure in the port inner engine and the wing commander,
flying in Halifax 'B', returned early due to a technical failure in the port
outer engine; Halifax 'W', piloted by Pilot Officer Deegan, ran into trouble
about halfway to the target when his port outer engine failed. With
difficulty in maintaining height he jettisoned the bombload and set course
for base. Soon the rear gunner warned the pilot that night fighters were
dropping flares in an attempt to vector the Halifax. Eventually a night
fighter did pick them up and as it closed in to about 1,000 yds the aircraft
was thrown into its defensive manoeuvre. This proved successful in
shaking off the night fighter but soon after the starboard inner engine went
completely unserviceable. With the prospect of returning to base on two

engines, the crew set about jettisoning any loose equipment so as to maintain height. Unfortunately in the confusion the trailing aerial was cut off by the bomb doors, making it impossible for the wireless operator to send out messages or receive fixes. The wireless operator attempted to repair the set, erecting a spare aerial to send out the necessary SOSs. Just after they had left the Dutch coast the port inner engine threatened to pack up and all the way across the North Sea at 5,000 feet the pilot nursed the engines, whilst the aircraft proceeded at 110 mph, almost stalling speed. Just after crossing the English coast an aerodrome appeared below and Pilot Officer Deegan immediately dove the aircraft toward the runway. Just as he touched down the port engine finally gave way, but the aircraft was brought to a standstill safely.

The other twelve aircraft reached and bombed the cloud-covered target, using the Pathfinder sky flares as their aiming points. Halifax 'S' enjoyed the brief company of a night fighter, and whilst fire was exchanged neither aircraft was damaged. Halifax 'P' piloted by Flight Lieutenant Murray sustained damage over the target but not by any enemy action. Just after they had dropped their bombload, a Halifax about 1,000 feet above them began to release its load, the incendiaries from which crashed through the tail plane and the starboard wing, and bent the aileron. The weight of the incendiaries sent the aircraft into an uncontrollable spiral dive, but after losing 2,000 feet the pilot managed to regain control. On the return flight the aircraft continually kept listing to starboard and whilst passing Emden the aircraft was further damaged by flak; one piece penetrated the window of the co-pilot's seat. Evasive action was attempted but proved impossible. Eventually the Halifax approached the English coast and landed safely on the first aerodrome sighted.

Bomber Command losses for the night consisted of 20 aircraft out of the 712 sent. An acceptable loss rate of 2.8 per cent. Mosquito diversions, bad weather and a long southerly approach to the target, contributed to the night fighters' and German controllers' difficulties.

With the arrival of 1944, 427 Squadron once more entered a quiet period. Bomber Command carried out raids on Berlin on the nights of 1/2 and 2/3 January: The force on 1/2 consisting of 421 Lancasters (28 lost) and on the next night 383 Lancasters (27 lost), 12 Mosquitos and 9 Halifaxes. Both raids suffered from scattered bombing and inflicted little damage upon the city. With 427 Squadron remaining operational with Halifax Vs it was not called upon for these predominantly Lancaster raids.

One person who did take part in the raid of the 1/2 January was Derrick Bell, on his 7th operation. Readers will recall that Derrick was part of Airborne Cigar 101 Squadron.

> We got in a muddle that night, the navigator went a bit wrong
> and we arrived over Berlin late. I can vividly remember as we

flew up to it, there were two layers of cloud, there was one
below us and one above, and it was weird, as though you were
flying along an illuminated corridor. As far as we knew we
were the only ones there, as we were terribly late. So we
bombed on what we hoped was the target. There was nothing
to aim at, I actually couldn't see the flames but could see the
glow on the clouds where the fires were. The Pathfinder
markers had disappeared, we were as late as that. We flew
back fairly uneventfully.

The return flight over Germany was uneventful but soon after Derrick
brought the Lancaster over Belgian occupied territory, they had company.

The first thing I knew about it, Larry the engineer said, 'Oh
something's hit us,' and the next thing the starboard wing was
in flames. I don't know what it was that hit us, but I think it
must have been a fighter. I discovered later that the Me 110
had upward pointing guns, it might have been that.

Derrick's aircraft had become another victim of the then unknown Schrage
Musik. Before Derrick was able to pass any instructions onto his crew,
however, events took over.

None of us baled out. I honestly think that four of us were the
luckiest people alive. The Lanc went out of control, we just
lost it, and I can remember as plain as anything saying, 'We've
had it boys,' or trying to say it. Then I knew nothing until I
woke up in mid air. The Lanc had obviously blown to pieces.
The crew at the front of the aircraft had been thrown out, four
of us woke up in mid air just in time to pull our chutes. I had
only got mine on one hook as that was all the time I'd had to
put it on . . . Anyway it worked.

From Derrick's crew, the bomb aimer, navigator, wireless operator and
himself had survived the explosion. The other four crew members were
killed, one of whom was a Canadian who was on his 89th operation. We
will be catching up with what happened to Derrick later.

It was not until 20 January that a considerable force of Halifaxes was
called upon for operations. The Lion Squadron detailed 16 aircraft for
another raid to Berlin, with only 14 becoming airborne because of last
minute cancellations. Two aircraft returned early, one owing to a starboard
inner engine failure and the other to the unserviceability of 'Gee'. The
remaining twelve aircraft proceeded to the target.

Arthur lifted Halifax LL169 from the Leeming runway at 1620 hours.
On arrival at the target it was found to be completely cloud covered, and

Arthur began the bomb run. During this period of keeping the Halifax straight and level a FW 190, probable Wild Boar, took its opportunity to make a solitary attack but no damage was sustained and the night fighter was lost. Despite all the activity, newly promoted Pilot Officer Nethery released the bombload of one 2,000lb high capacity and 4,320lb of incendiaries at 1939 hours from 20,000 feet on some Pathfinder red flares with green stars. Unfortunately not all the bombs released as 60 of the 4lb incendiaries were hung up. The return flight was uneventful and Leeming was reached at 2355 hours.

Again the results of the raid could only be guessed at by Bomber Command owing to the cloud cover. Reconnaissance was not possible until another four raids had been made on the city. Out of the 769 aircraft sent, 35 were lost. Despite a long northerly approach route and other diversionary raids, night fighters were directed into the bomber stream and had success. From 427 Squadron Pilot Officer Cook's Halifax EB246 failed to return and the crew of seven were killed. Flying Officer Cozens, a bridegroom of a month, attempted to land his Halifax LL191 at RAF Coltishall owing to a lack of fuel, but after three attempts he over skidded the aerodrome, crashed into some trees and ended up in a nearby field. The aircraft caught fire and a local farmer and his wife pulled three of the crew from the burning wreckage. The navigator was killed instantly and the flight engineer, the bomb aimer and the pilot all subsequently died from their injuries. The wireless operator remained on the dangerously injured list for some time, but the rear and mid upper gunners escaped uninjured.

This raid proved to be Arthur and his crews last as part of 427 Lion Squadron, for they were posted to 8 Group and Pathfinder Force. Exactly why the crew moved on is a little unclear. Their run-ins with the squadron's officialdom may have prompted their names being put forward for a transfer. However, when Arthur informed the crew of their selection for Pathfinders, his crewmates were happy to move on with him.

No. 427 Squadron continued on operations until the end of the war, which eventually totalled 232 bombing and 39 minelaying raids. It completed 3,309 sorties at a cost of 69 aircraft lost and one destroyed in a crash. The Lion Squadron had the distinction of having carried out the most raids in 6 Group, (along with 419 Squadron).

At the end of January 1944 Arthur Darlow and crew arrived at Navigational Training Unit (NTU) Upwood to begin their Pathfinder training. Their time flying in a Halifax had finished and they no doubt looked forward to the chance of flying the highly praised Lancasters.

CHAPTER 8

PATHFINDERS AND LEIPZIG

Soon after the appointment of Sir Arthur Harris to Bomber Command, the concept of establishing a target finding force was suggested. The basic idea was that high calibre crews who had demonstrated their ability to regularly find and bomb targets should be brought together to lead raids and identify targets to the main force. Harris opposed the idea, basically on the grounds that elite crews were better left to act as examples to their squadrons, rather than forming a select force. Arguments continued for some time until eventually Harris received a direct order from the Prime Minister through the Chief of the Air Staff. On 5 July 1942 Wing Commander D.C.T. Bennett was appointed to command the new Pathfinder Force. Bennett, an Australian, was noted for his navigational expertise, and he held a number of long distance flying records. He had commanded Halifax squadrons in 4 Group and was preparing to take part of 10 Squadron to the Middle East when the call came.

Upon formation, each of the night bombing groups was ordered to nominate a squadron to become Pathfinders. Initially the force comprised:

No. 156 Squadron	Wellingtons	1 Group
No. 7 Squadron	Stirlings	3 Group
No. 35 Squadron	Halifaxes	4 Group
No. 83 Squadron	Lancasters	5 Group
No.109 Squadron	Wellingtons	No particular group

Bennett began immediately to work on every aspect of the problems previously associated with Bomber Command operations: firstly, effective selection and training of crews; secondly, the obvious need for an enhancement of navigational aids; thirdly, developing a method of marking targets. Initially he concentrated a lot of effort on the navigational aspect. In particular H2S and Oboe which was being developed as Bennett formed the Pathfinder Force, received considerable attention.

Once the Pathfinders had successfully reached a target their next responsibility was to mark it in such a way as to be easily identifiable to the main bomber stream following behind. Target Indicators (TI) were developed, involving all sorts of combinations of colours in an effort to avoid enemy copying and decoys. Different colours of TI were designed for different purposes and changes of colour during raids should it become necessary. The TI had barometric fuses, in order to burst just above the ground and cascade on to the target. Their burning period was fairly short and continuity of marking by the Pathfinders was essential. In addition to the TI, sky markers were developed, consisting of parachute flares of various colours. If the target area had considerable cloud cover, making visual sighting impossible, H2S could be used to position the sky markers above the target.

Three systems of marking were developed, with codenames obtained by Bennett's asking some of his staff from where they had originated. Hence:

Parramatta: TI dropped blindly onto the target. Replenished and added to by backers up.

Newhaven: Flares dropped illuminating the target area and then TI dropped upon visual identification of the target.

Wanganui: Target area cloud covered and sky marking with flares.

If the codeword 'Musical' appeared on operational orders then Oboe-equipped Mosquitos would be carrying out the marking.

At the start of Pathfinder operations in August 1942 their success was limited, but after the enhanced training of crews together with operational experience, the squadrons became more effective. Oboe was available for operations in December 1942, enabling Bomber Command to bomb relatively accurately when there was complete cloud cover. Now Bomber Command had a means to mark targets with experienced crews, Oboe and H2S to assist navigation, and suitable pyrotechnics to light up the aiming points. In January 1943 the Path Finder Force (the designation of the force having changed) became a separate group, and Bennett was promoted to air commodore, the first Air Officer Commanding No. 8 (PFF) Group.

During all these events another major asset for Bomber Command was developed as Mosquitos began to be recognised as having considerable advantages in bombing operations. It was quick, could fly at high altitude, thus enhancing the range of Oboe, with bomb bays that could accommodate four 500lb TI. It played a considerable role not only in marking targets but, as already mentioned, in running diversion raids and smaller 'nuisance' raids. All these operations carried out by a plane that, at first, had no on board defensive capabilities except its ability to achieve high altitude and out-run the enemy. It is worth noting now that the regular use of the twin-engined Mosquitos would have an effect on the fate of our crew.

Arthur Darlow had his first taste of flying in Lancasters on 31 January 1944, in a ten minute cloud base test acting as second pilot. On 6 February, he completed his training, having only spent 14 hours 50 minutes on board a Lancaster. Amazingly only 1 hour 10 minutes of this was spent as first pilot. However the aircraft certainly impressed the crew, not only then but as they experienced it operationally.

> *Alex Nethery:* **What a beautiful aircraft!** As a comparison between it and other bombers, it was like comparing a Lincoln to a Ford truck. The Lancaster was a smooth and reliable machine. It could face a lot of battle damage and still go back for more. You'd just patch it up and send it out again. It was quite fast considering the bomb loads it carried and it seemed worthwhile to go on a raid with a Lancaster.[33]

In April 1943 the PFF received more squadrons, in particular 405 RCAF Squadron from 6 Group, to be based at Gransden Lodge in Cambridgeshire, and so it was there to which after completing their training period at Navigational Training Unit at Upwood, our crew was transferred on 7 February 1944.

No. 405 Squadron was the oldest Canadian squadron of Bomber Command, becoming part of 4 Group on 23 April 1941. From October 1942 to March 1943 the squadron had been posted to Coastal Command, to assist in the defence of the Atlantic convoys. There followed only a very brief period with 6 Group before the transfer to 8 Group, to be the only Canadian squadron in the Path Finder Force. The squadron was very proud of its selection and involvement in 8 Group, something made very clear to any new crews.

> *To The Budding Pathfinder Crew*
> *On Arriving At 405 Squadron Royal Canadian Air Force*
>
> Following the setting up of Path Finder Force it was decided that one Canadian squadron was to receive the honour of joining P.F.F. The squadron chosen for the job would have to be good, for it was realised that Path Finder Force took only the best, had a very exacting task to perform, and called for the utmost skill and determination from all its members. Keeness was essential, and such phrases as 'press on' and 'keep your finger out' were soon catch-words which, bantered from lip to lip at first in a jovial manner, were soon packed with sincerity, for they expressed the feeling of the P.F.F. crews who realised the immensity of the job they had been given. They were prepared to give their utmost and to do the job well.
>
> The Group motto 'We Stand or Fall by our Accuracy' does not need explaining – it speaks for itself.

---

[33] Quoted in *Two Wings and a Prayer, op.cit.,* p86.

This was the bill the chosen squadron would be required to fill, and the task, yes, and the honour, fell to 405 Squadron, R.C.A.F. . . . it fell into the job with the same keeness and determination so magnificently displayed by other squadrons in the group. The training was intense – many failed to make the grade – but those who did, formed the nucleus of what was to become in a few months time, the most reliable and conscientious squadron in P.F.F. Group.

Competition became intense, each squadron vying for the coveted honours, but 405 set a pace which was soon to outstrip all competition. As a result, the fame of the new squadron spread. On many occasions it was referred to by people of authority, as the finest squadron in Bomber Command.

This good name and reputation can only be held and maintained so long as you, the new crews, future Flight Commanders and Section Leaders, are willing to carry on the good work.[34]

The squadron was based at Gransden Lodge airfield, which crossed the county boundaries of Bedfordshire and Cambridgeshire. There were three runways, one of 2,000 yards and two of 1,400 yards. It was a relatively small station with accommodation available for 86 officers, 200 NCOs, 800 airmen and nearly 300 WAAFs. The numerical strength of the squadron at the end of January 1944 was:

	Aircrew	Groundcrew	Total
RCAF officers	42	3	45
RCAF airmen	31	222	253
RAF officers	10	1	11
RAF airmen	36	51	87
RAAF officers	3		3
RNZAF airmen	1		1
USA officers	1		1
Totals	**124**	**277**	**401**

It was a well dispersed station set amongst fields, and crew members were given a certain piece of advice upon arrival. The need for one particular item of equipment was made plain to the new crews:

On joining the squadron you will be given the usual arrival chit which you will proceed to get signed by each individual section thereupon scribed, leaving the Squadron Orderly Room to sign last of all. This arrival chit and the dispersed

---

34 Public Record Office AIR 27 1789.

nature of the airfield go well in hand, if you like gravel bashing, so my friend, after the first day, the word 'mechanised' really sticks in your brain; with sore feet and weary bones you will sleep dreaming of the luxurious Coronation Scot, Buicks and Rolls-Royces, and even luxurious air liners during your first slumber bid at Gransden.

Having had this wonderful night, you will realise anything mechanised is a wonderful invention, but unfortunately the only armoured vehicle issued to personnel on this station is a bicycle, so visit your Section Leader and persuade him to write out the necessary 'bumph' which will take you before the N.C.O. i/c Police. Now there is nothing to be afraid of, and it's worth making the attempt. By the way, it's a good idea too, to see the N.C.O. i/c Cycle Maintenance, sometimes he has cycles just finished repairs, and you can never tell! Remember, if you can't get one, don't be misled into the idea that you can ride anyone else's without official authority, it's strictly forbidden, not encouraged, and anyway it's a very serious offence.[35]

Allan acted upon this advice immediately and signed up for a bike. Proud of his new acquisition he rode off and had his tea. Unfortunately while he was helping himself to tea someone else helped themselves to his bike and he had to pay £4 19 shillings and sixpence for a replacement.

Arthur, however, was motorised:

> *Trevor Utton:* Arthur had a BSA 250, an ex post office bike . . . Pip had a Norton 500 which I subsequently bought but before that we relied on Arthur. The three of us, on this BSA 250, Arthur at the front, me in the middle and Pip hanging on the back somewhere, well the poor old thing went up and down the hills. We often went out on the beer like that.

Gransden Lodge lay only a few miles from the village of Gamlingay, a village with which Arthur had strong family connections, since his grandfather and grandmother both came from here. Two of his uncles' names were on the village memorial to those lost in the First World War. Arthur often took the opportunity to visit relatives in the village, including his cousin Minnie Darlow. To this day she remembers the smart young airman standing in her doorway, and the times the Lancasters flew over, one of which, every now and then, would fly that little bit too close to her house.

---

[35] Public Record Office AIR 27 1789.

Whilst our crew had been preparing for their new responsibilities, the Battle of Berlin raged on. On 27/28 January 1944, 515 Lancasters (33 lost) and 15 Mosquitos attacked the city; scattered bombing resulting in only a reasonably successful raid. On 28/29 January 1944, 432 Lancasters (20 lost), 26 Halifaxes (26 lost) and 4 Mosquitos took part in a successful raid. On 30/31 January 1944, 440 Lancasters (32 lost), 82 Halifaxes (1 lost) and 12 Mosquitos achieved another successful raid. On 15/16 February 1944, 561 Lancasters (26 lost), 314 Halifaxes (17 lost) and 16 Mosquitos caused extensive damage to the city.

The people of Berlin certainly suffered from the continued attention of the RAF, but nothing like the scale of the disaster in Hamburg occurred there. The 'Black Heart' carried on beating. The population now received a respite from attacks, but the bombers would be back.

At Gransden Lodge airfield, the dawn of 19 February 1944 was cloudy with slight mist. Operations were on and there was only local flying practice; ground training was stood down. Intermittent slight snow and rain continued for the rest of the day, but the weather became fair after 2300 hours.

The target for the night would be Leipzig. The city of approximately 710,000 inhabitants was the largest town in the Saxony region of eastern Germany, and also noted as the home of the Leipzig World Fair and for possessing the largest railway station in Europe. It was an administrative and commercial centre, with the main industrial development located on the outskirts of the town. The most important industry concerned aircraft production and Air Ministry Intelligence had information concerning the nature of the work carried out and its location. Importantly Air Ministry Intelligence also concluded: 'The main factories are situated outside the town and do not form a compact group of targets'. With regard to the city as a whole: 'Leipzig is predominantly a city of tenements and ranks with Hamburg and Berlin as the most densely peopled city in Germany. These large tenement areas are very vulnerable to bombing.'[36] Leipzig obviously lent itself to the concept of area bombing.

Bomber Command ordered a maximum effort, and 832 bombers eventually took off from their bases. Fourteen aircraft from 405 Squadron were detailed for the operation. This would be the crew's second time over the city, and their first as Pathfinders.

Crew:	Captain	W/O Darlow, A.E.
	Navigator	W/O Lorimer, G.A.
	Bomb aimer	P/O Nethery, A.
	Wireless operator	Sgt Burrell, A.W.
	Rear gunner	Sgt Copeland, D.

---

[36] Public Record Office AIR 40 1682.

Mid upper gunner	Sgt Utton, T.E.
Flight engineer	Sgt Richards, P.W.

Aircraft Type and Number: Lancaster III   V

Bomb Load: 5 x 2,000lb HC
Total: **10,000lb**

Zero hour for the raid was 0400 hours.

Navigation: The crew's planned route would take them to the Norfolk coast at Cromer then across the North Sea to the Dutch coast where red route markers were to be dropped. Then in to Germany and onto a direct course for Berlin. However before reaching the capital they were to turn southeast at a point identified by further route markers, and subsequently to turn once more towards Leipzig and into the bombing run. There would be two return routes; those bombing before zero hour + 8 minutes would come on the southern route and those after along the northern route. The southern route brought the bomber stream across Germany just north of Frankfurt and as it neared the Belgian border and some route markers, it turned to cross the Dutch coast, south of Rotterdam. The northern route took the stream just to the north of Osnabrück before turning on another set of route markers, to cross the Dutch coast just north of Leeuwarden.

Window was to be dropped at two bundles per minute within 50 miles of the target, in both directions, and at one bundle per minute for the rest of the journey.

Pathfinders

Time over target	Aircraft type	Marking Method
z – 2	30 Primary Blind Markers	If unable to see the target the Primary Blind Markers to mark blindly with red TI and the release point with flares, green with red stars. If the aiming point could be seen, then to retain their TI and release point flares and revert to the role of Supporters.
z – 2 & z – 10	55 Supporters at z – 2, 3 Supporters at z + 10	If unable to see the target Supporters to bomb blindly. If able to see the target to bomb visually or if markers down then bomb on the centre of the TI or the release point.
z + 1 to z + 18	14 Blind Backers-up (1 per/min, 2 at z + 3 0 at z + 2,4,12,16,17)	If unable to see the target the Blind Backers-up to mark the aiming point with green TI and

| z to z + 17 | 11 Special Blind Backers-up (1 per 2 mins, 2 at z, 1 at z + 17) | the release point with flares, green with red stars. If able to see the target they would revert to the role of Visual Backers-up. |
| z to z + 18 | 25 Visual Backers-up (1 per/min, 3 at z, 2 at z + 1,5,9,13) | If unable to see target and the TI dropped were obscured by cloud the Visual Backers-up would retain their own TI and bomb on the target or on the release point. If able to see the target they would aim their green TI at the centre of all TI seen. |

Main Force

Time over target	Aircraft numbers	Bombing Method
z to z + 4	138 Lancasters	To aim at the centre of all
z + 4 to z + 8	137 Lancasters	greens or at the centre of the z
+ 8 to z + 11	78 Lancasters	release point flares. They were
z + 10 to z + 14	130 Halifaxes	not to attack before zero hour.
z + 13 to z + 17	132 Halifaxes	
z + 16 to z + 19	77 Lancasters	

To coincide with the operation there would be various diversionary raids and special operations. A minelaying operation to Kiel Bay involved 49 aircraft, 15 Mosquitos were to raid Berlin, 3 Mosquitos to raid constructional targets in France, 16 Mosquitos to attack various airfields in Holland, 12 Mosquitos were involved in fighter patrols, 3 Mosquitos on meteorological reconnaissance, 5 aircraft from 100 Group on further special operations and 3 Mosquitos to raid Aachen.

Arthur's crew were detailed to act as 'Supporter' for the raid: Inexperienced Pathfinder crews placed at the front of the raid with the primary markers so that the initial markers were not the only aircraft above the target. Their role was to drop Window and jam flak radar, also dropping only high explosive bombs so that there would be no early fires, which could be mistaken for markers. The bomb weight of 10,000lb carried by their Lancaster exceeded by 4,760lb the previous bomb weight the crew dropped on Leipzig whilst in a Halifax at 427 Squadron.

Things began to go wrong for the bomber force early in the operation. The forecast winds were not the same as those encountered, which dispersed the bomber stream and caused many aircraft, in particular those with inexperienced navigators, to proceed to the target too quickly. Experienced navigators soon picked up the discrepancy between the forecast and actual wind speeds and made some correcting adjustments to their flight paths, by including doglegs. Some aircraft carrying navigation lights were seen over the North Sea on the approach to the enemy coast and reports came in that they were twin-engined. However it was thought that they might well have been friendly bombers orbiting in an attempt to lose time. There were in fact two collisions, one fifty miles off the coast and another south of Emden.

The German night fighter controller sent part of his force to the Kiel diversion, early in the night's operations. The subsequent Mosquito attacks on the Dutch airfields prompted the controller to recall his night fighters which happened to be present in the Hamburg, Heligoland area to join the rest of the night fighters as the main RAF bomber force crossed the Dutch coast. From the area south of Bremen to the target there was considerable fighter activity. Bomber Command estimated that 25 aircraft were lost to fighters prior to reaching the target. The plight of the bomber stream grew worse owing to its poor concentration. The route passed several heavily defended areas and some stragglers were probably picked off by flak.

At the target the situation worsened. Many of the crews who had not adjusted for the lower than forecast winds, were over the target before zero hour. The flak remained quiet and the searchlights off whilst those crews that arrived early orbited. Some main force crews actually bombed early using their own H2S. The target was found to be completely cloud-covered and as such sky marking was adopted. When the Pathfinders did mark, slightly early, all those bombers awaiting the start of the raid came in one rush from all directions and the attack developed very quickly. Again some aircraft were lost in collisions. When the searchlights were used they were unable to penetrate the cloud but did provide a backdrop for the fighters to pick up the bombers. The flak began taking relatively easy pickings from the congestion over the target with light flak attempting to snuff out Pathfinder skymarkers.

Initially the Pathfinders achieved and maintained an excellent concentration of skymarkers, which were bombed in preference to the groundmarkers that had disappeared into the cloud. However after z + 8 marking became less plentiful and the bombing began to be scattered, indeed it was reported by some crews that there were no flares burning between z + 11 and z + 15.

Arthur brought his Lancaster in over the target slightly behind schedule, having lost time en-route. Alex prepared to release the bombload.

> *Alex Nethery:* Five to eight minutes prior to bombing time I
> would leave my radar and go up front to turn on the bombsight
> and arm the bombs. While there I had to decide if I could
> bomb visually or not. If visual was not possible, I rushed back
> to my radar, moved the range from 100 miles to 10 miles and
> proceeded to bomb on radar.

On this particular night Alex bombed visually at 0401 hours, from 20,000 feet on two Wanganui flares in the centre of approximately twelve that were in a good concentration. Out of the bombing run, George gave instructions to take the aircraft on the southern route home.

After the bomber stream had split into two for the home run, there was fighter activity along both routes but predominantly on the northern route. But even this was minimal compared to the outward journey. Upon analysis of the operation, Bomber Command felt that the diversion raid to Kiel had had some effect, in that the night fighters were short of fuel by the time they reached Leipzig and so could not pursue the bombers further. However because of this, it was not really possible to assess the value of splitting the homeward route into two. All the 405 Squadron Lancasters were able to return to base, and Arthur touched down at 0638 hours.

Details of the effects of the bombing were unattainable until after a further attack by 184 American Flying Fortresses the next day. The 405 Squadron record has a signal received from Bomber Command's Air Officer Commander-in-Chief, i.e. Arthur Harris on 21 February 1944:

> I have received the following message from General Spaatz U.S.A.A.F. [begins] your great effort against Leipzig last night was a tremendous help to our successful mission today. The fires resulting from your bombing guided our planes to their objective and fighter opposition was minimised. I feel our joint blows against the enemy during the last 24 hours are a real step toward final victory. Please express my deep appreciation and hearty congratulations to all members of your command.[37]

Five out of ten of the most important factories in Leipzig suffered severe damage from the two raids, with at least another 30 war factories hit. The western part of the city was seriously affected, especially the industrial area east of the Plagaitz station where the largest wool-spinning factory and dyeworks in Europe were three quarters destroyed by fire. Business and residential property escaped lightly. (All this information is attributable to the Bomber Command report of the raid, which also quotes a German claim that 'British bombers made a terror attack against localities in Central Germany, hitting chiefly residential districts in the town of Leipzig'.)

In total Bomber Command lost a staggering 78 aircraft, made up of 44 Lancasters and 34 Halifaxes, on the raid to Leipzig, the highest loss in a single raid of the war to date. The raid highlighted the difficulties that Bomber Command was having, in evading the developing German night fighter tactics, in particular the Tame Boar operations, and there resulted major strategical changes. The loss rate of all aircraft for the raid was 9.5

---

[37] Public Record Office AIR 27 1789.

per cent, although the Halifax loss rate came to 13.3 per cent (indeed 14.9 per cent omitting those returning before reaching the enemy coast). As such, owing to the increasing casualty rates that Halifaxes were suffering, the older types, Marks II and V, were withdrawn from operations in Germany. Also Sir Arthur Harris, for the time being, all but broke off the campaign against that other distant target, Berlin, in response to the rise in German night fighter success, and lack of evidence of damage to the morale of the city's population. Instead he switched to more southerly targets and the less well defended southerly routes.

CHAPTER 9

SCHWEINFURT AND WINDS OVER BERLIN

There was little time for 405 'Vancouver' Squadron to recover from the long haul involved in the Leipzig raid. The next night, 20 February 1944, 13 Lancasters were detailed for a raid on Stuttgart including that of our crew. Again acting as supporters and with a bombload of ten 1,000lb MC bombs, Arthur lifted Lancaster 'V' from the Gransden Lodge runway at 0034 hours on 21 February. The load was released over a partially cloud covered target at 0402 hours on three red TI amidst moderate flak. The crew then enjoyed an uneventful trip back landing at 0650 hours. All 405 Squadron aircraft returned to base and reports from crews suggested a good 'prang' with fires still visible 150 miles from the target. In fact the bombing from the 598 aircraft that took part was somewhat scattered but considerable damage was caused, all for an acceptable loss of only nine aircraft.

No operations were scheduled the next day and on 22 February the crew completed a four hour cross country run. On the 24th operations were on once more, the target was Schweinfurt, where the Germans' main ball bearing factories were situated.

In September 1942, Albert Speer, the German Armaments Minister, had warned Hitler about the need for defence of the ball-bearing production facilities, which were of great importance to the German war effort. Hitler increased the number of anti-aircraft guns in the Schweinfurt area, but the Americans were quick to identify this 'bottleneck' in the German war industry and launched an attack on 17 August 1943. This famous raid reduced the production of ball bearings by 38 per cent and caused Speer to use up his stocks in maintaining armament production. However the American crews paid dearly for their daylight venture deep into Germany. The raid had been combined with a raid to the Messerschmitt works at Regensburg, and from the total of 376 Fortresses that took part in the raids, 60 aircraft and crews were lost.

On 14 October 1943, the Americans attacked Schweinfurt again, inflicting a second serious blow, the result being a 67 per cent loss of ball bearing production. But this achievement for the Americans was made, again, at a terrible cost as a further 60 of the 291 Flying Fortresses sent on this raid failed to return. The Americans made the decision to put a hold on further daylight attacks until suitable fighter escorts could be made available.

Director of Bomber Operations at the Air Ministry, Air Commodore Sydney Bufton was one of those who realised the importance of the attacks on Schweinfurt and prior to the first American raid he wrote to Air Marshal Bottomley highlighting the need for Bomber Command to follow up the American daylight raids. However Harris was to begin his offensive against Berlin and did not see Schweinfurt as a target of high priority. Indeed he viewed it as one of the 'panacea' targets as he called them: 'These were targets which were supposed by the economic experts to be such a vital bottleneck in the German war industry that when they were destroyed the enemy would have to pack up.'[38]

Harris could not bring himself to appreciate the importance of attacking such targets, which included the ball bearings factories. He was of the opinion that the Germans could easily disperse their factories and obtain supplies from overseas. He argued that in 1943 Bomber Command did not have the ability to find and hit such a small and distant target as Schweinfurt. However his seniors at the Air Ministry continued to press Harris to attack them. Harris continued to protest. On 27 January 1944, however, he received direct orders and toward the end of February 1944 Bomber Command and the 8th USAAF started to coordinate their attacks on Schweinfurt.

The first Bomber Command raid to Schweinfurt took place on the night of 24/25 February 1944. The day before a force of 266 USAAF B-17s (11 lost) raided the ball-bearing factories, and a Bomber Command force of 734 aircraft was sent as a follow up, split into two waves of 392 and 342 aircraft respectively, to arrive at the target two hours apart. There were also diversionary raids: 179 aircraft on a sweep over the North Sea, 110 aircraft minelaying in Kiel bay and the Kattegat, 15 Mosquitos to airfields in Holland, 8 Mosquitos to Kiel and 7 Mosquitos to Aachen. By combining the early diversionary raids with the two-wave attack on Schweinfurt, Bomber Command hoped to reduce losses by having the German night fighters drawn into the air too early in the night's proceedings.

At Gransden Lodge five Lancasters were detailed to be part of the first wave, nine Lancasters to attack in the second wave. Arthur Darlow and crew were detailed as part of the second wave, once more acting as supporters.

Crew:	Captain	W/O Darlow, A.E.
	Navigator	W/O Lorimer, G.A.
	Bomb aimer	P/O Nethery, A.
	Wireless operator	Sgt Burrell, A.W.
	Rear gunner	F/S Copeland, D.

[38] *Bomber Offensive, op.cit.*

Mid upper gunner   Sgt Utton, T.E.
Flight engineer   Sgt Richards, P.W.

Aircraft Type and Number: Lancaster III   V

Bomb Load: 5 x 2,000lb HC
Total: **10,000lb**

Zero hour for the raid, 1st wave 2305 hours, 2nd wave 0105 hours

Navigation: The crew's planned route would take them from base to Beachy Head then across the channel to Cayeux. From there across occupied France and into Germany past some red flares dropped 17 miles SSW of Saarbrucken, then a turn north east to Schweinfurt.

There were two return routes. The first wave was to return on an almost direct easterly route back to the French coast, looking out for some red route TI off track at Aachen and then across to Beachy Head and base. The second wave, including Arthur's aircraft, after passing through the target would turn around, returning to its last turning point before it attacked the target. It would then follow the same flight path home as the outward flight, looking out for some red flares dropped 15 miles north north-east of Strasbourg.

Window was to be dropped at the rate of two bundles per minute within 50 miles of the target in both directions, and at one bundle per minute for the rest of the route. Seven Mosquitos were to fly ahead of the first force and five in front of the second, dropping large amounts of Window.

For our purposes, only the details of the second wave planned bombing and marking are below. The first wave was planned as a Newhaven attack with emergency skymarking. The second wave marking method was mixed Parramatta and Wanganui.

Pathfinders

Time over target	Aircraft type	Marking Method
z – 2	12 Primary Blind Markers	To mark aiming point with greens and release point flares. If H2S u/s then to hold all markers and act as Supporters.
z – 2	43 Supporters	To bomb blindly or on a good DR, or if markers down then at centre of TI. They were not to wait for the Blind Markers.
z to z + 7	8 Blind Backers-up (one per min)	To keep aiming point marked with reds and release point flares.
z to z + 7	14 Visual Backers-up	To aim reds at centre of all visible TI with a 2 second

overshoot. If cloud obscured
they were to hold markers and
bomb blindly or on release
point flares on a heading of
50 degrees magnetic.

Main Force

Time over target	Aircraft numbers	Bombing Method
z to z + 4	124 aircraft	To aim at centre of all reds, or
z + 4 to z + 8	123 aircraft	if obscured by cloud then at
		centre of all flares on a
		heading of 50 degrees
		magnetic.

14 ABC aircraft throughout the attack

Arthur lifted his Lancaster off the Gransden Lodge runway at 2058 hours with a load of five 2,000lb HC bombs. On the outward flight it was possible to see the fires from the previous raid when they were about 60 miles from Schweinfurt. Arthur and the crew arrived over a partially cloud-covered target and released their load amidst the searchlights and moderate flak at 0105 hours, after Alex identified the target by some TI green dropped by the primary blind markers and by his H2S. Bomber Command later recorded between 50 and 100 searchlights in the area but they were inefficiently controlled, and the moderate barrage of the flak guns decreased in intensity toward the end of each of the attacks. The crew witnessed two rows of fires at the target arranged in a 'V' pointing north, with five green TI in the 'V' of fires. Following an uneventful return flight the crew arrived back at base at 0415 hours.

After analysing both the attacks it became clear to Bomber Command Operational Research that the raid had had limited success. In the first raid the initial marking had been good but it grew steadily worse, drawing further and further back along the line of approach, a classic example of creepback. This continued and eventually the centroid of the plot of night photographs was situated six miles to the south of the target. In the second raid the marking had again, initially been good, lying in a triangle (the 'V' witnessed by our crew) around the aiming point. But again subsequent backing up fell short and the attack drifted along the line of approach, with the main force aiming at the first TI visible.

Bomber Command Report On Night Operations,
Day Reconnaisance
Photographs obtained on the 5th March showed extensive damage to the vital ball bearing works of Kugelfischer, V.K.F. Werke I and II, Deutsche Star Kugelhalter and Fichtel und Sachs A.G. All these factories were gravely affected many

buildings being destroyed or damaged. Numerous incidents occurred among business and residential property in the town, and in the villages of Garstadt and Grafenrheinfeld, 5 miles SW and 2½ miles S of Schweinfurt. Much of this damage was, however, caused by the American daylight attack on the 24th February.[39]

Had the two-wave attack together with the diversionary raids worked? In the report on night operations, Bomber Command seemed to think so.

> A Bullseye exercise over the North Sea, and a mine laying operation to Kiel and Kattegat, caused a large force of fighters to be gathered and held in the north. As the first bomber stream approached Schweinfurt, the fighter controllers moved their forces southwards from beacon to beacon, covering the bombers' approach but always keeping to the east of probable targets. Only 15 combats took place on the outward route, 3 in the target area and 4 on the way home. Even fewer combats were reported by the second force; 4 on the way out, 9 over the target and 2 on the way home. The fighter controllers moved their forces from the Schweinfurt area to cover a surprise deviation to a new target. 12 aircraft of the first force were seen to go down in combat, one near Abbeville, one near Verdun, 5 near Saarbrucken, 3 between Saarbrucken and Schweinfurt and 2 over the target. Only 4 were lost to fighters during the second attack; one near Stuttgart on the way out, one over the target, and 2 on the first leg of the homeward route.[40]

In total 33 aircraft were lost on the raid, 22 in the first phase and 11 in the second. Bomber Command could put eight down to loss from flak and 16 to night fighters; reasons for the other nine were unknown. There were also four aircraft involved in collisions, two over the North Sea and two over England, but only one was wrecked. Another aircraft was destroyed in a taxying accident. From 405 Squadron only three aircraft involved in the first wave returned. Lancaster JB241 piloted by Flying Officer Jackson was attacked by a night fighter, and the aircraft subsequently exploded, coming down at Bermering, France. Three men were blown clear and became POWs. The other four men were killed. Lancaster ND526 piloted by Flying Officer Christisou was also attacked by a night fighter and came down near Weyer, France. Five of his crew became POWs and the other two men died.

The squadron had no time to mourn their losses, as the very next day

39/40 Public Record Office AIR 24 266.

operations were on again. As on the previous night, Bomber Command was
to send two waves of bombers, which comprised 594 aircraft, to attack
Augsburg. From Gransden Lodge, 11 aircraft were detailed to take part in
the first phase and three aircraft for the second phase, Arthur and crew were
scheduled to act again as 'Supporters' in the first part of the attack.
However, 42 minutes into the flight and whilst still over England there was
a complete intercom failure. Arthur changed course and took the Lancaster
out over the North Sea where the bombload and fuel from the number 1
starboard tank were jettisoned. The crew then returned to base. One other
aircraft from the squadron returned early; all the others attacked the target
and returned to base. Bomber Command lost 21 aircraft on the night in
what was a particularly damaging raid. The marking was accurate and the
old centre of Augsburg was completely destroyed.

The next few nights were quiet ones at Gransden Lodge in terms of
operational flying; Arthur took the crew on training flights, a 4¼ hour
cross-country and a one hour HLB (high level bombing) on the 29th. The
crews were kept on their toes, however, with plenty of ground training. On
1 March operations were on once more; 14 aircraft were detailed for a raid
to Stuttgart. Arthur and crew were to continue their now familiar role of
supporters. Taking off in Lancaster 'W' at 2354 hours, they arrived after
just over three hours' flying at an almost completely cloud-covered target
area. At 0307 hours Alex released the five 2,000lb HC bombs using the
H2S, from 18,700 feet. After an uneventful return flight Lancaster 'W'
touched down at 0705 hours and the crew's subsequent raid report
suggested a successful raid with the glow of fires still seen 90 miles from
the target area. In fact the cloud cover had adversely affected the accuracy
of the bombers, but some new damage was caused to the city. The cloud
cover did also provide some help to the bombers by hindering the activities
of the German night fighters. Only four aircraft out of the 557 sent on the
raid were lost. All 14 aircraft from 405 Squadron returned to base.

For the next fortnight the squadron enjoyed a period away from any
operational duties, with plenty of ground and air training. On 15 March the
squadron prepared for a return to Stuttgart, and 16 aircraft were detailed.
Arthur and crew in Lancaster 'W' were again supporters. They took off at
1935 hours with five 2,000lb HC bombs. There were navigational
difficulties on the way to the target. The plan was to pick up Lake
Constance, so as to make a timed run to the target. However this was not the
case and time was wasted turning south in an effort to locate the lake.
Eventually Arthur gave up and turned back on track. At 2311 hours the
aircraft approached the estimated aiming point, identifying a number of
green TIs on the ground. At 2312 hours some Pathfinder flares were seen to
fall. Soon Alex picked up the corner of a built up area on the H2S and upon
this, the bombload was released at 2316 hours, from 18,700 feet amidst
moderate flak. After an uneventful return flight the Lancaster arrived back
at base at 0227 hours. The crew's report mentioned scattering of the

Pathfinder marking, which proved to be the case, with little damage resulting as most of the bombs fell in open country. The crew report also mentioned 'red and white fighter flares seen over a large area'. The night fighters contacted the bomber stream just before Stuttgart was reached and exacted their toll. Out of the 863 aircraft on the raid 37 were lost, one of which came from 405 Squadron. Lancaster ME622 piloted by Flight Lieutenant Fyfe was shot down over the target area by a night fighter, four men were killed, the other three became POWs.

On 18 March 16 aircraft at 405 Squadron were detailed for a raid to Frankfurt and Arthur and crew were once more in Lancaster 'W' to act as supporters with their six 2,000lb HC bombload. Taking off at 1932 hours they enjoyed an uneventful outward flight arriving at the target area at 2154 hours. Alex released the bombload from 18,800 feet by H2S, checked by a timed run from Giezen. After an uneventful return flight they landed back at Gransden Lodge at 0036 hours. All 405 Squadron aircraft returned from what proved to be a successful raid; for accurate marking had led to the city suffering extensive destruction. Out of the 846 aircraft sent on the raid, 22 were lost.

On 22 March Frankfurt was again visited by the bomber force, and 14 aircraft from 405 Squadron were detailed. Arthur and crew were once more in the now familiar Lancaster 'W', as supporters, again with a bombload of six 2,000lb HC bombs. Taking off at 2221 hours, the raid unfolded in a similar fashion to the one a few nights earlier. At 2146 hours the bombload was released from 18,100 feet by H2S, again checked by the timed run from Giezen. On leaving the target the crew witnessed many concentrated fires with lots of smoke and also some spoof red TIs which had been dropped south of the target. Arthur landed the Lancaster back at base at 0215 hours and soon all the squadron's Lancasters returned. Of the 816 Bomber Command aircraft that took part in the raid 33 were lost. An acceptable loss rate for Bomber Command as once more the Pathfinder marking proved accurate with the amount of damage surpassing that of the raid on 18 March. Two nights later 162 B-17s of the US Eighth Air Force also bombed Frankfurt inflicting further damage. The city's diary records: 'The three air raids of 18th, 22nd and 24th March were carried out by a combined plan of the British and American Air Forces and their combined effect was to deal the worst and most fateful blow of the war to Frankfurt, a blow which simply ended the existence of the Frankfurt which had been built up since the Middle Ages.'[41] From 18,000 feet in the air, the men of Bomber Command would have not been able to see the effect of the raids upon the city but it would not be long before some of them would get the chance.

---

[41] *Stadtarchiv Frankfurt am Main, Chroniken s5/140, Vol. 6* p988 quoted in *The Bomber Command War Diaries* by Martin Middlebrook and Chris Everitt, Midland Publishing, 1996, p483.

On 24 March 1944, 405 Squadron prepared for a raid to the 'Big City' with the invasion of Western Europe by the Allies pending, which would mean a redirection of his bomber force, Harris had decided to risk one more attempt at lighting the fires in the Reich capital. This was another major operation for Bomber Command with 811 aircraft eventually taking off.

During the day the USAAF were to again attack Schweinfurt in southern Germany, and so Bomber Command planners chose a northerly route to the target, hoping to avoid the German fighters drawn south earlier in the day. Also a diversionary raid by training units would take place over northern France, suggesting further attacks on southern Germany. Mosquito raids to Kiel, Duisburg and Münster along with attacks on airfields were also planned to confuse German controllers.

Crew:	Captain	W/O Darlow, A.E.
	Navigator	W/O Lorimer, G.A.
	Bomb aimer	P/O Nethery, A.
	Wireless operator	Sgt Burrell, A.W.
	Rear gunner	F/S Copeland, D.
	Mid upper gunner	Sgt Utton, T.E.
	Flight engineer	Sgt Richards, P.W.

Aircraft Type and Number: Lancaster III   W

Bomb Load: 1 x 4,000lb HC
                 5 x 1,000lb HC
Total: **9,000lb**

Zero hour for the raid, 2230 hours (advanced during the operation by 5 minutes), duration of attack, 2225 hours to 2245 hours.

Navigation: The bomber stream would cross the North Sea to Denmark, across the Baltic and down to Berlin. After leaving the target the bomber stream would head due west with a slight turn to avoid the defences of the Ruhr, then across Holland and out to the North Sea.

Window was to be dropped by Mosquitos ahead of the main force over Denmark, which would then go on to the diversion raid at Kiel. Mosquitos attacking Berlin were to drop four bundles of Window per minute going into the target and two per minute going out. The main force aircraft were to drop two bundles of Window per minute within 50 miles of Berlin and one per minute for the rest of both routes.

Pathfinders

Method; Newhaven with emergency skymarking

Time over target	*Aircraft type*	*Marking Method*
z – 5	28 Blind Marker Illuminators	If less than 7/10ths cloud to drop green TI and white flares

		blindly, if more to release greens and release point flares (red with yellow stars). If H2S was unserviceable, all markers to hold their TI and flares and then bomb with the supporters.
z – 5	70 Supporters	To bomb blindly, if possible, otherwise after visual identification, or on a good DR, or at the centre of all TI or skymarkers.
z – 3	6 Visual Markers	To mark the exact aiming point with mixed salvoes of reds and greens.
z – 1 to z + 14	20 Blind Backers-up	Those detailed to attack before z + 7 to aim at the centre of all TI if a Newhaven was in progress. If cloud had prevented this, to drop skymarkers blindly. Later arrivals to drop both reds and skymarkers blindly.
z to z + 14	20 Visual Backers-up	To aim reds at the centre of mixed salvoes, or at the centre of all TI with a 2-second overshoot.

Main Force

Time over target	Aircraft numbers	Bombing Method
z to z + 3	125 aircraft	To aim at the centre of all
z + 3 to z + 6	125 aircraft	mixed salvoes in the early
z + 6 to z + 9	128 aircraft	stages of the raid, later at the
z + 9 to z + 12	125 aircraft	centre of reds. If TI could not
z + 12 to z + 15	129 aircraft	be seen, to bomb on the centre of skymarkers.

There would also be 26 'ABC' aircraft throughout the attack.

The main force received orders not to pay any attention to weaker and shorter burning red markers as these would undoubtedly be decoys positioned by the enemy. A Mosquito and a Lancaster were to act as master bombers broadcasting their advice and comments throughout the raid. These types of aircraft were becoming regular features of raids, carrying the responsibility of directing the bomber force and correcting, adjusting and re-concentrating the bombing. Wing Commander Lane of 405

Squadron was to fly the master bomber Lancaster, a special aircraft fitted with Merlin 85 engines, which gave it the ability to achieve higher altitudes and thus direct proceedings from above.

No. 405 Squadron detailed 15 Lancasters, including 'W' piloted by Arthur Darlow. 'W', detailed as a Supporter, was lifted from the Gransden Lodge runway at 1845 hours. George had been given his forecast winds for the route but early on it became clear that the actual winds were a lot higher than expected.

> *Alex Nethery:* Briefing Met. had said 50 to 60 mph winds. It
> was actually 100 mph or more. When my radar came on at
> 5,000 feet we were already in trouble.

Certain aircraft within the bomber stream broadcast to Bomber Command the actual wind speeds and directions from various points, by using their Gee and H2S. Bomber Command were then able to broadcast to all other crews the revised wind speeds relating to the previous half hour and a forecast for the next half hour. Navigators could make adjustments to their routes and many did but the result was that the bomber stream became very scattered. Bomber Command also signalled to aircraft that zero hour was to be moved forward by five minutes to allow for the new wind estimates. Even so, at the target many aircraft arrived early and were forced to orbit. Some had flown right over and had the dilemma of whether or not to turn back, involving considerable risk. Some had made correcting movements prior to the target and arrived on time. It would be fair to say that the bomber force was all over the place.

Arthur and crew ran into the target along what they thought was the scheduled flight path. However they found that the wind had drifted their aircraft west of the target. They changed course and came in due north. By the use of H2S, a wood was picked up north-west of the target and the bomb load was released from 19,350 feet at 2228 hours, south of the wood. After leaving the target area they witnessed ground fires over a wide area and recorded seeing a 'blob' of red and green TI dropped 15 miles south of the target. Wing Commander Lane arrived on time, trying his best to control the scattered bombing force. However all he could do was voice encouragement to crews: 'Those bastards wanted a war; now show them what war is like' was one of his reserved outbursts.[42]

The Berlin defences threw up slight to moderate heavy flak from 17,000 feet to 22,000 feet with moderate to intense light flak up to 16,000 feet. The searchlights were active, forming cones whenever breaks in the cloud allowed, or shining on the cloud base trying to diffuse the light and hence silhouette the bombers for the Wild Boar pilots. The Germans also ignited a considerable quantity of phosphorous on the ground, once the raid opened, in an attempt to further diffuse light amongst the cloud base.

---

[42] Quotation from *The Berlin Raids*, Martin Middlebrook, Penguin Books 1990.

Most of the losses on the raid, however, occurred on the homeward journey as the bomber stream became further spread. The diversionary raids had proved ineffective and the German controllers had picked up the bomber stream as it crossed the North Sea. But the wind hampered the Tame Boar operations as the bomber stream continued on its northerly approach. Once the bombers left the target area, however, the Tame Boar's task was made that much easier with bombers scattered throughout the night sky. Many bombers also strayed into flak defended areas, Leipzig, Madgeburg, Osnabrück, Münster, Kassel and the Ruhr. In terms of casualties the night proved disastrous for Bomber Command with 72 aircraft and men being lost (57 on the route home). The losses for Halifaxes was 13 per cent compared to 7.6 per cent for the Lancasters. Bomber Command put down 45 losses to flak, 18 to fighters and 9 to 'causes unknown'. Unfortunately this summary was somewhat off the mark. Bomber Command was still unaware of Schrage Musik and its potential. Indeed the intelligence report issued on 7 April 1944 summarised, 'The lack of concentration, which may have served to reduce possible losses to fighters, undoubtedly increased the loss to flak . . .'[43]

In fact the scattering of the force was one factor leading to a very effective Tame Boar operation, one that could and would be repeated. By the time the bombers left Berlin the whole of the German night fighter force was airborne, including those of NJG 1[44] mostly based in Holland, which had been kept down in the earlier part of the raid. The scattered bombers flew straight into the waiting night fighters and the carnage began. Despite the night fighter activity all 405 Squadron's Lancasters managed to return to Gransden Lodge.

Lancaster 'W' was one of the aircraft which brought back a night photograph of the raid and subsequent analysis by Bomber Command intelligence staff plotted their photograph as 10½ miles from the aiming point. They were not alone; of the 55 plottable night photographs showing ground detail only 11 showed any part of the target area.

> *Bomber Command Narrative of Attack:* A fair concentration of TI was achieved, 6 being plotted 1-2 miles E and SE of the aiming point, 2 on the Templehof airfield (2 miles SSW) and a group of 15, 2-3½ miles SW. Incendiaries extended over an area stretching from 1 mile N of the aiming point to 11 miles S and SW with the main concentration developing 3-7 miles SSW as the result of over-shooting by the main force. This was probably due chiefly to the powerful north wind. The enemy used many dummy markers, which may have contributed to the drift.

---

[43] Public Record Office AIR 24 268.
[44] Note; NJG1 stands for Nachtjagdgeschwader 1, meaning night fighter Geschwader 1. A *Geschwader* contained three *Gruppen*, a Gruppe contained three *Staffeln*; a Staffel was similar to a squadron but smaller, usually composed of about nine aircraft.

The raid as a whole had had limited success with the bombing spread all along the bombers' route over the target. Further investigation by Martin Middlebrook detailed in his book *The Berlin Raids* gives:

> The number of casualties is given as 47 people dead, 156 injured and 190 missing . . . and an estimated 24,000 people were forced to leave their homes . . . buildings hit [included] the Swedish Embassy, the Steglitz Town Hall, a theatre, the Mercedes Cinema, five hospitals, a church, a butter warehouse, a grain silo, the Kreuzberg Gasworks where there was a large fire in a gasometer, the offices of the National Milk and Fat Industry, three breweries, a Gestapo building, Himmler's bunker, three military establishments and one naval establishment . . . nine important war industry factories [were also damaged].[45]

Despite the losses of the 24th, squadrons only had a few days to recover. No. 405 Squadron was once more operational on the night of 26/27 March when nine Lancasters were detailed for a raid to Essen, one of which was later withdrawn owing to magazine trouble. Arthur and crew flying in Lancaster 'W' once more, one of those detailed, took off from Gransden Lodge at 2003 hours. Their bombload consisted of one 4,000lb HC Minol, six 1,000 HC (short-lived), 510 x 4lb incendiaries and 30 x 4lb 'X' type incendiaries, making a total of 12,160 lbs. Their role was once more to act as supporters. After an uneventful outward journey they arrived at a cloud-covered target and Alex released the load from 19,850 feet at 2159 hours on the glow of TI red and green below the cloud. Whilst over the target they witnessed a large explosion which lit up the sky for 12 seconds. After an uneventful return flight, Lancaster 'W' touched down at base at 0033 hours and all other 405 Squadron Lancasters also returned.

The Oboe Mosquitos on the raid had marked Essen well and there was considerable damage caused within the city. Out of the 705 aircraft sent on the raid only nine were lost. The German controllers possibly expected an attack deeper into Germany.

This raid marked the closure of the Battle of Berlin, which had involved 19 major raids to the city, but did not achieve its aims. The Luftwaffe Tame Boar operation was proving itself more efficient as time progressed. With pressure mounting on Harris to switch his focus of attacks to other targets, he decided to make one more raid deep into Germany. His decision proved unwise as the raid on Nuremberg on 30/31 March 1944 proved the most disastrous in the war with regard to Bomber Command losses. The Tame Boar operation tore into the bomber stream and the reckoning at the end of the night was 95 heavies missing, 12.1 per cent of

---

45 Martin Middlebrook, *op.cit.*, p290.

total force. There were 14 Lancasters involved in the raid from 405 Squadron but it did not include Arthur's. Thankfully for the squadron all the crews returned.

The raid ended an unhappy period for Bomber Command and Arthur Harris's, hopes of ending the war by bombing alone unrealised. Fortunately for Bomber Command crews, the focus of operations now switched toward preparations for the forthcoming invasion of northern France by the Allies.

CHAPTER 10

INVASION PREPARATIONS

On 17 August 1943 at the Quebec Conference Churchill, Roosevelt and the Canadian Prime Minister Mackenzie King met, to discuss the opening of the second front within Europe. It was agreed that Operation Overlord, the invasion of Europe across the English Channel, would become the primary ground and air effort in Europe in 1944.

It soon became obvious that a successful invasion on the north-west coast of France would demand considerable weakening of the German air force and at the end of January 1944 the Combined Chiefs of Staff issued a directive, giving 'Pointblank' new emphasis. The original directive issued in June 1943 regarding German fighter aircraft industry would receive even more attention, together with further attacks on the oil industry.

Overlord planners, however, envisaged another, concurrent, role for the bomber forces, the Transportation Plan, to prevent German ground forces reinforcing their divisions within an invasion area, by targetting the transportation system in the Western European occupied countries. In particular, bottlenecks in the rail system were identified, marshalling yards, regulating centres, servicing facilities, assemblies of rolling stock and locomotives. It was hoped that the destruction and disruption caused at these critical focal points would lead to a breakdown of the system as a whole, considerably slowing enemy military reinforcement. The plan involved targets from the Pas de Calais area down to Normandy, the Pas de Calais area receiving considerable attention to convince the Germans that this would be the Allied invasion area.

Bomber Command crews were able to identify with these clear military objectives. Targets would fall within the range of radar devices, assisting navigation and target finding and marking. Shorter routes and time over enemy territory afforded less contact with enemy defences, particularly the night fighters whose Tame Boar operations would have less reaction time. Sir Arthur Harris was not so enthusiastic about the diversion of his forces. He still wished to direct his capabilities to the heart of Germany, destroying its industry and weakening the civilian will to fight. However the Air Staff and Sir Charles Portal recognised and maintained that overall Allied strategy required bombers to act in an auxiliary role. After the war Harris wrote rather philosophically on the subject.

In April of 1944 I certainly had no illusion that the strategic bombers had done their work; it never occurred to me that we could reduce the largest and most efficient industrial power in Europe to impotence by a year's bombing with an average striking force of six or seven hundred bombers which were never certain to find the target if it lay east or south of the Ruhr. On the contrary, I expected that the damage we had done to German industry – and for the size of the force it was most impressive – would be repaired in five or six months if we gave the enemy any respite from strategic bombing, and so I informed all concerned. That respite we were now proposing to give him; there was no alternative if the most formidable military problem of this and possibly of any war was to be solved and Europe was to be invaded across the sea. Naturally I did not quarrel with the decision to put the bomber force at the disposal of the invading armies once the die had been cast; I knew the armies would not succeed without them.[46]

As implementation of the Transportation Plan began, Harris was conscious of and forecast the lessening risks surrounding operations in support of the preparations for D-Day and effected a change in policy concerning crews' operational tours:

> The risk, fatigue and strain in respect of operations carried out against short range and lightly defended targets in France, and short range mining operations where fighter defence is practically nil, is nowadays in no way comparable to those associated with long range targets in Germany. Under present arrangements those entirely different types of operation count as one sortie. The result is that some aircrews must inevitably finish their operational tour having experienced far less risk and strain than others, which is obviously undesirable. In addition, with the large amount of bombing of targets in France and occupied territory now being or about to be undertaken, crews will finish their operational tours too quickly, and the crew strength of squadrons cannot possibly be maintained. This especially applies to Stirling and Halifax crews, who will finish their operational tour much sooner than Lancaster crews, whereas the latter have to undergo far greater strain for the same number of sorties.
>
> In view of the above, I consider it essential to differentiate between the two entirely different types of operation, and to institute two separate methods of assessing operational sorties.

---

[46] *Bomber Offensive, op.cit.,* p191-192.

I have therefore given instructions that bombing and minelaying operations which are carried out in an area W of 7°E and N of 53°N, and W of 6°E between 53°N and 46°N should each be counted as one third of a sortie only. It is necessary to make a few exceptions to this proposal, and under existing conditions I propose that mining in the inner harbours of Brest, Lorient, St Nazaire and La Pallice should be counted as full sorties in view of the defences and opposition likely to be encountered.[47]

Trevor Utton on the change in targets: There was relief but there was also annoyance because the Germans were still defending these. We only got a third of a trip for those and that upset us all.

At a meeting on 25 March 1944 headed by Sir Charles Portal and General Dwight Eisenhower it was concluded that bombing operations should be divided between the German Fighter aircraft industry and the transportation system in France and Belgium. Specific targets were subsequently specified. On 29 March Portal reported on the meeting to the Prime Minister. Included in the report was the following:

There is one point, which I should mention to you now. In the execution of this Plan very heavy casualties among civilians living near the main railway centres in occupied territory will be unavoidable, however careful we may be over the actual bombing. Eisenhower realises this and I understand that he is going to propose that warnings should be issued to all civilians living near railway centres advising them to move. I hope you will agree that since the requirements of 'Overlord' are paramount, the Plan must go ahead after due warning has been given.[48]

On 3 April the War Cabinet met to consider the obvious and serious diplomatic issues surrounding the Transportation Plan. They informed Eisenhower of their concerns requesting that targets be selected on the basis of minimising civilian casualties. Lord Cherwell, Churchill's scientific adviser, was asked to look into the implications of the plan, and he concluded that in the time allotted the plan was unlikely to succeed, and that casualties to civilians would be in the order of 40,000 killed and 120,000 injured; the need for accurate bombing was highlighted.

---

[47] Harris despatch 8th March 1944, Public Record Office AIR 24 269.
[48] *Official History of the Second World War*: John Ehrman, *Grand Strategy* Vol V, August 1943 to September 1944, HMSO London 1972. Crown copyright is reproduced with the permission of the Controller of Her Majesty's Stationery Office.

The Defence Committee met on 5, 13 and 20 April reviewing the progress of the plan, which now included a revised list of targets in an attempt to limit civilian casualties. Estimates of casualties had been considerably reduced from the original 160,000 to 16,000 (10,500 killed, 5,500 injured). Attacks on nine rail targets up until 10 April had resulted in 1,103 civilians killed against the previous estimate of 2,540. Bomber Command losses of aircraft on the raids to the rail targets were significantly low during this same period, 2,055 aircraft having taken part with the loss of only eight.

On 26 April the Defence Committee met again, by which time 26,000 tons had been dropped on 32 targets, which meant one-third of the plan was now completed. Casualty rates were still below the estimates but photographic evidence suggested that bombing accuracy was not as expected, and the civilian population of the areas under attack was showing considerable unrest. Winston Churchill decided to refer the question to the War Cabinet once more.

On the 27th the War Cabinet met with Churchill, who expressed concern over the casualty rates, highlighting that it was the British bomber forces who were carrying out the majority of the operations, and therefore taking the blame. He proposed to discuss the issue with Eisenhower. On 2nd May Churchill received the following reply:

> I must point out that the casualties to civilian personnel are inherent in any plan for the full use of air power to prepare for our assault . . . It applies to the present problem and will equally apply to the future. It applies particularly to the proposed program of attack on M.T. (Motor Transport) Depots . . . and it will certainly apply to attacks on Headquarters and Communication Centres, which will be of vital importance immediately prior to the assault. Railway centres have always been recognised as legitimate military targets and attack on them is clearly obvious to the general population as a strictly military operation.[49]

Eisenhower reiterated the importance of attacking the rail targets to create time following the D-Day assault, pointing out that he didn't want his hands tied by limiting targets to those affording low casualties. Any such action would 'emasculate' the whole plan and Eisenhower concluded that any exclusion of targets meant 'the perils of an already hazardous undertaking will be greatly enhanced'.

The War Cabinet met the same day to discuss the letter and ministers

[49] *Official History of the Second World War*: John Ehrman, *Grand Strategy* Vol V, August 1943 to September 1944, HMSO London 1972. Crown copyright is reproduced with the permission of the Controller of Her Majesty's Stationery Office.

who opposed the plan were now only able to do so on the back of the most pressing disadvantages. However, reports were coming in that hostility to the bombing campaign continued to grow and ministers wanted to try one last time to lessen the impact of the plan upon the civilians. The question was once more referred to the Defence Committee, asking them to consider the implications of limiting all air operations in support of Overlord.

On 3 May the Defence Committee finally agreed that subject to the approval of the War Cabinet, the Transportation plan should proceed, ensuring that total casualties did not exceed 10,000. Two days later the restriction on targets was lifted and the issue was settled. The directive of 25 March was now officially adopted and the air offensive in the occupied territories intensified in the subsequent run up to D-Day.

Meanwhile, the bomber crews had continued to apply themselves to their orders. The Lille Marshalling Yards on 9 April were 405 Squadron's target; seven Lancasters were detailed but our crew was not called upon. Unfortunately this was one of the raids on which there were considerable civilian casualties; the target was damaged but 456 French people were killed. The next night the squadron sent seven Lancasters to Laon in a raid where little damage was caused. The squadron was unable to rest the following night, for ten Lancasters were detailed for a raid to Aachen that involved 341 Lancasters and 11 Mosquitos. Considerable damage was inflicted on the target at a cost of nine Lancasters, but all 405 Squadron aircraft returned.

The night of 18/19 April 1944 was certainly a busy one for Bomber Command. Over 1,100 aircraft were dispatched, of which over 800 visited railway marshalling yards at Rouen, Tergnier, Juvisy and Noisy-Le-Sec. Mosquito raids to Berlin and Osnabrück took place as well as over 150 aircraft laying 457 mines in the Western Baltic. Leaflet drops and resistance operations completed the night's activities.

Eight aircraft from 405 Squadron were detailed for the raid on Noisy-Le-Sec and eight aircraft for the raid on Tergnier. Lancaster 'W' was a visual backer up on the Tergnier raid, our crew's first operation in the preparations for D-Day.

Crew:	Captain	W/O Darlow, A.E.
	Navigator	W/O Lorimer, G.A.
	Bomb aimer	P/O Nethery, A.
	Wireless operator	F/S Burrell, A.W.
	Rear gunner	F/S Copeland, D.
	Mid upper gunner	Sgt Utton, T.E.
	Flight engineer	Sgt Richards, P.W.

Aircraft Type and Number:		Lancaster III W

Bomb Load:	2lb TI Green 'A'
	2 Ord TI Green 'A'
	10 x 1,000lb MC
Total:	**10,004lb**

Zero hour for the raid was 2330 hours, duration of attack scheduled for 2324 hours to 2336 hours.

Navigation: From Gransden Lodge the 405 Squadron aircraft would leave the English coast above Dungeness crossing the Channel to a point on the French coast about 10 miles east of Dieppe. From there a turn south-east and after crossing about 100 miles of occupied territory the bombers would be positioned south of the target. The line of approach crossed the target almost due north, and after bombing, the stream would turn due west. After about 55 miles the bombers would then cross the incoming flight path and turn to follow this back to base.

Pathfinders

Once over the target the Pathfinders were to use both Newhaven and Musical Parramatta. There was also a Master bomber on the raid acting as a visual marker, with the memorable callsign, 'stinkbow'.

Time over target	Aircraft type	Marking Method
z – 6	2 Musical Blind Markers	To bomb at 28,000 feet dropping TI green or red
z – 3	2 Musical Blind Markers	provided the run was satisfactory.
z – 5	9 Illuminators	At 14,000 feet to drop white flares and bombs on the TI, the first flare with bombs and the remainder at 10 second intervals. If unable to see the TI then reserve the bombs, drop the flares blindly on H2S, orbit the target and then bomb with the main force.
z – 3	3 Visual Markers	After definite visual identification, to mark the aiming point with mixed red and green TI, otherwise retain the TI and act as the main force.
z to z + 6	7 Visual Backers-up	To keep the aiming point marked with TI green firstly on the centre of mixed red and green TI, alternatively on the

| z | 5 Supporters | centre of green TI. To aim their bombs at the mixed red and green TI or red, or green TI. |

Main Force

Time over target	*Aircraft numbers*	*Bombing Method*
z to z + 3	71 Halifaxes	To aim firstly at mixed red and
z + 3 to z + 6	71 Halifaxes	green TI, and red TI, alternatively at the centre of green TI.

The Pathfinders' orders emphasised the need for accuracy on the raids and definite visual identification, obviously owing to the danger of dropping bombs in civilian areas. Orders were also passed to the main force bombers that if the TI were not seen the bombs were to be brought back, but allowing for a proportion to be jettisoned in the sea within five miles of the French coast, reducing the all up weight to the maximum landing figure.

Warrant Officer Darlow and crew took off amidst light rain at 2156 hours. Weather conditions over the target were reasonably good, clear above but with haze over the marshalling yards. Alex picked up a group of visual markers' red and green TI and at 2335 hours from 11,800 feet he released his TI along with one 1,000lb bomb. The TI were seen to fall on the north-east edge of the concentration. Arthur then circled for the bombing run and at 2338 hours the remainder of the bombload was dropped from 11,000 feet on a group of red TI believed to be at the edge of the centre of the marshalling yards. The crew later reported that all the bombing appeared to be around the concentration of TI but on the first run they had seen one green TI about one mile west, and one red and one green one mile east. They also reported one green cascading five miles north of the target area at 2344 hours.

Enemy ground defences were minimal but there was fighter activity. Bomber Command records one attack being reported and two fighters, a FW190 and an Me110 claimed as destroyed.

All eight aircraft from 405 Squadron returned to base and after analysing each crew's report the squadron operations record book recorded the following: 'Marking and bombing generally considered excellent with slight spread to West.'[50]

Unfortunately subsequent investigation using information obtained from other sources would not lead Bomber Command to reach the same conclusions.

After analysing the information received after the raid, it became clear that it was not a particularly successful one. Only three of the four blind

---

[50] Public Record Office AIR 27 1789.

marker Mosquitos opened the attack and their marking was inaccurate. The visual markers put their first mixed salvo 1,500 yards north-west of the aiming point, and the next two salvoes 700 yards south-west. The master bomber instructed the backers-up and main force to concentrate on the two southernmost salvoes. As a result most of the bombing fell on the built-up area south-west of the aiming point resulting in severe damage. Bomber Command records 126 hits on the yards. Indeed when Bomber Command plotted the night photographs taken, it clearly demonstrated the inaccuracy of the bombing. Reconnaissance photographs showed nearly 50 rail lines blocked, but apart from a turntable in the forward sidings and two buildings in the passenger stations, the installations and other buildings were not significantly damaged.

A partial success could be claimed for Bomber Command but at the cost of 6 Halifaxes and crews alongside the damage inflicted upon the civilian population of Tergnier.

Of the other raids carried out against marshalling yards that night, those on Rouen and Juvisy were considered very successful, with only one Lancaster lost on the Juvisy raid. The attack on Noisy-Le-Sec was also successful in terms of destruction and disruption to the marshalling yards. However, Martin Middlebrook records in *The Bomber Command War Diaries* that although 750 houses were destroyed, and more than 2,000 damaged, 464 French people were killed and 370 injured. Bomber Command lost four Halifaxes. All eight of the 405 Squadron Lancasters that took part in Noisy-Le-Sec raid returned to base.

The crew had completed their first raid to a military target in occupied France. The risk of being shot down had diminished considerably with the limited reaction time that the German night fighters now had. However, the importance to Bomber Command of accurate marking became the priority issue and on this particular night, 'friendly' civilian casualties and damage to civilian property were high. Churchill's fears were being realised. But how many Allied lives did these raids save on the invasion beaches of Normandy?

On 20 April 1944, 405 Squadron received orders to prepare for a raid on the railway yards at Lens, France. Fourteen Lancaster IIIs were detailed, including Lancaster 'W' to act as a visual backer-up. All aircraft took off, Arthur and crew at 2205 hours, with their load of five cluster 7 inch hooded flares and nine 1,000 MC bombs; their job was to back up the earlier visual markers to keep the target area lit up, then blow it apart. At 2344 hours they made their first run on the target, but because of a stuck distributor arm no bombs or flares were released. On the second run one green and one red TI were visible, and the flares and one 1,000lb MC bomb were released, but no ground detail could be seen. On the third run it was again too hazy to see any target details but after instructions from the Master Bomber the remaining eight 1,000lb MC bombs were released on some green TI. The defences at the target were negligible with no fighter activity, no searchlights and only heavy flak providing any opposition. After an uneventful return flight Arthur landed the Lancaster at 0105 hours, a round trip of just three hours. The yards had been accurately bombed and only one aircraft, a Halifax, was lost out of the 175 aircraft that took part.

On 22 April 405 Squadron prepared for two raids, one involving seven aircraft detailed for Düsseldorf and the other seven aircraft for the rail marshalling yards at Laon. Arthur and crew received their orders to act as backers-up on the raid to the rail yards. Loaded with twelve 1,000lb MC bombs, Lancaster 'W' left Gransden Lodge at 2221 hours and after nearly one and three quarter hours approached the target. The target area lay under a number of illuminating flares but no target indicators could be seen. At 0004 hours and 0005 hours the master bomber ordered, 'Do not bomb,' asking for more illuminators. At 0006 hours the crew witnessed a large explosion, later identified as the No. 4 shed in the yards. The target by now was well illuminated.

Arthur brought the Lancaster round for its second run, and six 1,000lb MC bombs were released at 0010 hours slightly to the north of green TI conforming to the master bomber's instructions. Arthur then brought the aircraft round for another run by which time the previous order had been cancelled and replaced. The remaining six 1,000lb MC bombs were released upon red TI on the ground. The bombing later proved very accurate causing severe damage to the yards, although at a cost. Both night fighters and flak took their toll. Lancaster 'Y' from 405 Squadron was attacked by a Ju88 over the target area and the rear gunner Sergeant McRea was killed instantly. Also Lancaster 'K' was hit by flak, the mid upper gunner Flight Sergeant Foulds being slightly wounded. Lancaster JB684 piloted by Flight Sergeant Saltzberry failed to return to Gransden Lodge. The aircraft was shot down by a night fighter and crashed at Condé-sur-Aisne, and all the men were killed. In total nine aircraft out of the 181 that took part in the raid were lost. The seven 405 Squadron Lancasters that raided Düsseldorf the same night all returned to base; it had been a successful raid in terms of damage caused to the target, but at a cost of 29 aircraft of the 596 that took part.

For the remainder of the month of April, Arthur and crew took part in no further operations. The squadron remained active however. On the 24th, 11 of the 14 aircraft detailed for a raid on Karlsruhe, attacked the primary target; two bombers attacked alternative targets and one returned early. Adverse weather conditions hampered the effectiveness of Pathfinder marking and most bombing fell outside the city. On the 26th, six of the eight aircraft detailed for an attack on Essen bombed the target; the other two jettisoned their bombloads prior to reaching the target. Essen suffered an accurate attack as a result of good Pathfinder marking. On the same night six aircraft were detailed and attacked the railway yards at Villeneuve St. Georges. The southern end of the railway yards was damaged, but there were also civilian casualties.

The last two raids of the month of April for 405 Squadron were on the same night of the 27th; Friedrichshafen with its tank component factories was one target, the rail yards at Montzen the other. Six Lancasters were detailed for the raid to Friedrichshafen and all attacked the target. All six returned and reported considerable fighter activity, in fact 18 Lancasters were lost from the force of one Mosquito and 332 Lancasters that took part. The raid was very successful in terms of bombing damage, and the American bombing survey team learnt from German officials after the war that this was the most damaging raid on tank production in the war.

Eight aircraft took part in the rather unsuccessful raid to Montzen, where only one part of the yard sustained damage. Unfortunately for the bomber crews, the German night fighters were able to intercept the force and a total of 15 aircraft from the 144 that took part were lost. Amongst these was the 405 Squadron Lancaster JA976 of Squadron Leader E.W. Blenkinsop, who had been acting as deputy master bomber. His Lancaster was shot down by a night fighter, crashing at Webbekom, Belgium. Of the crew of eight, seven were killed, but Blenkinsop was blown from the aircraft and survived. He managed to get undercover with the Belgian Resistance, but in December 1944 the Germans captured him. He was taken to Hamburg and into forced labour, subsequently dying on 23 January 1945 in Belsen concentration camp of 'heart failure' and has no known grave.[51]

On 3 May 1944 405 Squadron detailed aircraft to take part in an 84 Lancaster and four Mosquito (all Pathfinder aircraft) raid to the Luftwaffe airfield at Montdidier. This followed up on a USAAF attack of 1 May. Also on the 3rd, 346 Lancasters and 14 Mosquitos attacked a German military camp at Mailly-le-Camp. Arthur and crew became operational once more, this time detailed to act as 'practice bomber' on the Montdidier raid.

Crew:	Captain	P/O Darlow, A.E.
	Navigator	W/O Lorimer, G.A.
	Bomb aimer	P/O Nethery, A.
	Wireless operator	F/S Burrell, A.W.
	Rear gunner	F/S Copeland, D.
	Mid upper gunner	Sgt Utton, T.E.
	Flight engineer	Sgt Richards, P.W.

Aircraft Type and Number: Lancaster III   V

Bomb Load:	1 x 4,000lb MC Minol
	11 x 500lb MC
	2 x 500lb GP, LD
Total:	**10,000lb**

[51] Martin Middlebrook and Chris Everitt, *op.cit.*, p501.

Zero hour for the raid was 0020 hours.

Navigation: Heavies: from base the bombers would pass over Reading and onward to Selsey. From there a direct route to the target. After bombing a turn south and then another turn west back to the channel before turning to the English coast, over Reading and back to base. Mosquito navigation was at the discretion of their CO.

Mosquitos to carry 24 bundles of Window, to turn immediately to track 296T and dive down to 13,000ft releasing Window at 1 bundle every 10 seconds. Heavies to carry 100 bundles and Window at 2 bundles per minute while in the target area.

Pathfinders
Method: Musical Paramatta directed by a Master Bomber

Time over target	*Aircraft type*	*Marking Method*
z – 6 to z – 3	4 Musical Blind Markers (1 per min)	To drop red and green spot fires and TI green and red.
z – 4	8 Illuminators	At 11-12,000 ft to drop white flares and bombs on TI. The first flare with bombs and the remainder at 15 second intervals. If TI are not seen, to reserve bombs and drop flares only, on H2S, make an oval orbit and bomb as practice bombers.
z + 2	4 Illuminators	To act as previous Illuminators but only to drop flares if instructed by the master bomber.
z – 4	Master bomber and deputy	At 8-9,000 ft the master will direct on darkie frequency and if he considers necessary will drop other markers or instruct his deputy to do so using a single salvo and overshooting by 3 secs with a false bombsight setting as follows: to wind add 24 kts. The deputy will make a run as if to bomb at z but will drop TI white only if required. Callsign – Cannibal
z	34 Practice bombers	At 9-10,000 ft to be directed
z + 3	36 Practice bombers	by master bomber or aim at

the centre of the TI if no
directions are heard. Bombs to
be in 1 stick at 0.2 second
intervals with false height of
1,100 ft set. If the TI are not
seen, bomb to be brought back
but a proportion may be
jettisoned in the sea within
5 miles of the French coast to
reduce the all up weight to a
safe landing figure.

Newly promoted Pilot Officer Arthur Darlow lifted the Lancaster from Gransden Lodge at 2300 hours with a bombload designed to damage the targets buildings and pockmark the airfield's runways with craters, preventing their use. The crew arrived at a clear target area, no cloud, negligible flak and on their approach the airfield became visible as the illuminators dropped their flares. At 0018 hours the master bomber commenced his run and at 0020 hours instructed the other bombers 'bomb green TI next to my white [or may have been yellow, see subsequent narrative of attack] TI'. Alex duly obliged.

> *Bomber Command Narrative of Attack:* All 4 Oboe Mosquitos marked in good time, and the 6 illuminators had also attacked before H-4. The Master Bomber dropped yellow TI but these were less accurate than the Oboe greens, which the main force were ordered to bomb. Very few bombs appeared to fall outside the target area.[52]

Our crew witnessed one small building burning, billowing flames and smoke. They then returned to base uneventfully, believing they had taken part in a successful raid. Indeed considerable damage was caused to the airfield as subsequent day reconnaissance demonstrated.

> This target was attacked on 1st May by aircraft of USAAF, but most of their bombs fell in open ground S. of the airfield. Bomber Command's attack was centred on the northern half of the target, and many craters occurred on the landing ground. 5 aircraft shelters were destroyed, together with other buildings and huts. At least 46 direct hits were scored on various runways. Near misses were obtained on a stores dump.[53]

52/53 Public Record Office AIR 24 276.

A successful attack but at a cost of four Lancasters from the four Mosquitos and 84 Lancasters that took part in the raid. There had been little night fighter activity on this raid, most of them probably notching up their kills on the Mailly-le-Camp raid, where 42 Lancasters were lost. One of the Lancasters lost on the Montdidier attack was ND881 from 405 Squadron. Flight Lieutenant McDonald's aircraft was shot down by a night fighter and crashed near the target. The crew of seven were all killed.

On 6 May 405 Squadron detailed aircraft for a raid to the railway installation yards in the Gassicourt suburb at Mantes-La Jolie. Arthur and crew were again to act as practice bombers and they took off at 0057 hours on the 7th laden with twelve 1,000lb MC bombs. As they approached the target area, the scattering of the TI became obvious. However at 0214 hours the master bomber reported 'Red is spot on' and Alex released the load from 9,300 feet on the red TI. The bombing damage matched the scattering of TI that the crew had seen. There was considerable damage caused in the yards but also some bombing fell outside the target area and there were civilian casualties. Out of the 149 aircraft that took part in the raid, only three were lost. One of these was Lancaster ND617 of 405 Squadron. The aircraft blew up over the target and the pilot, Pilot Officer Borrowes DFC, was killed with his crew.

CHAPTER 11

'BALE OUT!'

In 1942 Lorna Hayes' a teenage WAAF, had lost her fiancé, who had been a member of a Stirling crew that went missing over the North Sea; all the crew were killed and only three bodies, not including Lorna's fiancé, were ever found. In May 1943 Lorna joined 405 Squadron at Gransden Lodge, as mess stewardess, apprehensive at first but subsequently happy to be amongst the more relaxed atmosphere of a Canadian squadron.

On an operational day Lorna would receive a list of those crews detailed for action. She then received a phone call requesting the crews' pre-flight meal at a certain time. After briefing the crews filed in to the aircrews' mess to sit down quietly to their bacon and eggs. Lorna had struck up a relationship with some of our crew, in particular Trevor, Pip and Allan (or Bert as he was known to Lorna), sometimes joining them, with Doreen, Pip's wife, for a trip to The Plough or The Crown and Cushion in Great Gransden. On one occasion Trevor persuaded Lorna to join him for a ride on a motorbike, starting from outside the mess to the end of the road and back. The WAAF skirt did not lend itself to its owner riding pillion, having a tendency to ride up over the knees, and the few men who saw the pair shoot off up the road had multiplied to a considerable number for their return.

At meals Lorna would often be standing at our crew's table chatting away. It became quite a friendship, and at one point Pip asked her:

'Lorna, If I don't come back will you go and see Doreen because if not she won't know that I'm not back.'

Pip was living off the base with Doreen in a nearby village but any telegram would have been directed to Doreen's home address. Lorna agreed to the request adding that it was irrelevant as he would always come back.

On 8 May 1944, the air and ground crews at Gransden Lodge busied themselves for operations. The mess stewardess received her list of operational aircraft and crews, one of which was Lancaster 'W', Arthur's 30th operation as first pilot. They were to bomb a railway marshalling yard at Haine St Pierre, between the towns of Charleroi and Mons in Belgium, and 405 Squadron detailed 14 Lancasters for the raid.

Crew:	Captain	P/O Darlow, A.E.
	Navigator	W/O Lorimer, G.A.
	Bomb aimer	P/O Nethery, A.
	Wireless operator	F/S Burrell, A.W.
	Rear gunner	F/S Copeland, D.
	Mid upper gunner	Sgt Utton, T.E.
	Flight engineer	Sgt Richards, P.W.

Aircraft Type and Number: Lancaster III   W

Bomb Load: 18 x 500lb HC
Total: **9,000lb**

Zero hour for the raid, 0325 hours.

Navigation: The bomber stream left the Norfolk coast turning left half way across the North Sea, and a long straight run to the target. After bombing, a few turns taking the aircraft around Mons and then a fairly straight run back to the English coast.

The Pathfinder marking method was to be musical Parramatta directed by a master bomber.

Pathfinders

Time over target	*Aircraft type*	*Marking Method*
z – 8	4 Musical Blind Markers	To mark the target with red and green TI and with red and green spot fires.
z – 6	8 Illuminators	To drop white flares on TI if seen or using H2S if not. Then to make an oval orbit and bomb as practice bomber.
z – 5	Master bomber and deputy	To direct on darkie frequency, callsign 'Chugboat'. To drop white and yellow TI if necessary. The deputy to make a run at z – 3 and drop TI white on visual identification of aiming point or as directed by the master bomber.
z – 4	4 Illuminators	As previous illuminators but only drop flares if instructed to do so by master bomber.
z + 1	28 Practice bombers	To be directed by master bomber or aim at centre of TI. If TI were not seen bombs were to be brought back but a

proportion could be jettisoned in the sea within 5 miles of the French coast to reduce the all up weight to a safe landing figure.

Main Force

Time over target	Aircraft numbers	Bombing Method
z to z + 6	75 aircraft	To bomb as directed by the master bomber.

There were many operations for Bomber Command that evening, in particular ten Mosquitos from the radio countermeasure and intruder patrol 100 Group were sent in support of the attack on Haine St Pierre. Other raids included attacks on airfields and coastal gun positions.

Lancaster 'W' detailed as a practice bomber took off from Gransden Lodge in good weather at 0214 hours on the morning of 9 May 1944, arriving after an uneventful flight at the target area around 0326 hours.

After the crews took off from Gransden Lodge, Lorna Hayes would retire to an armchair and blanket in a room at the back of the mess to await the return of her boys. Just before nodding off she would request one of her girls to wake her when the phone rang, a call that would give her 405 Squadron aircraft's scheduled return time, so arrangements could be made for the tired crews' post-operation meal. Lorna would then instruct the girls to have everything ready by the ETA and to awake her again about 15 minutes prior to the crews' return.

On arrival at Haine St Pierre Lancaster 'W' found the weather conditions favourable, with no clouds and good visibility from the moonlight. The four Oboe Mosquitos and eight early illuminators dropped their flares punctually. The master bomber gave instructions to the main force to bomb his yellow TI, and subsequently a good concentration of bomb bursts was observed. Good fires then obscured the target area and dimmed the TI, at which point crews were told to bomb at the centre of the conflagration. Several large explosions were seen and the master bomber estimated that 90 per cent of the bursts were in the target area.

Bomber Command's subsequent analysis of the German defensive measure concluded that the ground defences over the target were negligible, one searchlight, and the heavy flak very slight. There was however considerable night fighter activity. As the bombers approached Haine St Pierre the German Controller ordered some medium range fighters to the St Quentin area at 0301 hours. Subsequently some were brought northwards toward Ghent. About five minutes after the raid opened, twin-engined and single-engined fighters appeared. Four attacks along with several other combats were reported, and a Me 110 was claimed. Those listening in on the German fighter transmissions were able to pick up a fighter pilot reporting he was badly wounded and his plane was shot to pieces. Also a fighter pilot was heard to claim '*Sieg Heils*' at 0324 and 0330 hours, and he stated at 0335 hours that his total was four. Night fighters pursued the bombers after the raid, some even following their foe out to sea. A Mosquito of 100 Group claimed a Me110 near Chièvres (near Ath, Belgium) as it threatened three Halifaxes. In all nine aircraft, six Halifaxes and three Lancasters, out of the 123 that eventually took part, were lost on the raid, all it was believed, to fighter opposition.

The next morning a reconnaissance photograph was taken of the marshalling yards and it appeared the bombing operation was a successful one with considerable damage to the railway yards and locomotive sheds.

But what had happened on the ground beneath the bombers? The garden of Monsieur Godart in the rue du Quéniau, Haine St Pierre, was adjoining the marshalling yard, and he recalls:

> For many weeks the BBC broadcasting in French, had been urging people living in the vicinity of rail junctions to leave their houses. These broadcasts insisted on the necessity of the bombings as part of war operations. They had finished up mentioning that in order to save civilian lives, a bombing in the north-east of France had been carried out at low altitude, thus causing the loss of some forty bombers with their crews. [This undoubtedly was the raid on the German military camp situated near the village of Mailly, in which 42 Lancasters had been lost.] Moreover, the most recent bombing operation at Haine St Pierre dated back to 21 March and since then the German workers of the TODT organisation had already repaired a number of tracks.
>
> These [broadcast] instructions were followed by almost everyone concerned; many of them still occupying their houses in the day, but sleeping in the neighbouring villages. That wasn't the case with us: my mother-in-law who was a hard working women, was breeding two sheep and in our cellar we had a little provision of potatoes, not to mention the clothes and the furniture. As a precaution against any possible prowlers (and there were some) she refused to move to somewhere else. Moreover, she was sixty nine and had difficulty walking; she wouldn't have been able to run away at once like my wife and I intended to do and actually did.
>
> Beneath the marshalling yard, at about 8 or 10 metres below the level of the tracks, a stream flowed called the *rieu de Baume* which, at the end of its underground course, flowed four metres underneath the lane 'des fonds Gaillards' before flowing into the Haine river. Under the marshalling yard where the above mentioned Todtistes [workers for the German

Todt organisation which built the West wall, roads and other construction projects] were often working, they had converted the stream course into a comfortable shelter with vault and lighting, a wooden floor and benches. For their part, the coalminers who were numerous in the Coron area [blocks of houses belonging to the colliery] had done the same under the lane.

By a moonlit night, with my mother-in-law's consent, we tested a plan, taking her to the shelter under the lane, about 300 metres away. When she arrived at the entrance of the shelter, she very nearly wrenched her ankle. However about 150 metres from the Todtiste shelter, a Monsieur C. Loman [a fitter and his family living in a lone house] was determined, if necessary, to go to the German shelter under the station. You could easily reach it in a minute's time. So from the night after our attempt, my mother-in-law stayed with the Lomans' family. My wife and I anticipated the events, sleeping at home, nearly fully dressed with all our clothes on, upstairs (it was a mistake) with our best clothes and the little house keeping money, near the bed.

Two or three nights went quickly by. I used to get my alarm clock to ring every hour, because for a number of days I found myself in such a state of fatigue (undoubtedly because of my low blood pressure of which I was unaware) that I fell asleep as soon as I was in a lying position. One night, I awoke at midnight, then at 1.00 am, 2.00 am and it was then, I think, that I heard the purr of a lone aircraft. I wound up the alarm clock and straight away fell asleep again. I did the same at 3.00 am and went asleep again. That was the last time because at 3.15 am, my wife woke me up; the whole sky was floodlit. We didn't know for how long!

A second eye witness recalls:

At 3.15 am, a detonation, just one, broke the silence of the night. We sprang up out of bed, all of us, the refugees at our house included . . . Was it a shot from the German flak? The explosion or ignition of a flare dropped by some aircraft? We'll never find out, but actually, a flare in the sky was slowly coming down, just over the marshalling yard. One aircraft, a single one, was flying over Haine St Pierre and Haine St Paul. In every house, it was a general exodus. After one or two minutes, the whole sky was vibrating with a threatening, informal rumbling. Good Lord! they were coming in strength, it was for us. Soon scores, then hundreds of blazing flares were parachuted and it looked like daylight over our villages.

In spite of the existence of shelters, carefully camouflaged at the back of the gardens, people at the far end of Haine St Paul and Haine St Pierre, having no time to get dressed, ran away to the countryside in the direction of Péronnes, and the hamlet of Fanuelz . . . They kept running across the dewy meadows until they were out of breath. Soon the night was filled with an awful din lasting for at least a quarter of an hour, maybe more . . . Several of us found refuge at the family Ghislain or at close relatives in the hamlet of Fanuelz overlooking the Haine (river) valley. They had a ringside seat, but in this apocalyptic night, when a twenty-five centimes coin could be seen on the ground, events warned of tragedy.

Monsieur Godart continues:

Straightaway, we went downstairs with our belongings; my wife had the key to the front door through which we would leave the house. She had knotted a white handkerchief to the key in case it was dropped, but when she wanted to get the key out of the lock, the handkerchief didn't come out; it was jammed between the door and the frame. First waste of time: a few seconds. We ran down the rue de la Cavée to the south. After about 20 seconds, when we were nearly at the end of the street, my wife froze, urgently needing to urinate. Second unexpected event, I hadn't thought about it. Again some more seconds lost, but nothing fell from the sky. After the bombing we realised we had been out of the danger zone, nothing had dropped within a radius of 50 metres and only a few bombs dropped a little further down in a place we had not passed through. This is just to say that in the case of an emergency it is wise, as the airmen do, to get rid of unnecessary things.

During the air raid of 23 March at 17.30 with very clear weather, I had noticed that the formations, flying in a very obtuse V, were following one behind the other at more or less equal distance, dropping their bombs at regular intervals. The fall of the bombs made an easily audible noise, something like a rustle of leaves which the explosions ended. There was then a short silent pause. As there had been about fifteen waves of formations (twice), I learned how to pin myself to the ground as soon as I could hear the rustle, and to run immediately just after the explosions.

But now there was complete darkness, and there was nothing visible in the sky except the points of candles (flares), and nothing higher up, not even their parachutes. I tried to repeat what I had done on 23 March. There was some noise, even violent noise, but without steadiness and detectable rhythm. I think I remember pinning myself to the ground then standing up again and lying down again; and so on, getting my wife to do the same, and coming to a grassy field the other side of the Haine river, arriving there over a footbridge. We were neither deafened nor shaken about, almost all the explosions were happening behind us. Continuing these [dropping to the ground] movements we reached the *Rue Haute* [high street] in Haine St Paul, then a meadow where J. de Geyter, a chief lamp lighter [working at the coal mine] was walking about giving anyone glassfuls of spirit from a bottle stolen from the Wehrmacht. The moon was enormous, nearly full. The bombing was ending, leaving us unharmed . . . I think it lasted about 15 minutes (without the proceeding flare lighting).

Our second witness continues:

It was the hardest and most dreadful shock. Literally, everyone of us got sick of it. Even in the undamaged houses, people, women, children, screamed till the morning. Nerves were broken immediately. It was too much and everybody of course could not be a hero. That night there was danger everywhere as even over the neighbouring countryside, aircraft were flying at high or medium altitude, in all directions, some of them in difficulty. One of them . . . in flames was splitting the sky like a meteor before crashing down near Péronnes. Nearly unconscious, staring at the fires . . . we got back to the occupied houses in the area. Among us, there were some people in pyjamas, who had lost their shoes in the meadows or the sunken lanes.

All the crew in the aircraft seen crashing to the ground were killed. According to a witness, a Mr Douilliez, the aircraft dug an enormous crater not far from a roadway, the chausee Brunehault. The next morning some civilians requisitioned by the Germans began to clear away the wreckage. One of these workers tried to steal away, from a corpse, a briefcase full of bank notes. However a German sentry saw him and forced him to hand the case over.

Our eyewitness Monsieur Godart continues:

We returned home by the street: the front door was shattered, the backroom had avoided much damage, the other rooms were badly damaged, but not destroyed. The brickwork of the kitchen and the other annexes was, for the most part, knocked

down. The battens of the slate roof southside and the beams
underneath were broken. All the window panes were shattered
in little splinters. The plasterwork from the walls covered the
floors in several piles. The little shed housing the two sheep,
which were unharmed, had a 15 cm thick cement ceiling
which had sagged one side only. The house was uninhabitable,
it was declared disaster stricken class B.

The nearest bomb crater was in the *talus de la Cavée* [a road
embankment]. It was a crater, in a way of standard size,
similar to all the others, about 3 metres in diameter at ground
level. We had seen dozens of similar ones, near the houses and
at a distance of 40 metres between them. None of those bombs
had caused much damage. However one bomb dropped on the
pithead machinery of the *charbonnages du Houssu* [a colliery]
at about 60 metres, thus exploding at nearly 15 metres above
ground and sending its blast below the horizontal . . . Nearly
100 metres behind the house, in a meadow, then partly
covered with a slag heap (in 1948 this slag heap caused a
landslide which flattened four little houses) a bomb dropped
without exploding, just leaving visible a hole of more or less
40 cm in diameter at ground level. Around the end of 1945 or
beginning 1946, the bomb was removed by some soldiers of
the US engineers. Then I saw the bomb, partly freed, tilted at
an angle of about 45 degrees at the bottom of a hole of 6 or 7
metres depth.

Soon after, our cat rejoined us, all covered with dust. As
planned, my mother-in-law had taken refuge with the Loman
family inside the tunnel of the *rieu de Baume* [stream]
underneath the railway station. There she found many people
who had, like her, made the same plans. The explosions
overhead had not hit them. The stream course, between this
refuge and the *chemin des fonds Gaillards* [a lane] was partly
obstructed by many craters and its level inside the tunnel came
up, but not enough to bother the occupants, all of whom came
out unhurt.

I did not hear that anyone under the flare lighting had
suffered from nervous shock or serious fright. My wife and I
were not much concussed; probably because fright is reduced
when one has to get moving without time for reasoning.

The damage to the rail yards was considerable but some bombs did drop in
the town. One local report detailed:

The two main rail tracks were hit in thirteen different places
. . . [a number of] signals . . . were seriously hit giving the

general aspect of a successful bombing. A great number of wagons, either fully loaded or empty, were destroyed, damaged, derailed or entangled. What was left of the electric installations and lighting wiring was destroyed or badly damaged. A signalbox and posts, which had avoided previous bomb damage, were razed to the ground. One other signalbox was seriously damaged, and a signalbox and post shelter were shaken but still standing.

No moving train was hit but the marshalling yard was out of order for some time. There were no victims among the railway men but twenty-five local people were killed. Some houses in the vicinity of the rail station . . . were destroyed or damaged.

Also intelligence networks working for the Allies in the occupied territories were quick to report the results of the bombing to London: 750 bombs hit the marshalling yards between the bridge of Bouvy and the big railway bridge of Haine St Pierre: all the tracks were cut off and ten railway locomotives, hundreds of carriages, and a locomotive workshop were destroyed, amongst other damage. A German military train was hit, as was a train of German weaponry and another of fuel tanks. When the German Governor of occupied Belgium and northern France, General Alexander von Falkenhausen, came to Haine St Pierre on 15 May, he ordered that the two main rail tracks had to be repaired and ready to use by the next morning, otherwise the persons in charge would be sent to the Russian front. It was done. Other reports state that over a thousand workers were at once put to work at the station to clear away the tracks to Mons and Braine Le Comte.[54]

At Gransden Lodge just after the bombing of the rail yards, a young girl awoke the mess stewardess as requested 15 minutes before the boys returned. Lorna Hayes had a quick wash, put on some make up and tidied her hair. She switched on the radio, turning the dial to 'aircraft', so that she could hear them calling in prior to landing. Some of the crews began calling in, landing, and going off to briefing. Not all had called in as Lorna began preparations for the meal. It was a good sign if the medical officer came into the mess hall first, for he would stay on the airfield until all crews were back. As the clock moved round to 5 am, the crews began to file into the mess hall, but without the medical officer.

On this particular night the German night fighters of IV/NJG1 (4th Gruppe, Nachtgeschwader 1) were flying from St Trond in Belgium, together with I/NJG4 based at Florennes.

---

[54] Source of Haine St Pierre accounts *Les bombardements alliés de 1944 dans le Centre*, Georges Place et Paul Vanbellingen, Cercle d'histoire et de folklore Henri Guillemin de Haine St Pierre et Haine St Paul, translated by Jacques Nachez.

Flight Lieutenant Chase RAAF piloting a Lancaster from 405 Squadron became a victim of Leutnant Wolfgang Marstaller of I/NJG4, who a few minutes later became a victim himself to an RAF Mosquito. Marstaller and his crew survived the crash landing, but he was to be killed later on in the war. The entire crew of the Lancaster was killed.

The Halifaxes of Flying Officer White USAAF (425 Squadron) Flying Officer Martin (432 Squadron) both fell to the earth near Courtrai. Georg-Hermann Greiner and Hauptmann Adolf Breves, both of IV/NJG1, claimed bombers near Courtrai. Hauptmann Breves took off from St Trond at 0317 hours in an Me 110 and using Schrage Musik attacked what was probably White's Halifax. The port wing burst into flames and the fuel tanks exploded. However the defensive fire from the bomber's gunners was so strong that Breves was forced to turn away. At this point he lost control of the Me 110, but he eventually regained control, landing safely back at St Trond. It was his first kill.

The fire in the wing of White's Halifax had begun to spread to the fuselage and after losing approximately 3,000 feet White gave the order to bale out. Flying Officer White and one other member of the crew lost their lives, four other members of the crew became POWs, two men evaded capture. Greiner's kill was probably that of Flying Officer Martin's Halifax; the pilot and two other crew members were killed, two men became POWs and two men evaded capture.

The Halifax, piloted by Flight Lieutenant Mead RCAF of 431 Squadron, became a victim of Georg Fengler, again of IV/NJG1. All the Halifax's crew were killed. The Halifax piloted by Flying Officer Wilson RCAF of 431 Squadron was claimed by Leutnant Friedrich Potthast also of IV/NJG1. The pilot was killed, four of the crew became POWs, and two evaded capture. Leutnant Potthast was killed two weeks later.

Pilot Officer Hawkins RCAF, piloting a 432 Squadron Halifax, became another victim of the nightfighter ace Oberleutnant Heinz-Wolfgang Schnaufer. It is very likely that Schnaufer, needing two attacks, used Schrage Musik to send the Halifax burning to the ground. The pilot and two other crew members were killed. Two of the crew became POWs, and the two other airmen evaded capture. Schnaufer would eventually claim 121 British bombers during the war.

The 35 Squadron Lancaster flown by Warrant Officer Kemp and the 426 Squadron Halifax of First Lieutenant Smith USAAF both fell on this particular night, probable victims of a nightfighter. Only one man from Kemp's crew survived to evade capture, the pilot and remaining crew were killed. Similarly one man evaded capture from Smith's crew of eight, but the pilot and others were all killed.

These aircraft may well have been the victims of Uffizier Konrad Beyer, possibly part of NJG4 at this stage of the war, who received the credit for shooting down four bombers on this particular night. His kills are recorded as 0325, 0331, 0333 and 0337 hours, which would tie in with Bomber

Command's intelligence summary. It seems that Beyer was able to penetrate and stay within the bomber stream as he picked off victims.

In the night skies over Belgium our crew had successfully bombed the target and set course for the homeward route. Arthur increased air speed to 200 knots indicated, as instructed at briefing, as the moon was nearly full. Approximately ten minutes from the coast, Allan became aware of a bright green blob on the cathode ray tube display of 'fishpond'. An aircraft was apparently shadowing them about 1,000 feet below on the port side. Shortly after Don got a visual sighting and as the aircraft got closer he said 'It's OK Skipper, it's a Mossie.' At the briefing prior to the operation they would have been informed that Mosquitos of 100 Group would be flying in the bomber stream to protect against the German night fighters.

> *Alex Nethery:* Arthur wasn't quite sure obviously, none of us were and there was a minute or so's hesitation. At that point Arthur decided to take evasive action just in case this aircraft was hostile. Just as he threw the aircraft into a corkscrew manoeuvre, by throwing the stick over and kicking full right rudder, we were struck by cannon shots starting, I estimated, about 3 feet in front of me. They extended up the port wing, set fire to both motors and both gas tanks. Unfortunately [the corkscrew manoeuvre] swung the tail of the aircraft up into the cannon stream.

Pip had been looking through a hatch in the floor of the fuselage and he clearly saw an aircraft with two tail fins, identifying it as an Me 110 (the Mosquito having only one tail fin). As Pip called to the gunners, the Me 110 opened fire. As the Lancaster began to burn, Pip, believing the cannon fire had severed the fuel lines, worked the graviner switch but the fire continued to burn furiously, engulfing the port engines and wing tanks. Arthur, realising the hopelessness of the situation, gave the order to bale out.

One of night fighter pilot Uffizier Konrad Beyer's kills, at 0337 hours, is recorded in the German records as being in sector OH. Our crew's Lancaster crashed in sector OH and it is highly likely that our crew had become one of the four kills claimed by Beyer.

CHAPTER 12

'REGRET TO INFORM YOU . . .'

At Gransden Lodge, Lorna Hayes was beginning to realise what had happened to Arthur and his crew.

> When they didn't come back, I was terribly upset. It was the only time I ever cried, other than when I lost my fiancé. I had never cried over a crew, ever before. It was just a deep friendship that we had. . . . It was about eight o'clock in the morning and I had been up all night. I finished what I had got to do and went to see Doreen. She was living in a coach house at the bottom of the drive of this big house. I knocked on the door and a lady answered. I can see it now, the door opened onto the stairs which went straight up. Doreen came out of her bedroom in her nightdress and stood at the top of the stairs. She looked down saying, 'Pip's not back is he?' I said, 'No but I don't know if he's put down somewhere.' She became very upset. She got dressed, came down the stairs and we went up to the big house to phone her mother. I stayed with her until she arrived and then had to go back in the evening, ops were on.

Eventually the telegram came through to Doreen, as to the next of kin of all the crew.

> Regret inform you that your husband Sgt Richards P.W. is missing as a result of air operation 8/9 May 1944 stop immediately any further news is received you will be informed stop Pending written notification from the Air Ministry no information should be given to the Press stop

Two 405 Squadron aircraft had failed to return from the Haine St Pierre raid. The other was Australian Flight Lieutenant Chase's Lancaster, which had been downed by a night fighter; all the crew were killed. Also noted in the squadron operations' records book:

118

Crew	Time	Details of Sortie or Flight
	Up	Down
RAF 174017 P/O Darlow A.E., R.143080	0214	MISSING 'W' PRACTICE BOMBER
W/O Lorimer G.A., J.19356 P/O Nethery L.A.,		This aircraft failed to return from this operation and
RAF/1390377 F/S Burrell A., RAF/1814673		nothing has been heard from any member of the crew
SGT Utton T.E., R.182337 F/S Copeland D.J.,		since time of take-off.
RAF/1603266 SGT Richards P.W.		

On 9 May Squadron Leader Gordon Bennett, Commanding 405 RCAF Squadron, sent a letter to George Lorimer's mother. Similar letters were sent to all the crew's next of kin.

Dear Mrs Lorimer,

Before you receive this letter, you will have had a telegram informing you that your son, Warrant Officer Lorimer, has been reported missing from air operations.

On the night of 8th/9th May 1944, your son, along with his crew and other members of this Squadron, were engaged in action over enemy territory. Unfortunately, his aircraft failed to return from this operation. It is the sincere wish of all of us that he is safe.

Your son was very popular with this Squadron and was an excellent navigator. He is greatly missed by his comrades, and his loss is regretted by all.

There is always the possibility that he is a prisoner of war, in which case you will either hear from him direct, or through the Air Ministry who will receive advice from the International Red Cross Society.

Your son's effects have been gathered together and sent to the Royal Air Force central Depository, where they will be held until better news is received, or in any event, for a period of six months before being forwarded to you through the Administrator of Estates, Ottawa.

May I now express the great sympathy which all of us feel with you in your great anxiety, and I should like to assure you how greatly his comrades in the Royal Air Force admire the heroic sacrifice your son has made in the cause of Freedom, and in the service of his country and the Empire.

If there is anything further I can do for you at any time, please do not hesitate to write me.

PART 2

CHAPTER 13

LANCASTER DOWN!

Extract from a letter written 20 June 1944 from William Darlow (Arthur's father) to the next of kin of the crew:

Five weeks has elapsed since the Air Ministry informed us that our boys were reported 'Missing' from a bombing attack on the 8th/9th May last, and still no further news of them has been received.

I send my deep regrets and sincere condolences in your anxieties and sorrow and express the hope that some of them at least, if not all, have survived. The attack was made over French territory (Haine St. Pierre – Brest) and I feel certain that my son, who piloted the craft, would have done everything humanly possible to save the lives of his crew. I met them all at the end of last March – a grand team – with an 'each for all' spirit amongst them. Our earnest hopes and wishes must now be that all of them, or at least some, managed to survive, and may be prisoners or even still free amongst some friendly folk in France.

I sincerely trust that the knowledge of our boys devotion to duty and their efforts in the common cause will assist you to bear your present anxieties in the same spirit as they always carried out the tasks allotted them.

In Belgium, between Tournai and Mons, lie Péruwelz and Bon-Secours. Bon-Secours is renowned for its church, the Basilica of Notre-Dame de Bon-Secours (our Lady of Good Help) which stands at the top of a hill marking the border between France and Belgium. In recent history its shrine drew crowds of worshippers from all over Belgium and northern France to pray to the Blessed Virgin, requesting her help in restoring the ill or crippled to health.

During the First World War the two towns were overrun, by the invading

Top: Seven Young Airmen (left to right): ...ex Nethery, Trevor Utton, Arthur Darlow, ... Richards, Don Copeland, Allan Burrell, ...) Constable.

Bottom left: Arthur and Anne Darlow.

Bottom right: Arthur Darlow and his son, Eric.

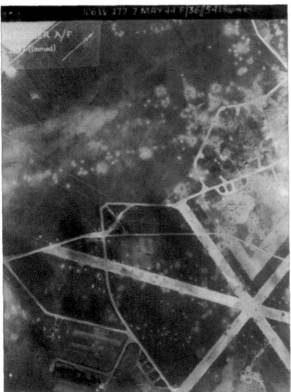

Hitlers Untergang bedeutet nicht den Untergang des deutschen Volkes

Darüber sagten die verantwortlichen Staatsmänner der Vereinten Nationen:

„Ausser den verantwortlichen faschistischen Führern braucht niemand in den Ländern der Achse die bedingungslose Übergabe zu fürchten. Die Bevölkerung der von der Achse kontrollierten Länder kann sich darauf verlassen: Bedingungslose Übergabe bedeutet nicht, dass sie Elend für Tyrannei eintauscht. Das Ziel der Vereinten Nationen ist, den befreiten Völkern den Weg zu öffnen zu einem freiheitlichen politischen Leben, das sie sich selbst aufbauen können, und zu wirtschaftlicher Sicherheit."
Roosevelt, 25.8.43.

„Es wäre töricht, die Hitler-Clique mit dem deutschen Volk und dem deutschen Staat zu identifizieren; die Geschichte zeigt, dass Hitlers kommen und gehen, der deutsche Staat aber und das deutsche Volk bleiben." *Stalin, 23.11.42.*

Wir führen keinen Krieg gegen Völker als solche. Wir führen Krieg gegen Tyrannei. *Churchill, 21.9.43.*

„Es liegt nicht in unserer Absicht, den wirtschaftlichen Zusammenbruch Deutschlands oder irgend eines anderen Landes zu verursachen. Ich sage das nicht aus irgend einer Vorliebe für Deutschland, sondern weil ein hungerndes und bankrottes Deutschland in der Mitte Europas uns alle, die wir seine Nachbarn sind, vergiften würde. Das ist nicht Sentimentalität, sondern gesunder Menschenverstand." *Eden, 29.7.41.*

Top: Arthur Darlow on his way to EFTS stops off at Mount Royal Memorial Pavilion, Montreal, Canada, June 3rd 1942.

(Steve Darlow)

Bottom left: Reconnaissance photograph at Montdidier airfield taken after the raid involving the crew.

(Public Record Office AIR242

Bottom right: A leaflet dropped by the cre on one of their raids.

Top: Aerial photograph of Haine St. Pierre Railway yards, taken 9th May 1944.

(Steve Darlow)

Bottom left: George Lorimer with Carmen, Jules and Jean (the young boy) Scherens. Clare Scherens (now Praet) took the photograph. These were the first group of people to help George evade capture.

(Jean Henrard)

Bottom right: The crashsite and wreckage of Lancaster ND347 at Bon-Secours. Photograph taken by The Resistance. The back of Raymonde Rock's head is in the foreground.

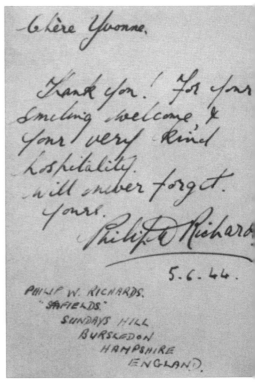

Top: George Lorimer and Alex Nethery in hiding at Raymonde Rock's house.

(Raymonde Rock)

Bottom left: George Lorimer (in hiding) with Raymonde Rock. *(Raymonde Rock)*

Bottom right: Note from Philip Richards thanking Yvonne Delmée who was one of those in the chain of Resistance activists who helped 'Pip' evade capture.

(Jean Henra

Top: Allies evading capture and Resistance members (left to right): John Trull, Belgian Resistance member, Jack Pierson, Philip Richards, Belgian Resistance member.

(Raymonde Rock)

Bottom left: Philip Richard's false identity card and travel permit.

(Peter Richards)

Bottom right: Arthur Darlow's POW identity card.

(Steve Darlow)

STALAG LUFT III SAGAN
51° 35'·8' N   4081/90
15° 19·5' E   221180

P/W CAMP   SAGAN
51° 37·6' N   4081/91
15° 21·1' E   246214
Neg. N° 41095

Above: Aerial photograph of Stalag Luft III Sagan and Belaria compound.

(Public Record Office AIR40229)

Right: Pages from Arthur Darlow's Wartime Log for British Prisoners.

lag Luft III A. Luckenwalde, 1945.

(Derrick Bell)

Accommodation in the Stalag – 500 per tent.
The square and some of the billets.
The dining table.

d. Church built by Russian POW's.

e. Liberating Russians.

f. Germans in the 'cooler' after the arrival
of the Russians.

g. Arrival of the first American troops.

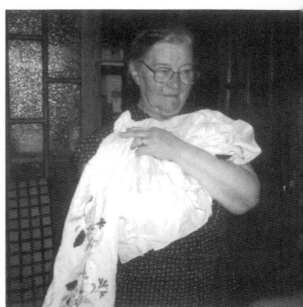

Top left: George Alexander Lorimer, 1947.

Top right: Clare Praet (née Scherens) with the blouse made from George Lorimer's parachute silk, 1996. *(Steve Darlow)*

Bottom: Rear Gunner Donald Copeland's headstone and burial site. Commonwealth War Graves in the communal cemetery, Chièvres, Belgium, 1996. *(Steve Darlc*

German army. Twenty-two years after they were liberated they were overrun again. Jacques Nachez was 12 years old, and living in the area, when the Germans came for the second time that century. He remembers it well:

On 10 May 1940, the German troops invaded our country and we appealed to our French and British Allies for help. The screaming of the sirens and the continual flying over of enemy aircraft forced us to go underground into the shelters. The radio was hardly optimistic and the crossing of the Albert Canal by German troops left us apprehensive about the strength of our defences.

That morning at about 10.00 am the first French soldiers, coming to assist in stopping the Germans, crossed the border at Bon-Secours. On 11 May and for several days, French armoured vehicles, tanks and guns pulled by lorries or horses, continued to cross the frontier into Belgium and take up position along the Dyle river (in the north east of Belgium). At dawn on the first day of the invasion, the German paratroops took up possession of the three main bridges across the Albert Canal. With these intact the road was wide open and the German troops and tanks poured into Holland and our country. The Belgian refugees, running away from the same enemy who had already occupied our country in 1914-1918, fled to France and as our town Péruwelz was on their way our streets became over crowded.

On 16 May, early in the afternoon, Péruwelz was bombed by three German aircraft, resulting in several fires. Some twelve houses were damaged, one totally destroyed. Two policemen and two civilians were killed, and another civilian was wounded. In Bon-Secours nobody was hurt. An unimaginable chaos reigned over the town where the mixture of civilian refugees and soldiers in retreat, blocked the streets trying to make their way to the French frontier. The bombing [of the town] gave the signal, the day after, for a near total evacuation of the population to France. Without knowing where we were going to, most of us found ourselves, a week after, in the Pas-de-Calais, not far from Dunkirk or Calais. We had been wandering for days and nights on the roads, mixed in with retreating soldiers who had lost their units, beneath the machine gunning of the diving Stukas, and were eventually stopped by the Germans.

On 28 May, the Belgian army, outrun by enemy forces, surrendered. After staying a week where the Germans had stopped us, we were allowed to return to Belgium. When we got back home we were pleased to find our houses undamaged, but they had been looted by refugees. We learned that the Germans arrived in Péruwelz and Bon-Secours on 20 May.

After the capitulation of Belgium and the fall of France, in the image of her Prime Minister, Winston Churchill, Britain did not give way to despair. She was our last salvation, our last hope to live free again. In June 1940, from London, on the BBC, in his famous speech 'L'Appel du 18 Juin' addressed to the French and Belgian people, General Charles de Gaulle told us to keep hope as we had only lost a battle but not the war. So people started to hope again in the final victory of the Allies against the German oppressor and in the joy of some day recovering our Freedom.

We had to prepare ourselves for a rigorous rationing, as food was becoming more and more scarce to buy. In December 1940, for each person:

the daily ration of bread (very bad) was 225 gms
the monthly ration of dry vegetables (such as beans and peas) was 200 gms
the monthly ration of butter was 200 gms
the monthly ration of margarine was 200 gms

In Bon-Secours and Péruwelz, lucky were the people who had a garden to grow potatoes, carrots and other vegetables.

The first months of the occupation were fairly quiet. September 1940 saw the first acts against the German telephone lines followed by reprisals against the population in taking hostages who were sent to prison in Belgium, or in Germany. Already on 2 September 1940, through public notices, the German military commander of Belgium and northern France (General Alexander von Falkenhausen) was notifying the population that in case of acts of sabotage:

1)   The military commander may put civilians in charge of surveillance missions. Those who intentionally or insufficiently, do not carry out their tasks will be sentenced to death.

2)   People hiding or giving hospitality to escaped prisoners of war or members of enemy armies at war with Germany (such as Allied airmen) will be sentenced to death.

3)   In minor cases (concerning numbers 1 and 2) of this notice and in case of impudence, forced labour or prison sentence will be given.

Little by little, the resistance organised itself, became more efficient and continued, throughout the war, to carry out all kinds of sabotage missions in collaboration with the Allied Intelligence Service. Some of the local people actively worked in the resistance. Others acted passively, but still with their lives on the line.

In the early morning of 9 May 1944 a number of the sleeping civilians of Bon Secours and Péruwelz were awoken by the air reverberating to the sound of roaring engines. Those quick enough to shake off their slumber were able to witness a burning aircraft illuminate the night sky as it screamed toward the ground, to explode in flames in their town. Some even witnessed a few parachutes descending through the, now peaceful, moonlit night.

The burning Lancaster crashed in a field to the side of the main road, Grand Rue, (now called Avenue de la Basilique) in Bon-Secours, killing a cow in the process.

> *Trevor Utton:* The port wing was on fire and Arthur called over the intercom to bale out. I undid the leather seat and got down into the fuselage picking up my parachute. I went to the back of the aircraft which by now was well alight, to the rear door about half way between the mid upper and tail turret. I opened the door, in and up and then turned to see Allan coming down the fuselage after me. As soon as the door was open out I went, and could see the wing was well alight. I remember the noise of the burning plane being replaced by the quiet of the night air. After a couple of seconds I could see what I presumed was Allan also coming out of the plane. The parachute opened and I looked down and saw what I thought was a manor type house, big grounds, and thinking this would be a good place to hide I worked the chute to eventually land in the garden, near a wall. I looked around and saw a lean-to type shed. I took my chute off and folded it and then took it with me into the shed trying to hide in a corner. After about two or three minutes the tallest German I ever saw with a rifle and bayonet came in and said ''Raus' [out] which I did. He and another soldier took me to the house.

Trevor, unfortunately, had steered towards and landed in the grounds of the Château Baugnies, which was located right next to the Ecole du Centre Filles where the local occupying German soldiers were quartered.

Allan Burrell called out to Arthur, over the intercom, that he was baling out. As he proceeded over the main spar and down the fuselage, he saw Trevor standing over the open door, then jumping. Allan followed, pulling his parachute cord, and having a few anxious seconds' wait until it opened.

Whilst descending, he witnessed the Lancaster crash into a ball of flames. He also had time to light up a cigarette.

> I landed in a street of terrace houses, the back gardens of which were divided by high brick walls – and when I say high, I mean about ten feet. Anyway, I landed one side and my parachute landed the other and I was left hanging about eight feet in the air. I eventually opened the release clasp and dropped to the ground. There was no way out of the garden and I approached the house and had some sort of thought about getting over the roof and into the street, but then there was a commotion outside, in the front, and eventually the Germans came in through the front door and out into the back garden. I tried to make myself invisible but they had a dog with them. This dog put his wet nose into my ear which caused me to move and that was the end of that! I stood up and from a range of about four feet one of the Germans fired his pistol at me. I felt the bullet zip past and I immediately put my hands up!

Unfortunately for Allan he had parachuted directly into the garden of a local German collaborator Monsieur Croquet. The Château Baugnies, where Trevor was captured, was about 300 yards from Monsieur Croquet's house. He telephoned the German quarters as soon as Allan came down, and it did not take them long to arrive to escort him away to join his crewmate.

Alex Nethery had also received the bale out order from Arthur:

> *Alex Nethery:* This is what I proceeded to do in a great hurry. I personally found my chute and put it on. I looked for Arthur's parachute until I realised that he was sitting on it, a backpack chute, that particular night. I went past Arthur with George right behind me. I glanced at Arthur, waved at him and had a look up at the terrible fire, which was raging on the entire port wing. There must have been at least 50 feet of flames out behind the aircraft. . . . The fuel used in those days was 100 octane and of course there was just no stopping it. As we went past, Arthur popped the fire extinguishers on the two port motors, which had a momentary effect on the flames but it was just a gesture. Going down into the front area where the escape hatch was in the floor, I was supposed to follow Philip Richards, the flight engineer, out of the aircraft with George behind me and finally Arthur would get out there as well. Unfortunately Philip Richards didn't have his parachute harness done up on the sides and he was standing to one side

of the open hatch doing up the sides of his parachute harness. So after a momentary pause I just put my head down and dove out of the aircraft first.

Once I left the plane I waited for the usual count of ten. If you pulled the cord right when you left the plane you'd tear the chute to shreds. So you waited for your speed to slow down by counting to ten and then you pulled the cord. I counted and went to my right to grab the handle, but to my horror it wasn't there! Then I looked down to my left and it was there, thank God! A parachute fits two ways. So I pulled the handle and out came the chute.

I was floating down and the bright moonlight was lighting my way. Now I could see I faced a major problem: our own Lancasters were right above me and I might get hit! But as they came over I could see that I was a bit too low for them. As I descended further, I'd say about 9,000 feet by this time, I could see what I thought was France. But as I went lower I spotted a canal and I was heading straight for it, so I started blowing up my Mae West life jacket. Then I tried to move the cords of the chute to one side to avoid hitting the canal. Canals had six foot high walls and if I landed in there I'd probably never get out. Adjusting the cords didn't seem to do any good, so I just left them. By now I faced another problem: I could see a forest beside the canal and that made me very nervous because I didn't want any sharp branches cutting through me!

It was a calm night with not a breath of wind. The ground was coming up very fast, almost too fast. My feet grazed the top of some trees and I hit – and I mean hit! – the ground just beyond the forest in a cow pasture about 50 yards from the canal.

I hit the ground with a thud and the chute came down and neatly covered my body. The fall knocked me out because I fell backwards after my feet touched the ground. The first thing I did when I came to, was bury my chute, just like they told us back in England. After that I checked for some cigarettes but couldn't find any.[55]

George Lorimer left the burning Lancaster just after Alex, by the front escape hatch. George landed with his parachute in the park of a property then called Château Debay in Péruwelz. As soon as he got rid of his parachute on the lawn, he quickly left. With German soldiers now active

---

[55] First part of quote from interview with author. Second part quoted in *Two Wings and a Prayer, op.cit.*

and walking about in the streets, he made his way from garden to garden behind the houses until he was out of the town. Then he started to think of what to do:

> I lay down in the grass to watch a house, which I thought of approaching. While I was doing so I was discovered by an armed Belgian or French guard employed by the Germans. This man was friendly and told me where I was, but did nothing to help me.

George then took a benny (benzedrine) tablet from his emergency kit and fell asleep. He continued to sleep as the sun rose and actually got a little sunstroke.

> I stayed in this area which was near the frontier until 2100 hours, when I decided to cross over into France through the forest of Bon-Secours.

This was actually a very good decision on George's part as the woods were known in the area as a place where members of the Belgian Resistance hid and the Germans were extremely reluctant to enter the trees in fear of being ambushed and shot.

> I reached the town of Bon-Secours at 2345 hours. I walked into the town and was seen by a German officer, but he paid no attention to me. After watching a lighted shop where a man was unloading goods, I went inside and asked for water. I was offered beer but refused this. Soon after a woman entered the shop and spoke to me in English. She then took me into the back of the shop and gave me some food. She said she could not help me, but had had contacts with American Air Force personnel who had been shot down in the area. I was also given 500 francs by a man in the store.[56]

Arthur landed about 200 yards from where the Lancaster crashed; he was one side of a fence, and his parachute the other. After retrieving and burying his parachute he started to walk along a nearby road in the opposite direction to the flaming aircraft. After about 100 yards he came to a T junction with the main road in Péruwelz, Boulevard Leopold III, and saw just to his left on the other side of the road a young woman standing behind some gates, beckoning to him.

Jean and Madeleine Henrard lived in the Boulevard Leopold III, and were obeying the curfew imposed by the occupying Germans. Jean heard the

---

[56] Public Record Office WO 208 3325, No. 2875.

Lancaster crashing and from his front window witnessed an airman para-chuting to an area between their house and the flaming wreck of the aircraft. Madeleine had also seen the parachute coming down, along with the explosion of the crash, and she went out and stood behind their 8 ft high gates peering into the moonlit night. After a few minutes Arthur caught her attention:

> *Madeleine Henrard:* I saw this airman on the other side of the road and I beckoned him across with my hand. As opening the gate would be noisy I told him to jump over a partially broken wall which was to the side of the gate. Germans were patrolling and so the noise of unlocking and opening the gates might have caught their attention. I told him to come in and gave him a glass of Dubonnet. He gave me a lot of papers and asked me to burn them as they were important. Then he had something to eat and asked me if he could sleep. So we took him into the house, prepared a bed for him and he slept the rest of the night.

Pip should have been one of the first to leave the Lancaster, and the probable reason for Pip's delay was that he had not heard Arthur order the bale out, since his intercom had become disconnected. However, as soon as he saw Alex and George preparing to jump out he decided to leave the aircraft. Pip retrieved his parachute and tried to get to see Arthur to see if he was all right but flames beat him back. While he stood next to the open hatch putting on his parachute harness, Alex and George jumped out. Pip sat on the edge of the front escape hatch with his legs and feet dangling out into the darkness. He had never parachuted before, but necessity eventually forced him out.

Pip came down on the roof of an outbuilding of a town house in the corner of the main square of Péruwelz, near the Town Hall. The property was owned by a Monsieur Ursmar Sauvage, who awoke suddenly owing to the noise, and realising something strange was occurring, immediately called for help from his neighbour Oscar Hainaut, the caretaker at the Town Hall. Monsieur Hainaut dressed, and still unaware of what was happening, he asked Monsieur Moerman, the Belgian armed policeman on night duty, to come with him. Monsieur Sauvage joined them and they found Pip suspended from the roof by his parachute, and trying unsuccessfully to release himself from his harness. They tried to reach Pip but none of the ladders was long enough.

At this time they were joined by Oscar's wife, Louise, who was a very active member of the local Resistance. Amongst other things she distributed a clandestine journal of the war's progress, which of course omitted to say that the Town Hall was becoming the centre for the Resistance movement in the area. Louise alerted her nephew Charles Hainaut (who aged nineteen was later killed by the Germans, on 3 September 1944, the day the area was liberated). After many attempts Charles managed to haul himself up onto the roof and help Pip out of his parachute harness.

Louise hid the parachute in a nearby garage and Pip was given something to eat by Monsieur Sauvage, together with an overcoat to cover his uniform. Pip asked about directions to France, but Louise advised that it was too dangerous at that moment, as the Germans were on high alert for the crew of the crashed aircraft. Instead she told him of a place of safety where he could avoid immediate detection. Louise went to wake her aunt, Madame Duez-Hainaut, who lived nearby, to explain the situation. Despite the fact that she was already concealing someone fleeing from the Germans, a *refractaire* (resistant to forced labour in Germany), she took Pip in. She gave him a glass of brandy to calm his nerves, but Pip, fearing it was drugged, tipped it into a flowerpot when she wasn't looking. Pip's caution, although sensible, was not necessary, for within minutes he was safely installed in her house and he slept the rest of the night under the stairs leading to the first floor.

Rear Gunner Don Copeland was still in the aircraft when it crashed and it is believed he had been killed, almost immediately, by the German night fighter's cannon fire. A local report says that the Germans left the Lancaster with Don in it for about three weeks. Don was taken to the cemetery at Chièvres in Belgium where he was buried and still rests today, alongside the seven members of Flight Lieutenant Chase's Lancaster, which had also been shot down on the raid to Haine St Pierre.

Jules and Carmen Scherens ran the 'Boucherie Lilloise' just behind the Basilica in Bon-Secours. Carmen spoke English as she had married previously an English Tommy, just after the First World War. Very early on the morning of 9 May 1944 they were awoken by the noise of a falling aircraft. Claire, her daughter from an earlier marriage, relates what happened.

> We saw the plane crash in the field near to the main avenue in Bon Secours, and prayed for the crew. The next day the word had got around that the Germans were still looking for some of the crew of the crashed Lancaster. I was just outside our house and actually saw this man [George] coming up the pavement at the side of the road. He still had his blue RAF uniform on. I wanted to call my mother but with the emotion of the circumstances I couldn't make any noise. I ran to my mother, who had lived in England and spoke English. We took him in, but at that time we didn't know if he was American, English, Canadian, whatever. We closed up everything and gave him some food. We hid him as soon as possible in case the Germans arrived, which they did about an hour later. We took his uniform, which was eventually hidden above the confessional in the Basilica.

When George had arrived, Claire's brother Bernard had rushed to the Reverend Ermel, a parish priest and considered a great patriot, to let him know about the presence of the Allied airman. He was an active member of the Resistance network who helped many prisoners of war who had escaped from Germany, and Resistance members to cross the French border, and quickly came to see George.

After getting George into some civilian clothes, he took him to a shed about a hundred yards away, behind a house next door to the Hôtel de France, where he could have a rest for the night out of reach of the Germans. In the morning Reverend Ermel accompanied by a Monsieur Fernand Bataille went back to the Château Debay in Péruwelz to recover George's parachute which he had left visible on the lawn. That afternoon Fernand's son Gerard, together with his friend Jacques Nachez, deciding possession of the parachute could prove dangerous, buried it under a pathway in the forest, inside a concrete drainpipe. (A piece of the silk parachute was cut away and kept by the Schuster's, and Claire still possesses a blouse made from it.)

With the Germans continuing their search around the area for the unaccounted crew of the crashed Lancaster, it was felt that George would have to be moved to a safer place. The Germans, quartered at the Ecole du Centre Filles in Péruwelz, usually had their evening meal at 6.00 pm, so the Reverend Ermel chose this opportune time to attempt George's transfer to a safer hiding place. He first got in touch with Zenon Lefebvre, a local farmer and subsequently famous member of the local Resistance movement, who during the war provided food for eighteen Allied airmen hidden in various places around Péruwelz. Using a code sentence 'A duck will soon be delivered' he telephond his intention of bringing George to him.

As George was unable to speak any French, Reverend Ermel gave him a *soutane* to wear, and dressed as a priest he left Bon-Secours, on a tandem, Ermel at the front, George behind, to rendezvous with Lefebvre. On the journey they came across a German patrol, and the disguise obviously worked as they were ignored. At a railway crossing they saw Lefebvre arriving hurriedly telling them to change direction as a German patrol was standing at the very place they were to meet. So they first went to the parish priest of the nearby village of Wiers and afterwards to a Dr Delcoigne's, where they waited an hour and a half, since the doctor was out delivering somebody's baby. On his return, the doctor invited George to get into the boot of his car. (Codenamed 'Clovis' by the Resistance network, the Doctor was the link between Wiers and Bon-Secours for evading airmen. He also would remove bullets from Resistance members who had been shot.)

During the journey they were stopped by an angry German patrol, obviously annoyed, probably because of their inability to capture those members of the crashed bomber crew who were still at large. When Dr Delcoigne produced his doctor's identity card, however, they were allowed to continue. They eventually arrived at the home of Ghislain Lermusiaux, where they met Raymonde Rock, who belonged to the Belgian underground.

CHAPTER 14

HIDING

Extract from a letter sent by Alex Nethery's mother, replying to William Darlow's letter:

> We are very grateful to you for the letter we received from you with regard to our son, and the other members of his crew and also thank you for extending your sympathy to us. We in turn send our deep regrets to you, as we well understand what an anxious and sorrowful time you are passing through. We have had no further word . . .Your letter has in a certain measure lightened our hearts and given us a little more hope that all is well with the boys. Alex had many times mentioned your son's name in his letters and spoken so highly of him, and we trust and pray that they are safe and will some day come back to us. Alex is our only son. My husband and myself, also his two sisters, loved him dearly.

When we left Alex, he had just landed to the side of a canal and had finished burying his parachute.

Alex Nethery: The time was about 4 am. What could I do? I was in enemy territory. The first thing I thought of was to walk to Spain, a neutral country, which was a mere 600 miles south, and from there get back to England. So I started walking south. I decided I'd walk by night and hide by day, and maybe find a friendly house and get some food.

I went up one of the embankments along a canal and noticed a footpath near the top. Then I thought I could walk the path during the day and get to a bridge or town. I was getting quite hungry and thirsty at this point. When I got to the top I became tired, so I laid down and fell asleep.

Sometime in the afternoon I was awakened by two young boys about 14 and 16 years old, who were staring at me. They must've known who I was because they probably heard the plane going down. I gave them some sign language to let them know what happened to me. They directed me to a cave at the side of the canal, then they let me know that someone would come for me at 11.30 that night. [These caves were actually some derelict limekilns.]

Just before dark an old man came to my cave to give me something to eat. It was two slices of bread with something in the middle that tasted like axle-grease. Actually rancid butter was more like it. The old man motioned on my watch that at 11.30 someone would be coming for me.

When the old man left, I left the cave and hid at another spot, but made sure that I could still see the cave. I wanted to make sure no Germans would be coming for me.

At 11.30 six men came and looked for me in the cave. When I could see that they weren't German soldiers, I came out and we all started talking. One of them gave me a bottle of beer which was my first drink of any kind for 34 hours. It was great! I could feel the moisture right down to my toes! But just then a farmer on a bicycle came and said a German patrol was coming our way. Everybody scattered except for myself and one other fellow. I guessed he was the one who was going to hide me.

We walked about two miles to his property and then he hid me in his tool shed. There I was, alone once again. The time was about 12.30 or 1 o'clock in the morning. I stayed in the shed a short while until I heard footsteps. My heart started thumping but, much to my relief it turned out to be the same fellow. I guess his wife gave him hell for leaving me in the shed and he came to get me and bring me into the house.

Inside, besides the family, were two big, fierce looking black dogs. The farmer and his wife didn't know English and I didn't know much French, but we somehow got along because they had illustrated pictures around the room and by pointing and using sign language we managed to communicate.

We sat down and I was served coffee – the cup, I remember, didn't have a handle – and I was given a flat lump of sugar. I watched and noticed that they stuck the lump in their mouths and then took a sip of coffee, I did the same.

We were there until about 6 am. They wanted me out of the house at that time because their kids would be waking up soon, and if they ever saw me they might blab around the school yard. So I was whisked out to some bushes until the kids left for school.

Shortly afterwards two people came to the house. They were from the Belgian underground and one of them was a lady, Raymonde Rock, and she spoke some English. I now found out that I wasn't in France like I first thought, but was actually five miles inside Belgium! [The man accompanying Raymonde was Zenon Lefebvre.]

By now I had replaced my Air Force clothes with civilian clothes and had been given a bike. Raymonde told me that she and her companion would bicycle along the canal foot-path, but I was to stay about a quarter mile behind so they wouldn't lose sight of me, or me of them, just in case a German patrol stopped me.

As we started I went only about 30 yards and the front tyre blew, but I kept going with the tyre flapping around the rim.

We went about five miles to a house near Raymonde's and I hid in a neighbour's garden [Lermusiaux] until dark. Once the sun went down I went to Raymonde's house, and when I got inside you'll never guess who was there! One of my crew members; George, the number one navigator. He made it, too, and he had cigarettes![57]

Raymonde Rock provided accommodation and hospitality to George and Alex for the next four months. She taught them things like how to use cutlery in a European manner whilst eating, in order not to give themselves away, but there were a few hairy moments. On one occasion George recalled walking down the stairs at Raymonde's, when he saw some people with German soldier hats, just beneath and behind the stairs. George slowly backed up the stairs.

Alex Nethery: There was little to do in Belgium whilst hiding there. Our orders were, 'Do exactly what you are told,' or be subject to court martial on return to the UK. I went outside the house once in four months to look at a pumpkin to see if it was ripe! We played cards, read slept and partied on Saturday nights. The four months seemed like twelve.

The hidden airmen occasionally witnessed the continuing air battle that still raged over the occupied territories.

Alex Nethery: Our location seemed to be on the flight path of returning bombers. White flares were often dropped to mark a turning point. Once every week or so we would see one of our planes going down in flames. We often heard the firing of machine guns and cannon. One night we watched in horror as five of our bombers were shot down in flames.

---

[57] Quoted in *Two Wings and a Prayer, op.cit.,* p83-85.

This was not the first time Raymonde had been involved in hiding an Allied airman. From the 18 April to 25 June 1943, she had given refuge to a US airman Lee Sanders, who was the gunner of a B17 Flying Fortress shot down near Antwerp. He was later to be caught by Gestapo whilst on an evasion line in France. Despite removing thirty teeth from his mouth the Gestapo did not glean any information from the American airman as to the names of his French and Belgian helpers.

George and Alex remained with Raymonde Rock, since the war situation made it seem prudent to keep them where they were.

Jacques Nachez: In the last week of August 1944 we saw the German army retreating and not looking as proud as in May 1940. On Saturday night, 2 September 1944, the GIs with a vanguard column of tanks arrived at Bon-Secours, down the hill on the French side. The morning after, Sunday 3 September, on my way to church, I was stopped by a Belgian gendarme (national police), our neighbour next door to us, who told me to get back home at once, as a German column was expected from Vieux-Condé (France). Thirty seconds later the gendarme was killed by a burst of machine gun fire from the Germans arriving from the forest and not from the other end of our street, as he expected. But for a matter of a few seconds I would have been killed with the gendarme.

The German column, preceded by a motorcyclist, continued its way in the direction of the basilica and turned right around it. The American tanks which were at the bottom of the hill, on the French side, shot at them with their guns. The German motorcyclist was killed and some of the German soldiers on the lorries were certainly wounded. A nun and a man were also killed by stray bullets. The column went on in the direction of Blaton, but didn't get far as the resistants were blocking off all the crossroads. The wall of the basilica was a little damaged by the shots from the US tanks; except for that no houses were damaged or destroyed during the war in Bon-Secours.

Alex Nethery: Listening to the BBC on the radio, at Raymonde's house, we had been following the Allied invasion. We had a map, some red thread and some pins and as the BBC announced the advances we would mark the pins up a quarter inch, then back an eighth, and this went on for a month before the breakthrough.

So we pretty well knew that the invasion forces were getting closer and closer to Belgium. Eventually we didn't get any news on the radio and there followed two or three nights when we could barely sleep for the roar of the German trucks

and armour going up the main highway, only half a mile away
from us. So on the fourth night there was silence, we figured
that the Germans were gone and it was now a question of how
far behind the Allies were.

The next morning around eight o'clock, Raymonde got the
word that the Americans had arrived in the town. George and I
were still in bed. She rushed out to meet them (her English
wasn't too bad). She got some cigarettes and some gum for us
and she returned announcing that the town had been liberated
during the morning. I got to walk out the front door for the first
time in four months, it was a fantastic feeling. From then on the
party started. Virtually every citizen in Péruwelz had saved a
bottle of something for the liberation and the party wasn't long
getting started. It seemed to go on for about 24 hours.

When the Americans liberated Bon-Secours and Péruwelz. Raymonde
assisted their vanguard by informing them of the presence of the enemy
barges on the canal and giving advice on adjustment of artillery fire.
Belgians, in still occupied villages, phoned through information on artillery
accuracy, some calls more urgent than others if shells were falling too close
to their own houses. Raymonde had risked her life a number of times whilst
active in the Resistance; she had a great loathing for the enemy occupiers
because her father had been shot by the Germans during the First World War.

George and Alex remained in the area for a while, driving around in a car
'requisitioned' by the Resistance.

Alex Nethery: After a couple of days of visiting and parties
we'd seen everybody and thanked them for what they had
done. George and I were anxious to get back to England so we
could let our families know we were alive. Raymonde
arranged a ride for us in a charcoal-burning car and we drove
to Paris. It was a horrifying site, the roadside was littered with
dead horses and wagons, burnt trucks, tanks; we didn't
actually see any bodies but it was a pretty desolate trip.
Raymonde had given us 500 francs apiece and George and I
decided we would celebrate with a glass of champagne. Well,
we soon discovered that a glass of champagne was 400 francs,
so that ended the celebration. We used the money to take the
metro around Paris to see the sights, buying a few postcards
and a couple of souvenirs. A few days later we finally caught
the DC3 back to England. It wasn't a happy flight other than
the fact that we were heading home. The war was still on, it
had six or seven months to go, and there were no parachutes
aboard this aircraft. We weren't happy. Luckily it was only a
short flight and we got back to England in good shape.

CHAPTER 15

EVADER

Extract from letter written 23 May by Pip's wife Doreen Richards to Violet Nethery, Alex's mother:

I expect Alex has mentioned 'Pip Richards' to you at sometime. Well, I am his wife (Doreen). Alex always called me 'Mrs Pip'. I know you will be feeling very upset hearing the news that they are 'missing'. But please try not to worry too much, as I feel sure they are safe . . . As you will probably already know they only went to occupied territory, which gives me more hope than ever. I knew all the crew very well and feel sure that if there was any trouble they would have baled out to safety . . . Please try to keep smiling. It is very hard I know. I find it very difficult myself, but I keep trying.

While Alex and George sat out their evasion, very different plans were made for Pip. Early in the morning of 9 May, at Madame Duez Hainaut's home, Pip was now sheltered and along with his helpers they relaxed, believing the present danger was over. However, penetrating the calm night, came the characteristic thud of German soldier boots outside in the street. There followed a quiet turn of the front door key and then all became silent. After a few moments there was a knock on the door followed by an anguished pause. Louise indicated the door should not be opened and no one moved. A few long minutes passed and eventually the Germans went away.

At about 5 am it was decided that Madame Duez-Hainaut should empty the ashpan on the road and have a look around to see what was happening outside. (During the war a lot of cobbled streets were in a bad state and full of potholes. These were filled with coal ashes.) She noted six Germans standing guard at various places in the immediate vicinity and a seventh walking up and down the street checking the buildings and roofs to the left and right. For Louise it was time to return to work at the Town Hall and she didn't want people to question her, even for something as trivial as her absence. She left the house nodding to the Germans innocently. A little while later she returned to her aunt's home with her husband. At about 6 am a whistle sounded summoning the German soldiers back to their barracks. Pip was roused and provided with some civilian clothes. Charles Hainaut had informed the members of his Resistance group and at about 10.30 am. Pip was transferred to another safe house in the town, from where he was collected by Hector Delangre, a stocky young Belgian farmer's son. Hector was an active member of the Belgium Resistance, party to numerous acts of sabotage such as blowing up railway lines, and disrupting telephone communications. After the war Hector's service was honoured with his award of the Croix de Guerre. Indeed Hector was to receive many commendations from Allied countries in recognition of his activities. Pip certainly held a high regard for this man.

Hector had to get Pip across the canal by a bridge, that Germans often patrolled, and they had to ensure all was clear. Once across the canal they followed a footpath, then crossed some fields to an old mill where Hector left Pip, asking him to stay until he returned. Pip decided to trust his new acquaintance. After several hours Hector returned and took Pip on to his family's farm in Baugnies village, where he met two Allied airmen who were already being hidden by the farmer: Jack Pierson was co-pilot of a USAAF B17 Flying Fortress shot down near Mons on 4/5 February 1944, and John Trull was the Canadian pilot of a Spitfire which force landed on 20 February 1944, at Pipaix near Baugnies village.

The Delangre farm had become, during the war, a famous safe house for many fallen Allied airmen, where they received the farmer's hospitality. On one occasion while they were all round the dinner table some German soldiers called asking for eggs. Hector happily obliged and they went on their way.

After staying there for two weeks, Pip was taken by Hector to Leuze, where he was handed over to a Leon and Daniel Delmeule, who than took him to Wattripont, to the Delmées' farm, another famous safe house. Here Pip, together with John Trull and Jack Pierson, met with Yvonne Delmée and her cousin Marie-Paule Tassart, who was to take on the responsibility for the airmen from here. She takes up her own story:

> When war was declared, I was 18, living at home with my parents and younger brother. When the war began we felt, wrongly, quite confident that Germany couldn't invade us. We had the Maginot line, a strong impregnable defence built between the German/French border. Unfortunately Belgium refused to carry it on along our border, they declared themselves to be neutral. For eight months nothing happened . . . The British forces landed in France and both the French and British armies were waiting and getting bored. Suddenly the Germans made a move. They never crossed the famous Maginot line, they simply violated Belgium neutrality and when that was done they just simply crossed into France. We

couldn't believe what happened. Chaos everywhere. . . . We couldn't do very much. The young men of 17 to 25 who were not prisoners of war had to go to Germany to work for 12 months in one of their factories. After six months they had a week home on leave but had to go back. Lots of them decided that they didn't want to return and that is where we started trying to help them, because if they did not go back they did not have papers or food coupons. Therefore we formed a group trying to find food for them and eventually false identity cards proving they had done their time in Germany. That is how it all started, just helping our boys.

Meanwhile, in Belgium, one of Marie-Paule's aunts was doing more than that. British and Allied air crew, shot down over Belgium, were helped by the population if they could get to them before being found by the Germans, and were hidden for a few days in some safe houses until taken away down an evasion line. Her aunt's house was one of these safe houses. She continues:

At home we carried on as best we could. Food was difficult to find and all sorts of small black markets were flourishing. Believe me, they were necessary just to survive, as of course the army were scooping the cream. The Germans were not too much trouble, to tell the truth. Leave them alone and they left you alone. That is to say, the general public of course. We knew quite a bit of what was going on if you tried to fight them in any way. But what could we do? Precious little. The German officers would slow their cars down when they saw a pretty girl on the pretext of asking the way . . . and we took great pleasure in giving our most charming smile and sending them in completely the wrong direction. Of course after a while they cottoned on to it. The boys would, when possible, put some sugar in their petrol tanks, but it soon became too precious to waste like that. Anything will do, water, grit, anything in the tanks, slash the tyres. All that didn't help very much but just gave us some small compensation for our pride being so hurt to have the enemy in our town. Sometimes they would walk three abreast to force us to get off the footpath. Only little things but very annoying in the circumstances, and so it went on.

Marie-Paule explains that although they had heard of the Resistance and of joining the Maquis, they thought of that as being for the men only. Then one of her cousins contacted her. He had been taken prisoner in 1940, and become friendly with a British POW, George Beeson, who like him wanted to escape. They decided to try their luck together and after three weeks they reached Paris where an old lady gave them shelter for a few days. Marie-Paule takes up the story:

> Now my cousin was OK, he ended up safe at home with his family, but what to do with George Beeson? He wanted to get back to Britain. Easily said, but hard to do. Through the grapevine he knew of my aunt in Belgium . . . First we had to fetch George Beeson from Paris. My cousin [who had just escaped] was very tired and weak and so didn't want to go back to fetch him from Paris, so I volunteered to do it. I took leave from my office work and went to Paris to meet George. Now we had to get back to Lille. George had no papers, of course, and we were afraid of checks on the train. One time we locked ourselves, together, in the toilet and when the Germans knocked on the door I opened it slightly and showed them my identity card, while George stayed behind the door. We arrived safely in Lille despite the train we were on being shot at [by Allied aircraft] with all the German soldiers running away.
>
> For the next move my mother and I travelled into Belgium . . . to Aunt Genevieve's house (she was a widow with two daughters of 18 and 20 [Pauline and Yvonne Delmée]). As soon as I explained the reason for my visit she told us she couldn't help, as she was herself in trouble. The escape line was broken. Three men had been arrested, one shot and for the moment nothing could be done. Moreover my aunt, who usually had one airman at a time to hide for a couple of days, now had three of them, one American, one Canadian and one Briton [Jack Pierson, John Trull and Philip Richards respectively] for over three weeks and simply could not cope with regard food. She was in a dreadful state and great danger. There was only one thing to do: take the three men back with me.
>
> Again we had no papers and this time we had to cross the Belgian-French border. This we managed by going the back way . . . through fields where you can have one foot in Belgium and then one in France. To cut a long story short we arrived at home. My dear old father thought I was mad. 'You realise,' he said, 'that if those men are found here I'll be shot as head of the family and you'll go to a concentration camp, and the men will only be made POWs.' Yes, we knew all that but what else could we do. My dad said OK, he was a very kind-hearted man and ready to help and take the risk.

Now Marie-Paule and her family not only had George Beeson but three other evaders, trying to feed them on no rations. It took some time to find the right people who could help them. First they needed false identity cards, so Marie-Paule and her brother took them, one at a time, to town to a shop where they could have their photographs taken. None of their charges spoke any French, and the electric tram, the only public transport in Lille at the time, was always crowded. Marie-Paule explained to them that when she got off they must do the same, but the tram was so packed that when she moved Pip Richards could not disentangle himself from a bunch of German soldiers around him. She motioned to him quickly and a German officer smiled at her and shouted something to his men. Gallantly they made way for Pip to join Marie-Paule. In the confusion Pip mumbled 'thank you', but luckily they didn't realise what he said. After that she decided that on their identity cards they should be described as deaf and dumb.

> After Pip it was George Beeson's turn. You see, we only had one pair of shoes (the right size) between them. Then there was Jack the American. He was a very big fellow and the only suit, if we can call it that, was home made out of cheap cotton material, with home made dark blue dye. Well on the way we had a downpour, and as he sat on the tram a big blue puddle started spreading around him. As he stood up to leave we noticed, with horror, that sleeves, trouser legs, indeed the whole suit had shrunk so much that Coco the Clown had nothing on him.
>
> Now it was all getting desperate. Food, food, food was the problem. They were all young healthy men used to plenty of good food in the services, and they had like us to tighten their belts. But more and more they wanted to get back to England. There was nothing we would have liked better ourselves but how?

Marie-Paule's cousin, who had escaped with George Beeson, was ready to help again if he could. The Canadian, John Trull was all set to try to get to Spain and then, of course, her family had a few names and addresses, where evaders and escapers could get shelter. Her cousin decided to go as far as the Spanish border with Trull, then if all went well she was to follow with Beeson, and a young woman with Pip Richards. They had to wait a few days to know if it was OK to proceed, but instead they had a message that the pair were stopped in Lyon; they had made a run for it, and John Trull had been taken to the Maquis. Her cousin had returned to Paris.

> What to do now? Things were getting worse at home. The Germans were requisitioning houses to find any soldiers or Maquisards and we were really nervous. I decided that regardless we had to try for Spain or to reach the Maquis in the

south of France. The other lady said she would come too. So she left first [with Pip] and the next day I followed. We had an address in Paris where they would give us a day's rest, food and tickets to continue our journey. When I arrived there with George Beeson, Pip Richards was still there and the young lady had vanished back to Lille. She took fright and decided she couldn't go on. What to do now? The people there couldn't keep us more than a day as too dangerous. So there I was with two deaf and dumb men on my hands.

From that address we went to a *bordel* [brothel]. These people did a lot to help the Resistance, doing a lot of business of course with the Germans. The two men were taken to one room, and I was given the room of one of the 'girls', very pretty by the way, all pink. I was told of course that I wouldn't be disturbed. I was in about five minutes when the door opened and a pretty girl said, '*C'est toi la nouvelle?*' (Are you the new girl). I told her no and after that locked my door. We stayed there for five days while they were arranging ticket permits to travel to Lyon. We used to go out twice a day for fresh air and exercise walking separately a few yards from each other. If one was stopped the other two were to carry on walking as if nothing happened. Nothing did luckily.

At last the papers were ready and off Marie-Paule went with her two deaf and dumb men! It took them two days to reach Lyon:

We had several checks on the train but they were so crowded and, quite frankly, as long as you produced a piece of paper they didn't look very interested, as long as your photo was on it. So all went well. In Lyon we were met by our contact and taken to another *bordel* for one night, then to a flat for a couple of days. Lyon, you remember, is where John Trull was caught out. We decided, like previously, that we didn't know each other, so if one was arrested the other two had a chance. Well Pip was only 23 and looked very young. In a waiting room, George Beeson sat on one side and Pip on the other. I stood up. To tell the truth I was nervous for I knew that Lyon was a big centre for the Resistance and that both Gestapo and the French Milice (that was a special branch of the police co-operating with the Germans in the south) were very active. Sure enough, within ten minutes two men in civilian clothes and dark glasses entered the waiting room, looked around and went straight to Pip asking for his papers. The check was really for young Frenchmen who didn't do or finish their 12 months work in Germany and didn't have the paper proving they had

done their time. Pip, being deaf and dumb, would not have had
to go but they looked at his papers. Then one of them went
behind him and clapped his hands. Pip straight away jumped
and looked back . . . They took him away. Just then our train
arrived but of course we didn't catch it. Instead we followed,
at a distance, Pip and the two men outside the station, only to
see them disappear into a car. What to do now? We retraced
our route to our last shelter and told the people what happened.
They told us that if it was Gestapo they could do nothing. If
however it was the French Milice, lots of them were helping
the Resistance on the quiet and there was a chance.

Marie-Paule was not to see Pip again during the war. She left George
Beeson with the local Maquis and he was still with them when the
Americans liberated the area.

Pip was taken away and put in a cell for the night. He had considered
jumping out of the car but thought better of it. His captors had already
missed one obvious indicator of his true identity, for they had not looked at
Pip's wallet, which was English and had one pound ten shillings inscribed
on the leather. The next day he was taken to a courthouse and placed in a
courtroom. Pip's false identity card had his occupation as a carpenter and
his hands were inspected. Eventually his French and German inquisitors
decided to release him. Whether or not anyone in the Resistance had
managed to influence anyone in the Milice is unknown. As Pip left the
room someone shouted 'Oi' but he resisted the reflex to react. The man
muttered something in French, Pip believing it translated, 'He's not deaf',
but he was released.

Now what was he to do? He had lost contact with Marie-Paule. Should
he go back to the station? No, they might follow him and pick up Marie-
Paule and George if they were still there. He began to walk out of Lyon. For
the next three days he walked without food into the Cevennes mountains,
eventually coming across an old lady who gave him a cup of coffee and
some bread. She knew someone in the local Maquis, who took him in.

The Maquis were often involved in skirmishes with the Germans, and on
one occasion the group returned boasting of a shoot out with some soldiers.
They telephoned someone from another group to tell them their news.
However this other group had also been involved in some shooting at the
same place and at the same time. Needless to say, there had been no
Germans there. Pip was invited to join them on a number of occasions, but
declined for obvious reasons. After he had been with them for several
weeks a number of Americans parachuted into the area. A captain, sergeant
and ten others met with the Maquis offering money and helping to coordinate their efforts in support of the forthcoming invasion. They had
millions of francs, which they were giving out to all the Maquis members.

Pip was offered a considerable amount, initially declining, but finally taking a small amount. He then joined an American OSS section on some of their operations, and his excellent service with the group was noted in a personal testimonial.

On 15 August 1944, the French and American armies landed in Provence in the south of France. Pip was in Aizac when the American forces liberated the area at the end of August, and it was not long before he was evacuated by air to Italy, where he spent a couple of weeks near Naples awaiting official confirmation of his identity. He took advantage of the Italian sunshine, relaxing and swimming, and writing one very important letter.

> My own Dearest Doreen,
>   I am safe in Italy & going crazy to see you. I expect I will be in England in about a week. I have been worried all that time about you, wondering how you took it when I didn't come back. I will finish now Darling, I am so excited I can't write. I have so much to tell you.
>   Bye Bye, for now Sweetheart all my love forever.
>   Your loving husband, Pip.

Despite the sunshine and relaxation, however, Pip was not well. He was suffering from yellow jaundice, but kept it quiet at his debriefing by military intelligence in case they would not allow him to fly back to England until he recovered. On his return to England he had to go to London for another debriefing, after which he went to Waterloo station to catch the train home. He still did not have a proper uniform on and one of the service police confronted him saying. 'You're improperly dressed, sir.' Pip's succinct reply was, 'Well you know what you can do? You can go and get bloody stuffed.'

CHAPTER 16

CAPTURE

Anyone caught helping evading Allied airmen could expect immediate death by shooting or at the least deportation to a concentration camp, but those who elected to help the German occupiers were not free from retribution, particularly once the war ended. Monsieur Croquet had been a major factor in Allan's quick capture, and a local man, codenamed Eugène, an active and subsequently famous Resistance fighter in the Péruwelz area, relates his fate:

> [Croquet,] a postal employee, had already been implicated in the denunciation of Belgians during the first world war. He was involved in the deportation of people, upon hearsay evidence and he had a very bad reputation. Since the invasion of 1940 he had restarted. He was involved in the arresting of an English parachutist who had fallen in the gardens of the rue de Sondville [Allan Burrell].
>
> I decided to visit him at the Postal Bureau at Quevaucamps to settle the score. I went with four or five men. But, typically, we came across an obstacle. All the post offices and all the banks had closed their counters. All the accesses were blocked. . . . so I made a plan to open the doors.
>
> The traitor in question had entered before us. We arrived a little too late. We spread ourselves outside the office. We told him that we had come to take the money. In fact it was to do away with Croquet and to do it with style . . . The police were there and were watching us and so that they would cause us no trouble we took them aside and disarmed them. They remained quiet.
>
> Then a woman arrived. I had lived with her before. She recognised me and was very happy to see me. I was now identified before all the witnesses. That would not be the first or the last time.
>
> We kept on trying the door but it would not open. Money was passed to me through the letterbox, a couple of thousand francs. What a mix up! I saw a cart with horses, and an idea

went through my head. I shouted 'Good, very well, you refuse
to open the door! We will open the door with horses.' The door
finally opened. We all moved down the corridor but a second
door was closed. 'There we are then,' I said, 'Its very simple.
I will go and get something to open it. If I can't open it I will
throw grenades into the room. I feel sorry for the people who
are in there.'

It was not long before I heard a noise. The door opened. I
then saw, to my satisfaction, my man sat behind his desk. I
said to him 'You know very well that I have come for you.
Everything that has just been happening has been an act. It's
you that I came looking for today. I know that you are a
Christian, you should go and see your priest and then I will kill
you. We have many things to reproach you for.' He then
confessed.

Did he think he could obtain indulgence on my part?
I don't know. In any case I was going to complete my mission.
I wanted to finish it without a hitch.

He went to see his priest and I shot him. We left. We drove
on a couple of hundred metres. We threw the policemen's guns
on the side of the road and warned the Basecles brigade to
recover their precious goods. That was all that mattered to
them.[58]

Whilst Pip, George and Alex were evading the Germans, the other
surviving crew members did not fare so well. When we left Arthur he had
been taken in to the Henrards' house and was sleeping in an upstairs room:

Madeleine Henrard: As I woke up early in the morning, I saw
the German soldiers near the house. I went and shook Arthur
to wake him and showed him the German soldiers. He went
downstairs and to an underground bombing shelter in the
garden and I gave him some breakfast. The Germans
approached the house and rang the bell so I took Arthur's dish
and went to put it in the basin. The Germans continued to ring
the bell and I opened the door, then several soldiers entered the
house. One went directly to the bombing shelter where he told
Arthur to come out and put his hands above his head. The
Germans searched and emptied the house.

Her husband had left the house prior to the Germans' visit, to tell the local
Resistance people about Arthur, so that they could bring him some clothes

[58] Translated from Bachy, P. *Vie et Mort du Val de Verne*, Amicale des Resistants de
Péruwelz et environs, 1979.

to change into. Jean did not want to be at the house anyway, whilst Arthur was there. Jean had served in the Belgian forces earlier in the war; he was wounded and received the Croix de Guerre during the Allied retreat in May 1940. He later became a prisoner of the Germans, but after he had spent a month in gaol in Mons the Allies launched the unsuccessful Dieppe raid, and believing that a full scale invasion was beginning, Jean's captors released him. He was now classed as an escaped convict and, without doubt, if he had been caught with an Allied airman sheltering in his house, he would have been shot. Madeleine was now worried that Jean and the Resistance members might turn up with the clothes for Arthur while the Germans were at the house.

> As I had two little boys who were now crying for their milk, I told the Germans that I had to go and get the milk for my children. I was actually breast feeding at the time but needed an excuse to get out of the house. I cycled with a milk churn to Péruwelz where I met the Resistance people and told them to go away. As I had told the Germans that I needed milk, I then went to Jean's parents, who had goats, explaining the situation and the fact that I must have some milk. When I returned to the house the Germans checked to make sure I had come back with some milk. I had someone working at the house at the time, looking after the children.

The Resistance made arrangements for a Monsieur Maurice Deplus to escort Arthur to Raymonde Rock's house. Here he should have stayed with George and Alex until the Liberation, but it was not to be.

> *Madeleine Henrard:* The German soldiers pinned me up against the wall with a machine gun, and wanted me to say that I had hid the airman. The soldiers stayed at the house until that night but I said nothing and the woman working at the house at the time also said nothing [coincidentally her name was Arthurine]. She had a husband who at that time was a prisoner in Germany and was therefore bitter towards the German soldiers. Arthur was taken from the house at 10 o'clock that morning and he signalled to me, with two fingers, the V for victory. I signalled back with a V and the soldiers saw this perhaps thinking that I was indicating there was another airman. So the soldiers ransacked the house again. There was a woman collaborator with the soldiers acting as a translator and I remember her abusing me and spitting at me.

Arthur was taken to the town gendarmerie. A few houses up from the Henrards lived another German collaborator, whom the Henrards believed directed the German soldiers to their house. This person was officially tried after the war and shot.

Trevor Utton was led by the German soldier across the grounds of the Château Baugnies to the German quarters at the local school for girls. He was taken up to a room, where two German officers were sitting behind a table spread with papers, presumably ready for an interrogation. Not long after, Allan was brought into the room as well. For some unknown reason one of the German officers gave Allan a sharp blow to his head. Both were held and interrogated until the early morning. From there they were transferred to the town gendarmerie where they were to join Arthur.

At about 1730 hours they were led out to a lorry and told to climb in to the back, which was already occupied by three coffins. The German soldiers accompanying them informed them that the coffins contained the bodies of their crewmates. Of course we now know that this was not the case, but Arthur, Trevor and Allan were none the wiser. If the coffins were occupied they probably contained the bodies of some other crew who were shot down the previous night. Each of the Englishmen had to sit on one coffin, along with a guard armed with a machine gun. There were also two other armed guards in the van. Arthur intimated to Trevor and Allan that they should there and then, try and get away, but he was dissuaded by his crewmates who decided that this was not the right moment, and spending the rest of the war as POWs would be preferable to the likelihood of getting killed in trying to overpower five armed guards. Perhaps there would be other opportunities, so for the time being Arthur followed his crewmates' logic.

The lorry took the airmen to the town of Ath, about 13 miles to the north of Bon-Secours and Péruwelz. Here they were handed over to the Luftwaffe, searched and put in a cell, where they spent the night locked up. Allan recalls receiving a visit from the German night fighter pilot, who had claimed their Lancaster as a kill, a young man of about 20 years of age, who was quite respectful to his victim.

The next morning all three were placed in a closed van and taken to Brussels where after being interrogated further, they were placed in solitary confinement in a stone cell in the courtyard.

On 13 May the three POWs were entrained to leave Brussels. After a wait of over nine hours they departed at 2145 hours. The route took them via Aldenburg, Cologne, Karlsruhe and Mainz to Frankfurt. Whilst on the train Arthur suggested that they make a bid for freedom. His plan was to go to the toilet and on his return they were to overpower the guards and jump off the train. Once more Allan and Trevor, no doubt considering the damage a machine gun could inflict, talked him out of it.

On their train journey they witnessed at first hand the destruction the German cities had undergone. Allan recalled seeing vast areas of devastation, often with nothing left standing. As they arrived at Frankfurt, which had been recently bombed, the welcome to the English airmen was not pleasant; shouts of *'Terrorfliegers'* (terror flyers) came from the hostile crowd, and the prisoners were grateful to be surrounded by enemy guards who could protect them.

After a short tram trip, they arrived at the Luftwaffe POW Transit Camp. Durchgangslager Luftwaffe or Dulag Luft was located in the small town of Oberusel, north of Frankfurt. All captured airmen were brought to this one place for interrogation and then dispatched to the various POW camps. Each airman on arrival found himself in a separate cell, containing a table, chair and bed. Each prisoner received what appeared to be a Red Cross form, the 'Arrival Report Form'. The Reception Officer at the camp would tell him that if he filled it in their families back in England could be notified all the sooner. The form, however, did not stop at the name, rank and number information the fallen airmen were required to give under the Geneva Convention, but it went on to ask about squadron and group details. The Germans also attempted to butter up their captives by providing or offering good food or trying to befriend prisoners and make them lower their guard. A number of Germans who spoke perfectly good English were disguised and placed amongst the prisoners, again to try and gather information.

At this stage in the war Bomber Command had become aware of the various ruses and interrogation techniques used at Dulag Luft. A very small number of airmen had, by then, escaped from their POW camps and returned to England. Their information was relayed to operational squadrons, often with the escapee touring stations and giving lectures. As such incoming prisoners, later in the war, knew something of what to expect and were rarely caught out.

The German interrogator had at his disposal a wealth of information to use to his advantage. He had access to the *Beute und Nachrichten Abteilung* (BUNA, 'Information through Booty'). Into this went everything recovered from the crashed aircraft and dead or surviving crew members. Also information gathered from intelligence agencies was fed in. It was often the case that the interrogator used his prior knowledge to lead his captive into disclosing further information.

Around the time Arthur, Trevor and Allan were passing through Dulag Luft another young RAF man by the name of Gordon Puttick, shot down on 13 May 1944, became a POW.

> *Gordon Puttick:* I was flying high level photo reconnaissance Spitfires and on my 54th trip over Europe I was shot down by anti-aircraft fire. I was flying at 31,000 feet to obtain photographs of an airfield and was going on to Hanover and other targets. A shell or piece of shrapnel blasted a big hole in my starboard wing and only by holding full left stick and rudder could I keep the aircraft straight and level. Also the engine started to overheat and soon became very hot.

Eventually I had to bale out at around 28,000 feet. I blacked out through lack of oxygen and was free falling when I 'woke up', fortunately still a long way up. I pulled the ripcord and the chute opened with a loud bang. As I neared the ground I saw five or six soldiers pointing guns at me. I landed close by and they quickly captured me.

They were older Wehrmacht, like our Home Guard. Their first words were *'Englander oder Americana'*. When I said *'Englander'*, they said *'Gut, gut'*. I was taken to a canal crossing, which was occupied by young German boys, who were manning a light flak post. They were quite friendly, saying 'For you the war is over. You are a brave soldier,' and various other comments. They brought me some sour milk and dabbed some iodine on a slight cut I had on my shoulder.

Several hours later, a small van collected me, with an armed guard and I was taken to a nearby airfield, given some food and then locked in the guardroom. Next day I went by the local bus to Lingen Railway Station. The station master confronted me on the platform, shook his fist and shouted *'Terrorflieger'*, which was echoed by the crowd who were waiting for the train. Fortunately it arrived at that moment and the guards quickly bundled me into a compartment. We travelled through the Ruhr to Cologne where we stopped for the night in cellars near the cathedral . . .

[At Dulag Luft] I was put into a cell, number 20c, which was about 10 foot by 6 foot and contained one wood framed bed with a kind of hessian mattress on it, and that was all there was. A high level window gave light but there was no way of looking out. I was locked in and the only means of attracting the guard's attention was by moving a small lever, which activated a signal-like arm in the corridor. When the guard, in due course, saw it, he asked what you wanted, and if it was necessary to go to the toilet he would open the door and accompany you. Three times a day we had a watery soup or a piece of bread and sometimes some peculiar beverage called 'coffee'. This tasted like varnish and for the rest of my stay, after the first day, I drank only water.

Every other day I was taken to the interrogator who tried to get me to tell him information about the squadron etc. I gave him name, number and rank and I remember on one occasion I very innocently said, 'Well you really don't expect me to tell you anything else, because under the Geneva Convention I am not allowed to say any more!' One day he produced a bread roll and buttered it in front of me. I anticipated some trick. He offered it to me and I was feeling very hungry, so I thought so

what, I may as well take it, I don't intend saying any more. I
ate it in front of him. He said nothing more and let me go.

Once there was a burly man in the room dressed in a long
rain coat and trilby hat. He didn't say anything but just kept
close to me. The interrogator quietly informed me that I was
stupid not to answer a few simple questions because I might
end up in a concentration camp. After all I was alone in a
photo recce Spitfire and could be considered a spy. This was
blatant nonsense of course but I was tired and hungry and
wondered what this Gestapo-like bloke was going to do.
However with the naiveté of youth I told him again that I
could only give name, number and rank whatever he said.

Soon after that I was released. Still having said nothing. I
was in the cells for 11 days, not long compared with some but
I felt like singing with sheer relief when I stepped outside in
the warm sunshine.

Arthur, Allan and Trevor avoided the prolonged interrogation that Gordon
had undergone. It may well have been here that they learnt about Don's
fate, but their morale may also have been boosted with the knowledge that
the other three crew members had not yet been caught.

Arthur, Allan and Trevor did not spend long at Dulag Luft, arriving on
14 May and then moving on to the nearby holding camp at Wetzlar, before
being entrained at 1600 hours on 15 May. All the departing prisoners were
packed into box-cars marked with '40 hommes – 8 chevaux' (40 men – 8
horses) and began their journey east. Allan and Trevor became separated
from Arthur at this point. Often the cars were overcrowded and men had to
stand or sit on a floor probably not cleaned since it last held livestock, and
compounded by poor ventilation. There was normally enough food and
water, when supplied, but no sanitary facilities and men would have to wait
until a suitable stop and then go to nearby woods.

After covering a distance of about 300 miles, which involved being on
the train for 47 hours, Allan, Trevor and Arthur arrived at Sagan station.
Following behind our men was Gordon Puttick. He too had been moved on
from Dulag Luft to the holding camp at Wetzlar, where he eventually
embarked for Sagan, his travel conditions better than that of our airmen.

Gordon Puttick: This was a canvas camp [the holding camp at
Wetzlar] and we waited around for a few days until a train was
available to take us to the POW camp. Whilst we were there
the American Fortresses bombed an industrial site nearby. We
watched the bombs falling and exploding until we were
quickly hustled into the tents. The next day we were marched
through the town amidst shouts and fist shaking from local
residents. We boarded the train, which had wooden seats

rather like the third class seats of years ago.

Traveling through Leipzig we saw trainloads of men in striped pyjamas. We threw them cigarettes when we could but the guards threatened to shoot so we had to stop. At that time of course we knew nothing about gas chambers and concentration camps. We eventually arrived at Sagan.

From the station at Sagan, the tired and dirty prisoners walked to the POW camp through the adjacent woods. In a short time they stepped out into the open and got their first glimpse of Stalag Luft III.

Stalag Luft III lay approximately 90 miles to the south east of Berlin, in the province of Silesia. The camp was about a half mile south of the town of Sagan, which lay on the Bobr River, a tributary of the Oder, and was set amongst a clearing in a dense coniferous wood. In April 1942 the POWs at the camp at Barth were evacuated to Stalag Luft III, Sagan. Initially the camp consisted of four distinct areas. A large area on the west side was for the Germans, called the '*Kommandantur*'; in the north east corner was the '*Vorlager*', containing the 'cooler', sick quarters, bathhouse, coal shed and storage buildings, and several barracks for Russian prisoners who were used as camp labour. To the south east lay the officers compound, called east compound and in the lower centre of the camp was the NCO's compound, called centre compound.

In the autumn of 1942 the Germans began work on a new compound situated to the west of the *Kommandantur*. It was briefly known as west compound until another compound was built to its south. The two new compounds were then given the names north and south compounds.

As the war progressed, and the number of bomber sorties over Western Europe increased, the population in the camp steadily grew. As 1943 drew to a close, nearly every barrack in every compound was full. Two further compounds opened in early 1944 to provide relief. On 10 January 1944 some 500 British prisoners were taken from east and centre compounds and transferred to Belaria compound. This new compound was situated 3 miles west of Stalag Luft III. West compound, the largest at Stalag Luft III, was the last to be opened by the Germans, receiving its first group of prisoners on 27 April 1944. A Red Cross report of 22 May 1944 recorded the number of POWs as 5,482 officers and 967 other ranks.

Allan, Trevor and Arthur, on arrival at their new residence, were searched and de-bugged. Then Allan and Trevor were transferred to east compound and Arthur was taken by ambulance to Belaria.

Allan and Trevor looked out onto their new home. In front of them were eight wooden single-storey barracks, built about one foot off the ground, which were their accommodation. The barracks all had twelve large rooms and they would have to share their room, in double tier bunks, with at least seven other POWs, and more as time went on, with the camp's population growing. Each room had one large window, shuttered at night, and a small stove to provide heat, if there was enough fuel. Each barrack had another three small rooms, a kitchen, a wash room and a lavatory. The supply of water, however, was very poor during warm weather as the camp was situated on high ground and the pressure of water to east compound was the first to fall as the other compounds, water demand increased. Along with the barracks there was a large cookhouse, a bathhouse, two pit latrines and a fire pool.

The compound was enclosed by a perimeter fence consisting of two barbed wire fences about 7 ft apart and 9 ft high, with a 2 ft high barbed wire entanglement between them. The fence was lighted from dusk to dawn, except when there were air raids, at which time the number of sentries doubled. At each corner of the fence were sentry towers from which searchlights and machine guns scanned the compound. Fifteen yards inside the perimeter fence was a warning fence, a wooden rail two feet high. At places the warning rail was moved in another three yards where ground microphones had been located. These were placed $32\frac{1}{2}$ yards apart along the perimeter fence at a depth of 3 yds. Any slight disturbance caused by tunnelling would register in the microphone and be transmitted by cable to a room in the *Kommandantur* where a 24-hour watch was maintained. The space between this and the perimeter fence was 'No Man's Land' with yellow sand spread across this forbidden area so crawling POWs could be easily seen. Allan and Trevor would quickly have discovered from fellow POWs that should they cross this fence or even touch it they would be shot at. Any balls rolling into this area required a sentry's permission to recover. There had been a number of cases of POWs being shot at retrieving balls but nobody had been hurt. There was also an anti-tunnel ditch, 7ft deep and 6ft wide, inside the perimeter fence, the over flow of water from the wash houses allowed to drain into it.

Sentries patrolled outside the fence, pacing between the towers, and at night other sentries patrolled in the woods, as did two *Hundführer*, armed guards with specially trained dogs, one inside and one outside the perimeter fence.

The compound had a small sports field where POWs could play football, rugby, cricket, volleyball etc. They had even been allowed to have the field flooded in the winter so they could play ice hockey. In October 1942 three rooms in one of the barracks had been converted into a theatre. One of the common rooms became a library.

> *Trevor Utton:* It was a new world, you wouldn't be in the mess
> that night having a few beers. There were all the wooden huts
> in rows, it looked orderly, sparse, sandy covered ground and
> bags of wire. You then realised that this was it, you were in a
> prison camp. Up to then you had been in transit or in the
> transit camp, which was like the Dorchester compared to

where we ended up. [At the transit camp] they fed us well and
they tried to impress us and get information out of us at the
same time.

Belaria compound lay on a hill affording the occupants a view over the
town of Sagan. It was set on the north side of the Sagan road, amidst flat
arable land with a few trees, exposed to a strong wind that reportedly kept
the camp a healthier place to live in.

When Arthur arrived at Belaria the camp consisted of six wooden blocks,
lifted off the ground by brick supports. Each block was divided into a
number of rooms, one initially set aside as either a common room, library
or lecture room, but four were soon converted to living quarters as the
camp's population grew. A fiction library and reference library/reading
room remained, doubling up as common rooms. In the compound were two
washhouses and two washrooms with provision for cold running water
only, and no baths or hot showers. Block 3 contained the camp hospital.
The theatre and camp kitchen/store were the only other buildings in the
compound. Allotments were tilled by prisoners, and there was a small
sports pitch. To the east of the compound was the *Vorlager* but this was to
be resited when the compound was enlarged.

On 1 November 1944, four more blocks were added to the west of the
old compound and a new larger sports pitch. These new blocks also had
brick supports but the space between the floor of the barrack and the
ground was boarded up. There were however small gaps left for certain
German guards, the 'ferrets', to crawl in and search beneath the barracks.
The *Vorlager* was moved to the western edge of the camp.

Belaria was enclosed by a similar system of perimeter fence and warning
fence (wire) as that of east compound. The differences were that there was
no patrol outside the fence, no sand spread between the warning fence and
perimeter fence and there were no ground microphones. As in east
compound, POWs were informed that they were not to cross the warning
wire. A Red Cross report of 6 November 1944 records one POW testing
this rule.

F/Lt J M Riley was shot through his right hand on August 13th
1944 after having touched the warning wire. Apparently the
warning wire at this point is quite close to a rather narrow by-
pass and when F/Lt Riley passed by with one of his
colleagues, he touched the warning wire involuntarily. The
guard on the nearby tower carefully sighted his rifle for some
seconds and fired the shot, wounding F/Lt Riley in his right
hand. The camp commander, when protesting, mentioned that
the order, which has always been known to all POWs for the
sentries to shoot at any POW touching the warning wire, was
still in force and that F/Lt Riley was actually holding the wire

when the shot was fired. Here again, as in so many cases, it is one word against the other.[59]

By the time our three Englishmen began their stay behind the barbed wire, Stalag Luft III had been up and running for just over two years. In that time the camp occupants had established an administrative and organisational structure to look after their own interests. Discipline enforced by the Germans was nothing much, with Appelle (roll-calls) twice a day. Although occasionally the prisoners could all be rousted out of an area whilst a search was undertaken.

The prisoner with the highest rank was given the title Senior Allied Officer, a position recognised by the Germans. As the camp grew and the prisoners were segregated by nationality the Germans recognised a Senior American Officer who represented centre, south and west compounds and a Senior British Officer who represented east, north and Belaria compounds. Next in line came the compound commanders, the highest ranked officer from the main nationality represented in that compound. This person controlled the administrative system in the compound and attempted to maintain order and discipline. There were the odd exceptional POWs who did not feel obliged to obey, but in the main the men responded to any orders given. The compound commanders would also liaise with the Germans, the protecting power, the Red Cross and other compounds.

The compound commanders were assisted by a next tier of men, who were given specific responsibilities. There were the intelligence, security and escape officers. Certain men were put in charge of the camp's basic administrative duties such as the mail office, the Red Cross parcel and personal parcel stores, the libraries, the kitchen. There were also men who organised activities for their fellow prisoners such as sporting events, religious services or theatre shows.

The block structure lay beneath and complemented the compound administrative organisation. Each block had a commander and men who took administrative responsibilities to match those at the compound level. Finally, within the blocks were the individual rooms which had room commanders, who were the final link in the information chain between the individual and the compound as a whole.

Trevor Utton: When moved into [the camp at] Sagan . . . you were allocated your rooms, your hut. You would get in and everybody wanted to know how long the war was going to be and what was happening. It was a completely different world . . . We had a room in which there would be perhaps a dozen bunks, wooden bunks with wooden bedboards and straw palliasses. It was completely foreign to anything we had seen

---

[59] Public Record Office WO 224 63A.

before and we thought, well, what happens now? It wasn't until probably a week that we realised this was your routine, you wouldn't be going down to the shops or into the mess for a pint. There wouldn't be any women or anything. This was your whole world, this room, this hut.

It was an officers' camp and we as NCOs were put there and had jobs to do for the officers. We were the barrack room orderlies. I used to take in the washing and I inherited a scrubbing board and a bucket. Now, I'd got nowhere to put the equipment except at night when we were locked in the hut. There was a night latrine, which was a trough, and a closet, which needed cleaning out daily, so I volunteered for that. I then had somewhere to put my washing. I had a laundry in the loo. I was given two jugs of hot water in the morning to wash the loo out. So I would use one for the loo and one for washing . . . You had to fill your time, you had to do something.

We each had a room that we had to keep tidy for the officers. All the NCOs were in one room, and all the officers in another room. Each NCO had a room he looked after, cleaned it in the mornings, went and got the coffee each morning, generally be a dogsbody. But for that we had the privilege of being in a decent camp. Certainly it was a better camp than the privates in the army had.

When Arthur arrived at Belaria, the camp consisted of only the six barracks. Arthur's diary recorded the nature and inhabitants of each.

Block I. or Tuck's Mansion
In this block resides the well known fighter 'ace' W/Cdr Tuck DSO, DFC and two bars.

The block consists of 12 large living rooms, 2 block seniors rooms, kitchenette and night abort. Each mess containing 12 'bods', does its own cooking, having $1/2$ the kitchen stove for $1/2 - 3/4$ hour per afternoon.

The men in this block have been troubled to such an extent by bed bugs that they were forced to sleep in tents, whilst the menace was removed. During this time the camp was deprived of $1/2$ the small sports pitch.

Block II
Block Senior Officer W/Cdr Parcelle. This is situated in the north-east side of the park. Has nothing of particular interest in it. Inhabitants were guests of Blocks 3, 4, 5, and 6 for two days, whilst the block was being deloused. The block commander was RAF attaché in Japan pre-war.

Block III

Block Senior Officer F/Lt Morgan. The Camp Hospital takes up half of this block, being under the charge of Captain Monteuuis RMC. More serious cases are taken to SAGAN, but even then, the hospital is over crowded, and under equipped. This block faces the main gate, and so one room is put aside for the Duty Pilot who records the movements in and out of the Goons (Kreigie name for Germans). The Food – Acco [food/cigarettes exchange system] is also situated in the same room, and is the camp's stock market . . . Clothing is also issued from this room, when stocks are available, which is very rare.

Block IV

Block Senior Officer W/Cdr Mehang AFC. Nothing of particular camp interest in this block. Headquarters of the Canadian element. Houses S/Ldr Hughes, DSO, DFM, who has 78 opo. to his credit and is a 'Pathfinder', Flying Officer Carmody, RAAF cricket captain, and Len Whiteley the camp band leader, late of Billy Cotton's Band.

Block V

Known as the 'Flagship' as the SBO [Senior British Officer] S/Capt Macdonald DFC and BAR, AFC, and other senior officers reside here. The Adjutants Office and the Educational office are combined in room 17. The Educational system is very good, books can be sent to Geneva for, and examinations of every type can be sat for. Naturally materials such as rulers, rubbers etc, are very scarce, and ink is not allowed into the camp.

Block VI

Senior Block Officer W/Cdr Ingle DFC AFC. My own living block situated on the southern (road) side of the camp. The men in rooms 3 to 7 have windows looking onto the Sagan road, and with a good view of the southern landscape, and 'Eckersdorf' a little village suburb of Sagan. Road traffic consists mostly of cyclists traveling from Sagan to the local Luftwaffe aerodrome.

> Block Adjutant; f/o Noble
> Block Quartermaster: f/o Grimbly
> Block Rations Officer: f/o McKay
> Block Sports Officer: f/lt Jackson

Arthur also detailed the occupants of his room recording the location of their shooting down.

Room 7 Block 6, Occupants:

F/Lt D F Hutchinson RAAF, Sydney Australia. [Wireless Operator flying in a Martin 187 Baltimore, part of R.A.A.F. 454 Squadron. Shot down on a daylight raid to Crete 23-7-43. The aircraft bellylanded in a minefield, leaving explosions behind as it skidded to a halt. Douglas Hutchinson helped and dragged his 3 crewmates clear of the aircraft just before it blew up. All were injured and one of the crew died. 'Hutch' started off in centre compound in the main camp before being transferred to Belaria in January 1944.]

F/Lt W B Deall RAF, Qdzi, Southern Rhodesia. [Spitfire pilot and previously a crocodile hunter, Florence 20-5-44.]

F/Lt A N Orr RAF, Glasgow, Scotland. [Rear Gunner with 78 Squadron who had a very difficult bale out from the rear turret of his Halifax. The aircraft was shot down on the Pilsen raid of 17-4-43. From the crew of seven, the pilot died and the rest of the men became POWs.]

F/O F G Smith RAF, Sidcup, London. [Navigator with 102 Squadron. Shot down by a night fighter on the Hamburg raid of 24-7-43. From the crew of eight Frank was the only one to survive.]

F/O W E Gibbes, RNZAF, Auckland, New Zealand. [Observer, Hamburg 3-7-43.]

F/O C A Lepine DFM, RCAF, Montreal, Canada. [Wireless Operator, credited with having completed two tours with 150 and 617 'Dam Busters' Squadron, and a tour as a staff instructor. Shot down by a night fighter on the Munich raid on 24-4-44 just after leaving the target. One of his colleagues was killed, the rest of the crew all became POWs. Charlie only becoming a POW after a long evasion attempt eventually caught attempting to cross the Rhine into France.]

F/O G W Baillie RAF, Salisbury, Southern Rhodesia. [Pilot, Dieppe 9-5-44.]

F/O G W Puttick RAF, East Grinstead, Sussex. [We have already met Gordon, a Spitfire pilot in photo reconnaisance. Shot down by anti-aircraft fire at 31,000 feet. Osnabrück 13-5-44.]

F/O D J Bell RAF, Nottingham, England. [Lancaster pilot, 101 Squadron, shot down on the Berlin raid 2-1-44. Derrick and three others survived of which only one managed to evade capture. The other four men in the crew died.]

F/O G L Gaunt RAF, Derbyshire, England. [429 Squadron Navigator shot down in a Halifax on the Aachen raid of 25-5-44. Two other members of the crew became POWs, the other four men were killed.]

Rather a mixed and motley crowd. Please note difference between PILOT & B PILOT. Former means fighter pilot and latter bomber pilot. This is done to comply with the wishes of f/o Bill Baillie, a 'Tiffee' [typhoon] Type.

As well as the name of Gordon Puttick in the list of Arthur's roommates, who has already been mentioned, appeared that of Derrick Bell from 101 Squadron who we met earlier. Below is an account of Derrick's movements after shooting down up to his arrival at Belaria. When we left Derrick, he was attached to his parachute by just the one hook.

I landed in some trees, hanging down. It's funny the ideas you get because it was almost as soon as I opened the parachute that I hit the trees and I thought 'Oh crikey I'm in some sort of a net, crafty blighters they have put up a net several thousand feet high'. Then of course I landed in the mud, it was amazing, minus a flying boot, minus if you can believe it two pockets which were sewn on the outside of my flying suit. They had gone. I had no pockets anymore, it was extraordinary. I wasn't wounded.

I couldn't get the parachute down to bury it cause it was all tangled up, so I tried to get as far away as I could. I hid up in some woods for a day, and just as I was getting up to move on, somebody saw me. He gesticulated and pointed up through the trees. There was a farm there and it was here that I was put up for the night. My lasting impression was that there was a great big dish of butter on the table, which of course we didn't have in England. They turned me out the next morning cause they were frightened, they were an old couple.

I was walking across some fields in broad daylight and once again somebody saw me. I didn't know whether to go back or forwards or what. I didn't know who they were. Anyway they beckoned and I went to meet them. He shoved me in an empty house and that night somebody came and fetched me and took me to another farm. It was there that I met up with my bomb aimer.

We met the local head of the Underground, Dr Verstraeten; he lived in Beaumont, a marvellous chap, terrific. He had the advantage of being a doctor and could have a motor bike, so he used to go about all over the place and fraternise with the Germans. Well he had got us in one of his bedrooms. There was a Flying Fortress shot down one day and the doctor even brought the Germans with one of the wounded back to the house while we were upstairs. He had got a wife and two children, one was six and one was ten. They obviously never breathed a word, although they knew who we were.

The doctor was a mild little smiling man gentle as anything, and he told us about the people that were working for the Germans, the informers. I asked how they dealt with them. He said:

'Oh, we go and get them. Then we take them to the wood and we say 'Well if you tell us all you know we won't shoot you, we'll let you go.' So they tell us all they know and then we shoot them.'

We met the chap that did it, big burly fellow that nearly crushed your hand when he shook it and his girlfriend was this great big tough girl as well. I wouldn't have liked to have fallen into their hands.

The doctor was trying to place us, for a few months, in an escape line. We went to various farms and houses each for about a fortnight, and sometimes back to the doctor's. Then the doctor had to go into hiding, cause they found him out, and one or two of the people that had hid us also were taken. Fortunately they all got away with it. The doctor was never caught.

The bomb aimer and I were free for five months. We eventually in some way decided to make our own way. Obviously we lost touch with the doctor and he was really the be all and end all for us, we did as we were told. [Now] we didn't know what to do.

Eventually two blokes came and fetched us and took us to Lille where we stayed overnight with a woman, in a big house. I never thought about it at the time but the whole of Lille was full of German soldiers and to find an empty house seemed very strange. The next morning these blokes came round for us, took us to the end of a road and left us. We were supposed to walk along to the other end and a car would be waiting for us. Well, we did this and sure enough another car was there. We hopped in the back and he drove off. We were just out of Lille, not very far, when we turned a corner and they [probably Gestapo] were across the road waiting for us and of course we were taken prisoner.

The funny thing is, we were all in civvies, as our uniforms had been destroyed. We all had identity cards, I was Eduard Léon Egide Jordens. The chap that was driving disappeared; he was taken separately. So I think it was a set up. Otherwise what was to distinguish him from us? Three people in civvies, two people they obviously knew about. We couldn't prove our identity. We said we were in the Air Force, though we had nothing to prove it, and they accepted it. So they knew, somehow.

I was kept in Lille gaol for about a fortnight and then they took us to Dulag Luft for interrogation. I was there about 10 days, I suppose. It wasn't severe, the interrogation. They kept bringing me back for a few days and asking the same questions. They wanted to know where I had been for four or five months and any names. I couldn't give them the names obviously.

From Dulag Luft Derrick was entrained for Sagan, being fortunate to travel in a rail carriage as opposed to the more usual horsebox.

The thing I do remember about the journey was the devastation as you went through the cities, everywhere. All the buildings, the empty shells everywhere. It was horrific . . . Well one chap was frightfully annoyed and I didn't blame him, he thought we were gloating. We were not gloating at all. We were amazed. You could tell he would like to have stuck his bayonet into us.

After arriving at the camp, Derrick was marched to Belaria whilst his bomb aimer remained in the main camp.

CHAPTER 17

PRISONER OF THE REICH

In the evening of Allan, Trevor and Arthur's arrival they would have made their debut in their compound's roll-call. All the prisoners paraded onto the sportsfield, except in bad weather when the count was made in barrack corridors. On the field the prisoners aligned in a hollow square, the occupants of barracks lining up in files, five men deep, on the same place on the field everyday with their barrack and roommates. There was a space between each block of men representing a barrack, a smaller space between the occupants of each room. German armed guards spread along the outside of the square, watching the assembled prisoners for anyone trying to move around and disrupt the count. Any sick prisoners were allowed to stay in their rooms where their number was counted. Armed guards were placed around barracks to prevent any sick prisoner, suddenly rejuvenated, from moving around the barracks and getting counted twice.

Before the parade the barrack leader, a POW, prepared a chit detailing the number on parade from each room, the number of sick in each room, and the number of personnel working in either the sick quarters, *Vorlager*, theatre or kitchens. A total was arrived at and a chit given to the Senior British Officer's adjutant.

Meanwhile one German walked behind each row of prisoners and one walked in front, counting each room in turn. This was then compared to the adjutant's chit and if there was a discrepancy there was a recount. Other Germans counted the number of sick in each room, the numbers of men working in the *Vorlager*, sick quarters, kitchen and theatre and which room they were from. The counters returned to the parade and compared the numbers they had with that of the adjutant. Again if the counts did not agree the process was repeated.

If the weather had led to a count in the barrack corridors, armed guards stood at the end of the rows of barracks, chits drawn up and numbers absent checked.

With all this procedure, the prisoners used whatever ruse they could in attempting to turn the roll-call into a farce. They never formed up properly, kept moving around, created disturbances, and sick prisoners made every attempt to be counted and then move on to another barrack to be counted again.

Allan Burrell: We used to have counts in fives. We would put the tallest prisoner at the front and back of the five, with the smallest man in the middle. He would crouch down when counted one way and then stand up when counted from the other way. You would hear '*fünf, fünf, vier, fünf*' on the first count then '*fünf, fünf, fünf, fünf*' on the second.

But tension occasionally ran high due to the POWs antics during Appell. Gordon Puttick in Belaria recalls:

On one occasion I broke off a bit early in order to have a pee, and as I came back I came face to face with the German Commandant. He must have thought I had skipped Appell and immediately went for his pistol. I managed to convince him that I had only visited the lavatory and he reluctantly let me go. I must admit I was in a cold sweat for a few minutes.

The Germans carried out their count with the means they had, in only extreme circumstances bothering to make a second count, accepting the adjutant's figures or falsifying their own. This bemusing of the German captors no doubt kept the prisoner's spirits up, but there were other ways of maintaining morale. At Belaria and east compounds there were the theatre shows, sports events, lectures and even a library. At Belaria:

Derrick Bell: I didn't find it boring because we had a wonderful library, very good and I used to read quite a lot and I got a great interest in Biology and there was a wonderful book called *Everyday Biology,* quite a simple book. They also had what became my favourite book, *David Copperfield,* which I read at least three times while I was there.

There were concerts provided by Len Whiteley's 'The Lower Silesia' swing sextet. Prisoners were even able to see feature films, two of which were *Male Animal* with Henry Fonda and Olivia de Havilland, and *The Spoilers* with John Wayne and Marlene Dietrich. It was possible to send and receive letters to loved ones back at home. Arthur wrote numerous letters to Anne and his parents and other relatives. He also wrote to Don Copeland's sister in Canada. Arthur even sent a letter to his bank back in England. In October alone Arthur received 26 letters, 12 of which were from Anne. In east compound Allan received numerous letters from a girlfriend, some of which mentioned the unfamiliar term 'doodlebugs', the flying bombs that terrorised London and the south-east from the summer of 1944.

News from home may not always have been good news, however. Bad news was particularly stressful to the POW, who was far from home and not in a position to do much about it. Just after Arthur had been shot down,

Anne had had a miscarriage and became quite ill. Arthur probably would
have known she was pregnant as she was three months into the pregnancy
when he went missing. The stress caused by Arthur being posted missing
was undoubtedly a contributory factor in the miscarriage. Arthur probably
received the news whilst at Belaria, though there are no entries in his POW
logbook and the letters between Arthur and Anne can no longer be found.

Sometimes the POWs were let out of the confines of their compound:

> *Gordon Puttick:* On one or two occasions, having given our
> parole we were allowed out of camp, under guard, and
> allowed to walk in the countryside for about a mile. I recall
> that we walked over fields towards a little village called
> Peterdorf. The field smelt a bit pongy, because all the 'night
> soil' from our latrines was spread over them. A large barrel-
> like vehicle drawn by horses took the mess from the camp and
> labourers, probably slave, used long handled scoops to throw
> the stuff all over the land. Once someone tried to escape by
> hiding in the vehicle, known as the honeywagon, but he nearly
> asphyxiated and didn't get away.

The prisoners at Belaria and east compounds had managed to put together
radioes, by which BBC broadcasts could be picked up. News bulletins were
written out and copies passed, through compound security officers to
security representatives from barracks. The news was then read to the
POWs and the paper burnt.

> *Derrick Bell:* We got information because there was a radio.
> Occasionally that was found and confiscated, but before long
> they got another one together, because the German guards, the
> ones who used to come around, hadn't got any cigarettes and
> we had plenty. The American Red Cross parcels were full of
> cigarettes and for a packet of cigarettes they would do
> anything.

One other time honoured way of keeping spirits up was not overlooked by
the prisoners. At Belaria some of them used to brew up 'Kriegielager' made
by fermenting raisins followed by distillation. Sanitation at Belaria was
pretty good, but at night the only facility available was a toilet in the corner
of a room with twelve occupants. Of course this could lead to differences
of opinion between those who could and those who could not control the
effects of the 'brew'.

> *Derrick Bell:* Awful stuff, vicious stuff. It really used to make
> them so high and they would then want to go in the middle of
> the night. Arthur slept above Charlie Lepine in the bottom

bunk, who used to pass wind a lot but never made a noise and periodically Arthur used to turn on him, because he got the full benefit as he was in the top bunk. One time he couldn't stand it anymore. Arthur had a good turn of phrase, and said 'For Pete's sake Charlie, stop it. They come out in moccasins and hit you on the head with a hatchet'.

On one occasion the occupants at Belaria were treated to a flying display by aircraft from the local Luftwaffe aerodrome:

Derrick Bell: We had the dentist from the local FW190 aerodrome come in to us. One day the FW190s shot us up, they came right across low flying, super low flying. The dentist said to one of the boys who was having his teeth done, 'There what do you think of that low flying yesterday'. 'Oh, low flying,' he said, 'ridiculous to call that low flying.' Well the next day they came over and they nearly went between the huts. It was really superb the flying they did then. They really did fly low.

Belaria compound had a newspaper, *The Log*, in which events both in and outside the camp were recorded. There were updates on situations at the camp, e.g. regard food parcels, regular gardening features, reports on sports events, theatre and concert reviews, news received from home and news received regarding the war situation. Constant updates on the war's progress, particularly the Normandy invasion, obtained through letters, radio transmissions, recent POW arrivals and translations of German publications, no doubt kept spirits high. In one case these spirits resulted in a rather interesting forfeit, published in *The Log*, for the loser of a bet concerning the date of the Allied invasion of Western Europe.

The Belaria Crawl
In a brief interview with the principals and their envoy plenipotentiary some illuminating information was obtained. It appears that the 'crawl' was on settlement of a wager over the probable date of the invasion; May 31st having been the 'deadline'. Our readers are reminded that the preservation of dignity was the first consideration of the protagonists and their staffs who made the arrangements.

The Envoy Plenipotentiary, in reply to a question, assured us that feeling of the utmost cordiality existed between the principals. The winner remarked that, delighted as he would have been to lose this wager, he was of the opinion that we should see the invasion before the end of this month. The crawler endorsed this opinion and added, as a last remark before dashing off on all fours; '*All is lost, save honour; I have been double-crossed by Eisenhower.*' On the sound of the alert by the Master Herald, the crawler assumed the prescribed position, preceded by the Master at Arms, flanked by the Guard of Honour and followed by the Winner, the Master Buckler, the Envoy Plenipotentiary and the representative of the Fourth Estate. Another fanfare was sounded, there was a tense hush, then a crash of cymbals, the signal to start, from the Master Starter. The large crowd roared and the long awaited Belaria crawl was under way. The crawler made good time over the first lap, 5 mins 31.2 secs. At the first corner he was greeted by the Master Victualler and was suitably refreshed by courtesy of the winner. The Fourth Estate was suitably and properly victualled.

The required procedure was carried out on the second and third laps, with due regard for dignity and ceremonial. The home stretch was crawled to the strains of 'Blaze Away,' the principal sustaining a smooth gait and easy rolling action; he finished the feat to acclamations of the onlookers, having done the last lap in 4 mins 16.2 secs, making a total crawling time of 21 mins 36.2 secs. – a record likely to stand for some time. The crawler's final remark was brief but to the point: '*I am sure,*' he said, '*That if there had been 15 more days in May, it would have been a different story.*'

The Resident Physician, Dr. Everard Monteuuis, then carried out an examination in chambers and advised the crawler to take things easy for a long time and to have an immediate and complete change of air.

The serving of refreshments, supplied to all participants by courtesy of the crawler, marked the conclusion of a most satisfactory event. Everyone now looks forward to the repeat performance, with embellishments, scheduled for next October.

One item in particular that regularly appeared in *The Log* was 'The Diary of P/O Pepys P.O.W' written by Squadron Leader J. Pestridge, RAFVR. The diary looked somewhat jovially at camp life.

Monday, 5th June, A.D. 1944: During the *Appell* this morning did see the guards in the *Vorlager* wearing their gasmarks, a premonitary symptom, for to be mindful of an invasion is one thing, but to be expectant of gas is an odious matter. At this time did we learn of the foreclosure of the sports field, some rumoured for the building of heated showers, and a swimming place, but it was all a falsity, for nothing was further from the minds of the builders.

Monday 12th June: This evening did ensue a worthy sight: there is one of our number who insists on violating the air with the screech of his practice on the bagpipes, during the day our ears are tormented by the melancholy shrieks and squeals of the pipes, which, I learn, turns Scottish men fighting mad. Driven to desperation, our brave Senior Belgian Officer led the Legion of Tuck Tenements in opposition against this strident cacophony. But they must needs retreat, for the would-be piper, an Antipodean to boot, blew so hard as to drive them away. Now our gallant Allies, so adept at sabotage, are concocting a satisfactory end to this bag of wind.

Monday, 3rd July: Another Monday, how the weeks do fly, for it was this day last week that we lost our theatre, the wash-houses, aborts and classrooms, too . . . This evening two inhabitants of Tuck Tenements, that verminous Augean stable of the compound, did make a protest by choosing to sleep out of doors; but our guards, perturbed lest they take cold, took them to the cooler – a seemingly illogical proceeding – however due to the recent arrests and storage of our Red Cross food, the cells were full; so our two conscientious objectors were returned to their tenement, there being no gain to either side.[60]

At the end of the day the POWs would retire to their rooms and their bunks. Gordon Puttick recorded in his POW diary:

Everyone considers his part of a bunk as his own private territory. Sometimes during the day or more often during the dark hours before sleep, little groups of people gather around a particular bunk to discuss their favourite topics or to plan some future event. Derrick [Bell] and Bill [Baillie] might call on Charlie [Lepine]; at other times Charlie will be seen sitting on Derrick's bed, the two engrossed in some moot point of mutual interest.

Up to this date 13-9-44 we are allowed to stay out of doors until 22.00 hours. Darkness comes before this time, but when the lights of the outer perimeter are switched on it is recognised as a signal for everyone to use the set inner paths. When at last the doors are closed and the blackouts placed at the windows, then is the time to bring out the indoor games. At one time Monopoly will be all the rage, but this generally after wet miserable days. Chess is played occasionally by

---

[60] *The Log* Stalag Luft III Belaria newsletter, Squadron Leader Bryce Cousens. Published by Bryce Cousens. Printed by Burr's Press, Cheltenham.

some members of the mess while others play battleships (their
own adapted versions usually); draughts and dominoes are
played less frequently. Of card games bridge is at present most
popular. 'Casino' is another card game popular in its turn.
'Golf' is played with a special pack of cards and follows
through a game of golf with cards to represent the various
aspects of the game. Totopoly (the racing game) is usually
played on damp afternoons. Discussions lead sometimes to
experiments as for example the planning of a house. At such
times pencil and paper is produced and many designs
scribbled down. Often these drawings will lead to discussions
mostly concerning the likes and dislikes of the 'architects'
involved. A certain amount of studying is done in the room but
concentration is difficult since only on rare occasions is the
room quiet for any length of time. Serious work is usually
done in the libraries. Small paper aircraft or darts sail across
the room to land on the back of someone's neck or come a
cropper on the opposite wall, 'kerbap' as Bill would say.
'Kriegies' become surprisingly playful at times, and take part
in the most childish pranks, such as hiding someone's
chocolate, mock battles with imaginary guns, talking in an
affected manner, and so on . . . On the other hand some very
sensible and enlightening suggestions, plans and ideas are put
forward and once again playfulness is forgotten and a truly
serious atmosphere is created.

Such was the everyday life of the average POW.

A main priority for the air force officer POWs at Stalag Luft III was to
consider escape. It was their duty to make every attempt to return to their
service. Upon entry to the camp new prisoners were assembled and briefed
by the Senior British Officer in their compound. Details of the escape
organisation were explained, although no names were given out. New
prisoners were told to not be too inquisitive and to ignore anything out of
the ordinary.

In Stalag Luft III there was an established chain of command through
which any escape plans were supposed to get clearance and probable help.
There were the odd exceptions who tried to go it on their own, but in the
main the process was a coordinated effort. The German captors directed
considerable resources toward detecting escape attempts, and the prisoners
saw this as one of the main reasons to maintain them, despite little success.
The German intelligence branch, the 'Abwehr', placed specially detailed
Luftwaffe personnel in the compound from early morning to late evening.
They were unarmed, wore dark blue overalls, Luftwaffe field service caps

and leather duty belts. The 'ferrets', as they were called, went anywhere they liked, crawling under huts, digging spikes in the ground, peering through windows and eavesdropping.

The senior Allied officers in the camps recognised escape as a means to maintain the morale and self esteem of the POWs, but even if someone were able to get out of the camp, the journey across Germany and occupied territory still had to be tackled. Failed escape attempts could see the perpetrators undergoing a loss of privilege or even subjected to a stint of solitary confinement in the 'cooler'. The German captors at Stalag Luft III recognised their prisoners' duty to escape, and so the punishment handed out could be seen as moderate. However just before Arthur, Allan and Trevor reached Stalag Luft III, an escape attempt had been made that would seriously alter the relationship between the German guards and their captives.

On 23 March 1944, 80 men escaped the confines of north compound through a tunnel. Four were recaptured at the mouth of the tunnel, but the remaining 76 got away. Only three of them reached England. The remaining 73 of the men were all recaptured, but not before causing considerable embarrassment and disruption to the German authorities. However, the Germans were to exact a heavy price for being so inconvenienced. The infamous Sagan Order was issued by Hitler, which resulted in fifty of those men recaptured being shot. In his POW logbook Arthur copied down a verse inscribed on the walls of the cooler by Flight Lieutenant Bretel:

> If you can quit the compound undetected
> And clear your tracks nor leave the slightest trace
> And follow out the programme you've selected
> Nor lose your grasp of distance, time and place.

> If you can walk at night by compass bearing
> Or ride the railways by light of day.
> And temper your elusiveness with daring
> Trusting that sometime bluff will find a way.

> If you can swallow sour frustration
> And gaze unmoved at failure's ugly shape
> Remembering as further inspiration
> It was & is your duty to escape.

> If you can keep the great Gestapo guessing
> With explanations only partly true,
> And leave them in their heart of hearts confessing
> They didn't get the whole truth out of you.

If you can use your cooler fortnight clearly
For planning methods wiser than before
And treat your first miscalculation merely
As hints let fall by fate to teach you more.

If you scheme on with patience & precision
It wasn't a day they builded Rome
And make escape your single ambition
The next time you attempt it, you'll get home.

[This verse] was copied from the walls of the cooler where F/lt
Bretel after a vain attempt to escape had spent a fortnight
'cooling off'. His last attempt to get home cost him his life for
he and a large group of his fellow escapees were shot.

On 6 April the tragic news about the massacre reached the occupants of
Stalag Luft III, and added to the news concerning Russian successes on the
Eastern Front, led to most escape plans being temporarily suspended. On 6
June, however, the camp received news of the Normandy invasion. In east
compound the prisoners heard the news over German wireless, the
loudspeaker of which was on the kitchen building. The Senior British
Officer at Belaria adopted a similar policy to the other SBOs in the
compounds at Stalag Luft III.

After the news of the shooting of prisoners at Sagan, an order
was issued, after a consultation, that no escapes were
permitted until a period of six weeks had elapsed to see what
the future action would be by the Germans towards recaptured
British escapers, when the matter would again be reviewed, in
the light of subsequent knowledge. This policy was constantly
under review, and at no time was general authority for escapes
given, but at the end of the six weeks any one who had an
extremely good chance of escaping, and who was clearly
informed of all the hazards which he was running, and
especially in view of the fact that the War was drawing to a
close, was given authority to escape.[61]

It was hard to contain some men who maintained the glimmer of hope that
they may get home before everybody else. After all in 1944 some men were
edging towards their fifth year in captivity. Also to some it was their way
of keeping their spirits up. During Arthur, Allan and Trevor's period at
Stalag Luft III both east and Belaria compounds had tunnels underway.

---

[61] Public Record Office WO 208/3284 StalagLuft III Belaria report compiled by Senior
British Officer and heads of the Escape Committee after the war.

Derrick Bell: Huts at Belaria were built on stilts so you couldn't tunnel and periodically the ferrets, the roving guards that used to wander about with a shovel and a feeler, used to crawl under the huts and everywhere. You would do daft things like wait until he was underneath, because you could hear them crawling about, and then everyone would jump up and down on the floor and roar. We did have, although I didn't have anything to do with this, a tunnel going. It was between two huts, end to end and it was right by the perimeter wire.

This was between Block 6 and the store/camp kitchen hut on the southern edge of the camp.

Derrick Bell: They had a tunnel going right in the open. You could walk across it anyday. They were very clever, they were all the old lags who had been trying all their [POW] lives. They had chairs made out of wooden Red Cross boxes. Great big armchairs with a hollow bottom.

The plan involved tunnelling 50 feet to a position just the other side of the perimeter fence, exiting into a ditch. The front of one of the chairs was open, covered by a rug, from which the prisoner could enter the tunnel. The other chair covered the removed trap lid, which was a box 18 inches square full of soil with grass growing on top.

Derrick Bell: During the summer, we had a marvellous summer over there, a chap would go out and sit down at the table in the middle and play cards or chess or something. The guards were going up and down the wire all the time, but there was a time when the guard was at the other end. So then they whipped underneath, took the lid off and went down, and dug until it was Appell time and we had to go on down to parade. Then up they'd come, replace the trap, smooth it all over, pick up the chairs and nobody ever knew.

The men worked on the tunnel until December 1944, by which time the tunnel extended 20 feet. Progress had been slow owing to the problem of dispersing soil, and to only being able to go into the tunnel when the weather was suitable, so that men sitting outside in armchairs would not arouse suspicion. Then came rumours of a move to another camp.

Derrick Bell: It didn't get far enough before the winter came and you couldn't sit in the snow and play cards. There was someone in the room opposite us involved. He was a wonderful violinist but he had his violin taken away, as a form of punishment; one time he was covered in dirt and they knew he had been digging. The trouble was the cooler was full all the time; there was a waiting list. They knew there was a tunnel somewhere because they used to find earth. It got a bit difficult to dispose of earth. The roofs of the rooms fell in sometimes and people were showered with the soil. You got less bedboards by the week, as the bedboards were used as props in the tunnel, so you ended up sleeping on three bedboards.

In October 1943 three men had escaped from the confines of east compound in the famed 'wooden horse' episode. From beneath a vaulting horse being used by 'enthusiastic' POW gymnasts, the tunneller's had dug themselves an unofficial exit. A disguised trapdoor enabled entry and exit into the tunnel. The success of the escape method was not lost on other POWs. During the winter of 1943/44 a trapdoor was sunk in the east compound sportsfield where the POWs paraded for roll-call. During a count, two feet of sand were removed, a trapdoor retrieved from beneath a greatcoat, placed in the hole and the sand replaced. During subsequent roll-calls the trap was raised and a tunneller entered the lengthening shaft. As previously described the general disorder during roll-calls helped the POWs keep the entry and exit of tunnellers secret.

The tunnel was christened 'Margaret'. The trap was 100 feet from the perimeter fence, and covered a 4 ft shaft. At the bottom, a chamber was excavated enabling two men entry into the tunnel and ample working space. They would go down during early morning roll-call, remaining there throughout the day until evening roll-call. During this period underground, the trapdoor was in place, with tunnel ventilated by airholes to the surface. If bad weather led to a roll-call in barracks the POWs would engage in a game of rugby. A scrummage over the trapdoor allowed the tunnellers the cover for their entry. Games of rugby took place in even the worst weather, accustoming the German guards to the POW's love of the game. The tunnellers remained above ground if the morning's weather was bad, a game of rugby started up as soon as there was a change for the better. It was essential to get the men out of the tunnel during evening roll-call as a night underground during the winter in Silesia would be of very little benefit to a POW's health.

Once the tunnellers were down fellow POWs shuffled their feet over the earth above the trap. In the evening they came back, the men who were placed over the trap coming out early, always accompanied by other groups so that their continual eagerness for roll-call would not become suspicious. As the POWs were all wearing greatcoats, sand from the tunnel was placed in small sacks hitched beneath the coats and taken away for dispersal. Shoring boards could also be carried to the tunnel beneath the coats.

By March 1944 the tunnel was almost completed. On the 23rd came the breakout from north compound, and the news of the massacre. With escape attempts officially put on hold, 'Margaret' remained unused, and in October news reached the prisoners that in light of the current war situation, escape was no longer considered a duty. Still there were some covert activities in the camp but many now began to plan for what the new year might bring. In particular 'Margaret' was completed and a plan devised for a mass escape. In the event of a complete rout of the German forces, the POWs were fearful that they would be exterminated. All compounds prepared for this eventuality: POWs were given responsibilities to overpower the guards, take control and embark upon a mass escape to reach Allied armies.

CHAPTER 18

EVACUATION

At 10 am on 12 January 1945 the Russian army began its drive from the river Vistula across Poland to establish a front line on the river Oder. The Germans were driven back by the superior numbers of Russian forces, who exploited the open landscape of Western Poland the same way the Germans had at the start of the war, and there was little time in which to evacuate the POW camps. As the month drew to its close the Russians edged toward the Oder and Sagan.

On the morning of Saturday 27 January 1945 the German commandant at Stalag Luft III received an order from Berlin, stating that prisoners were to remain where they were. That evening the order was reversed; at 1830 hrs Stalag Luft III was given notice to vacate the camp. Varying reports placed the Russians between 30 and 45 miles away. In east compound some of the Allied prisoners were enjoying a theatre production, when the adjutant interrupted, 'I'd be moving if I were you. We leave at 11.00 pm.' A mad rush ensued as prisoners gathered what they could. Food was stuffed into bedrolls, sledges that had either been made when evacuation rumours started, or now quickly constructed, were piled high with supplies for the march. However the Germans kept delaying the evacuation. Finally south compound left at 2300 hours, west compound left at 0030 hours on the Sunday morning, north compound at 0345 hours closely followed by centre compound, and east compound at 0600 hours.

At 2130 hours on the Saturday evening the occupants at Belaria had been given 30 minutes' notice of the evacuation. *The Log* records the events:

> This was the usual timing, however, and we finally paraded at 0015 hours on the morning of Sunday the 29th [actually the 28th]. This was a lucky delay as it gave us time to make sledges upon which to tow our kit, enabling us, of course, to carry much more. The greatest ingenuity was shown in constructing these vehicles and everything from coal boxes to Red Cross armchairs went into their making.
>
> It is impossible to describe our feelings when we were to march and I won't attempt to do so, but the immediate reaction was interesting. We had never been in such a situation before.

We were about to leave behind an accumulation of books, equipment, food, clothing, cigarettes, etc, which had been accumulated during the past five years, and officers who had hoarded every safety pin, nail and bit of broken glass were to be seen trying to give away thousands of cigarettes, brand new clothing, and all other things which they could not carry but did not wish to burn or leave for the Germans. We felt that this move indicated that the war was very nearly over and were accordingly in the highest of spirits.

The 0015 hours' parade was eventually dismissed at 0145 and we were told that we should really be going in about an hour and a half, so we went back to our quarters and rechecked boots, pack, etc, and had a good meal. One very bitter aspect of this move was that our much looked forward to British Red Cross Xmas parcels which had arrived late were to have been issued the next day. Of course we never got them.

We eventually left at 5 am on the Sunday, a very strange procession wound its way across the German countryside . . .[62]

Arthur was only a bystander as his fellow prisoners departed. He had succumber to a bad leg whilst in the camp and had to move into the hospital block and await transport. The hospital party was eventually made to march to Sagan camp on the Sunday, however and Arthur pulled his 180lb snow sleigh carrying anything he deemed worthwhile. They arrived at the deserted north camp where they were to join up with other sick prisoners from the main camp. In total there were about 500 prisoners left behind, considered to be too sick to be moved. They were accompanied by a few medical personnel, clergy and healthy prisoners who had volunteered to stay and help the sick or wounded. The previous healthy occupants had moved out quickly, and such was their haste that a considerable amount of food was left behind. For the next few days the sick party certainly did not go hungry. However on 6 February they too were moved out.

At 6 am on Sunday 28 January the men of east compound started to move out. Each man collected a food parcel, but there was still a surplus of supplies. Tins and half-eaten food littered the camp, something of which the local Germans took full advantage. As the column passed through the gates they could see the road ahead littered with surplus items, as those from the other compounds, who had left previously, realised the task ahead and lightened their loads. As the column progressed it became obvious that the main concern was going to be the weather. The snow on the roads had been compacted somewhat by the previous marchers and proved suitable for men pulling sledges. However it frequently snowed, sometimes turning

62 *The Log* Stalag Luft III Belaria newsletter, *op.cit.*

into a blizzard, with the ice-cold wind whipping across the column. It was not long before some men began to suffer from frostbite.

Any attempts by the Germans to guard the column of prisoners were soon abandoned. Orders had been issued that they were to shoot anyone attempting to escape, but it was not long before they too began to suffer from the cold. With heads bowed, concentrating on the feet of whoever was in front, they paid little heed to what the prisoners were doing. Not that they needed to worry, the prisoners had been given orders by their superiors that escape in the current circumstances would be a wasted effort. Only a very small minority took its chances.

On the first day of the march the column of prisoners from east compound made slow progress. It was not only the weather and weight of the sledges that slowed them down. They came across columns of wagons and civilian refugees, for as the Russians advanced, refugees from the Ukraine fled west. Also evacuees escaping the Allied bombing campaign were being sent east. These victims of the war were able to mingle with the prisoners in places. Some of the prisoners exchanged goods with these refugees.

> *Trevor Utton:* When on the road we saw the refugees. You could chuck a blanket up on their cart and they would throw back half a loaf of bread.

The local inhabitants also took pity on the POW marchers.

> *Derrick Bell:* One thing I remember about that march, which was very touching, was a woman who we marched by. She rushed out with a jug of milk and gave it to us. The guards didn't do anything.

After covering a distance of 10 miles the column of prisoners from east compound arrived at 5.30 pm at Halbau. There was a considerable delay in finding billets and the column was left standing in the street for a further four hours. Many of the men were now feeling the pain of the extreme cold. Some civilians attempted to get hot drinks to the prisoners but the SS troops present did all they could to prevent them. At 10 o'clock they eventually ended up in a large school and a church. The church was the smaller of the two at Halbau, the other already occupied by American prisoners, and was very cold. The next day the men from east compound remained in Halbau, but those in the church were moved to the school, where some of the rooms had been evacuated by the Americans; who had been marched on. The school had central heating and the prisoners enjoyed its relative comforts.

From Halbau the POWs from east compound followed in the trail of those from north compound. They passed through Freiwaldau and after an

11 mile march arrived at Leippa. Again they had a wait before eventually being billeted at a church and school at the western end of the village. The men in the church found conditions crowded, and prisoners had to spend the night sitting upright in the pews.

The following day the column continued the march, a further 20 miles, and by evening ended up at Muskau. They were billeted in a large glass factory consisting of high brick buildings surrounded by a wall. The factory was still operating, with the furnaces still burning. The men seized the opportunity, some sleeping against the main boiler. Men also took the opportunity to dry off their clothes and do some cooking. The kitchen still functioned and there was hot soup provided.

The warmth raised the spirits of the men, but they were soon to receive information to bring them down to earth again. The next day it became apparent that the snow had begun to thaw and the roads became slushy. Sledges were no longer of any use and the men would have to carry anything they required. Also the British columns were told that they were to be divided.

The column of prisoners from north compound and half of those from east compound were ordered to march that night for Spremberg; it marched 11 miles of the journey, and reached Grunstein at 6 o'clock on the morning of 2 February where it rested until 11 am. The prisoners then continued the 7 miles to Spremberg, arriving in the early afternoon. From there the men were taken to Tarmstedt, 15 miles north-east of Bremen.

The other half of the prisoners from east compound, including Allan and Trevor, joined up with the column of prisoners from Belaria, who included Gordon Puttick and Derrick Bell. They were to follow up a day later and be entrained, so it was rumoured at the time, for Nuremberg.

The men from Belaria and those who had joined them from east compound arrived at Spremberg and were taken to a large German tank corps depot, where they were locked into the empty tank sheds. They received a half litre of hot liquid, containing no meat or solids but a slight cereal flavour. The men did not wait long before they were on the move once more. *The Log* records:

> We entrained during the afternoon into empty cattle trucks and at 1630 hours we were locked in – 50 to each, which made it quite impossible for us all to lie or sit down at once, so we took it in turns to do so.

> *Derrick Bell:* There was filthy straw in these cattle trucks. One of the chaps, I don't know how he managed it, picked up an oil lamp. He was determined to have it lit and it was hanging from the roof swinging from a hook and we were surrounded by straw, if that had fallen off, well!

The Log continues:

> Seven hours later the train left the station and we were told
> that our destination was Luckenwalde, a large Stalag, 32 miles
> south of Berlin and about 60 miles from our present position.
> Next morning we were still going, with frequent stops in
> railway sidings, and we arrived at Luckenwalde station at
> about 1700 hours.
>
> It was just beginning to get dark and the Germans had great
> trouble in counting us before marching off to the camp. When
> they had done so four times with different results, none of
> which was the figure they expected, we marched off in the rain
> to the camp where we spent an hour and a half standing
> outside the gates waiting for admission – there was no
> apparent reason for this. When we finally got into the camp at
> 2000 hours we were searched, deloused, etc, until 0600 hours,
> the next morning, when we were shown our new barracks.
>
> It is impossible to describe the revulsion and disgust we all
> felt on seeing them – they were squalid and sordid buildings
> with great patches of damp all over the inside walls and
> ceilings. The doors would not shut and most of the windows
> were broken. Three-tiered beds in sets of 12, accommodating
> 200 men in each room, were indescribably filthy, with dirty
> and half filled paliasses. There was nowhere to cook our food
> and the water was turned off so that we could not even wash.
>
> During the train journey from Spremberg the Senior British
> Officer of our party was visited by a German Foreign Office
> official who, without giving any reason, asked for a statement
> from the British that the Germans had made every attempt to
> improve conditions on the march and that we were quite
> satisfied with their behaviour in this respect. This was
> undoubtedly an attempt to offset the indignation shown by the
> world press over the whole incident, and, with typical German
> propaganda methods, it was implied that the giving of such a
> statement would greatly improve our living conditions at the
> new camp. The statement was, of course, refused.[63]

The Allied POWs from Sagan were not the only ones who faced the
prospect of a stay at Luckenwalde:

> *Derrick Bell:* Luckenwalde was a terrible place, we didn't
> know till afterwards how terrible it was. We realise now we
> had the best treatment. The Russians there and the Poles and

---

[63] *The Log* Stalag Luft III Belaria newsletter, *op.cit.*

the other people, even some Italians, had a rough old time. I had a photograph of some people standing up against a wall waiting to be shot. We [the British] were ignored, I don't even think we had a roll-call. Just this enormous bowl of soup everyday. It was pretty foul. You could have a wash but there were hundreds and hundreds in the compound and hardly any washing facilities, certainly couldn't have a bath. The best you could do was stand on this stone sink and sit under the tap.

Trevor was able to celebrate one of the important milestones of life whilst at the new camp.

Trevor Utton: It was while we were at Luckenwalde that I had my 21st birthday and the lads got together, four or five of them and gave me a present of about 10 cigarettes. And that was far better than any silver watch, incredible.

The sick party who had remained behind at Stalag Luft III whilst the healthy men departed, were marched to the station at Sagan in late afternoon on 6 February, with Arthur still dragging his laden sleigh. Here they were once more to enjoy close company with their comrades as they were packed into cattle wagons. Arthur was one of 48 men and 8 guards crammed in, several men laying down owing to leg and spine trouble, the majority having to stand. The doors and windows remained shut and the ventilation was terrible.

They left Sagan station at approx 2300 hrs and from then on there was continual stopping and backing up. On Wednesday, 7 February, in the mid afternoon, they reached Dresden, by which time many of the men had been sick owing to the lack of air. The only water available was that obtained by the German guards from the locomotive, and this was causing diarrhoea and sickness. If they had been there one week later, they would have had other things on their mind as the city was flattened by the bombing raids of 13/14 February.

The next day they passed through Chemnitz, Newmark, Plauen. The German guards allowed the doors to be open a couple of feet and the bomb damage at Plauen could be clearly seen. They travelled on to Hof, but then had to retrace part way to Plauen in the evening because of an air raid on Bramberg. On Friday and Saturday, 9 and 10 February the train, with its sickly passengers, eventually passed through Hof and Bramberg. In the 25 hours this took, the prisoners were only given one stop, without water, in a small marshalling yard. By the evening Arthur, too, was sick.

At about 1900 hours on 10 February the train pulled into Nuremberg. The idea was for the prisoners to sleep (if possible) overnight before marching, the next day, to camp.

Arthur's POW logbook:

Extremely uncomfortable in carriage, cramped, thirsty and dirty. No one allowed out of truck for toilet or sickness. Decided to escape conditions, and made successful break at 0300 hrs, Sunday Feb 11th.

Prior to the evacuation at Sagan, the BBC had made a broadcast to POW camps, received over the hidden radio sets, informing them of the current situation of the war. No doubt ample opportunity would arise to make a bid for freedom on any marches. But with the war coming to a close, it would not be worth taking the risks involved in an escape bid. The broadcast requested that men should stay together for safety reasons and for ease of identification. However south compound and Belaria did not receive the message before the evacuation.

Arthur's POW logbook:

Very cold out in the open; have one Red [Cross] box and water bottle. Only hope to find enclosed truck making in Swiss direction.

1400 hrs: So far unobserved, am very tired, leg giving me trouble, and shoulders and buttocks aching with cold and dampness. Have inspected nearly 300 trucks, but found only 1 going my way, to Crailshulm, 50 kms away. A coal wagon, open and very wet. Encamped, but had to move out, as believed station official had spotted me. Walked around m. yard [marshalling yard] and met wagon party of Polish cadets, working for 'Goons'. Was offered work with them for 14 days, and a trip to Augsburg. Couldn't afford to wait that long owing to rations. Was advised not to await truck transport, as yards were in bad state and very small chance of a wagon going my way. Decided I'd made a big enough nuisance of myself to the German officials and decided to make for camp. Feeling pretty nigh done in. Poles directed me to camp and I set out from m. yard. Tramped through Wehrmacht camp and helped *soldaten* (*sic*) on with his pack. Continued on through village and then out across woods towards camp. Picked up by Hauptmann outside camp about 1900 hrs, and placed under arrest and put in cooler for the evening.

After his night 'cooling' off Arthur entered the main camp. He was soon to come to the conclusion that conditions at Sagan were paradise compared to his new situation.

CHAPTER 19

MISERY AT NUREMBERG

Before the arrival of the officers from Sagan, the camp at Nuremberg, now renamed Stalag Luft III, had been the main camp of Stalag XIII D. This was formerly occupied by Serbs, Poles, Russians and French, but they were turned out into some outlying barracks to make room for the new inmates. The camp was laid out on the former grounds of the Reichsparteitag for which the toilet and washing facilities had been built long before the war. When the war started wooden barracks had been built between these facilities offering one wash house and one abort house per three living barracks. The area made available for the resituated Stalag Luft III consisted of five compounds numbered 3, 4, 5, 6 and 7. Prisoners in compounds 5, 6 and 7 could intercommunicate while the others were kept separate, a measure designed to keep new POWs away from the old POWs. Compounds 5 and 7 had about 12 bungalows for 150 men each, compound 6 had three huts less, compounds 3 and 4 had only about 4 to 5 huts, those missing having been destroyed by fire some time before the arrival of the Allied officer airmen. In compounds 3 and 4 tents were already being erected to accommodate new arrivals from Dulag Luft. Each compound had a small sports area.

Some of the barracks had rooms accommodating 25 to 35 officers in each, some were divided into two large halls with 65 to 75 officers in each, and in other barracks there was just one large hall with up to 150 men in each. There were usually triple or two tier wooden or iron beds available but some men had straw sacks to sleep on. More than a thousand men were actually sleeping on the floor. There was very little furniture, and although there were some wood or coal burning stoves in all the barracks, no fuel was provided. The POWs started to demolish some of the latrine barracks and washhouses to get the fuel, to which the Germans strongly objected. Parties of POWs were allowed out into the nearby forests to cut wood, whilst others dug out tree stumps which were more often than not too wet.

The washhouses were in very poor condition, and overcrowding had led to about 450 men having to share two water outlets. For the first month or so at the camp there was no soap issued. The latrines were badly worn out. Seats had been installed in two rows over a sewage trench but all the wooden material had disappeared and the trench was completely open.

During the first month only 50 rolls of toilet paper were issued for more than 5,000 men.

Cooking of food proved extremely difficult due to the shortage of fuel, which also meant very little, if any, hot water available for washing. The amount of food available fell way below what the POWs were supposed to receive. Arthur recorded these conditions in his POW logbook.

<u>List of German rations supposed to be issued weekly</u>

Potatoes	2125 grams per week
Bread	1750 ,,
	(160 grams Knackerbant (*sic*) in lieu of 250 gms bread)
Meat	200 grams issued in soups
Barley	60 grams ,,
Dried Veg	120 grams ,,
Flour	30 grams ,,
Sugar	140 grams
Cheese	37^1/2 grams
Jam (Ersatz)	140 grams (or 100 grams Cheese in lieu)
	(We can expect up to 50% loss of cheese)
Peas	120 grams in soup
Margarine	174.4 grams
Salt	112 grams
Tea	10.3 grams
Millet	Nil

Jam, Tea, Millet not seen so far.

Minimum number of calories required by the human body to sustain life, (i.e. person to lie in bed all day and only go to the toilet) is approx 1700 per day.

Clerks require 2000 – 2500 calories per day.

German rations issued amounted to <u>811</u> calories per man per day.

From 30th January till March 1st (day of 1st Red Cross issue) personnel of Nürnberg POW Camp lived on a maximum of <u>1181</u> calories per day. 30 – 50% of this food (i.e. vegetables, barley and flour) were mainly uncooked, owing to shortage of fuel.

Weather was very cold (snow falling), and aborts were partly broken down to afford fuel for cooking and heating purposes. Coal non-existent.

There was another major concern for the POWs, 'friendly' fire. Much of the free space in the compounds was soon taken up by splinter trenches which the Allied officers dug themselves. This was allowed only after the Senior Officers had given their parole for the whole camp not to make any escape attempts from these splinter trenches. The reason for the trenches is made clear by reference to Arthur's POW logbook.

Feb 20-21-22:   Heavy daylight raids on Nürnberg [Nuremberg] by USAAF.

Feb 26:   8.30 pm RAF . . . Mosquitos raided Nürnberg. One hut (112) had side wall blasted off floor. [Bomber Command had sent a force of 38 Mosquitos to raid Nuremberg on the night of the 26th February.]

The prisoners at the camp decided to make a complaint about the conditions. On 13 March 1945 the camp was visited by a Red Cross delegate who made the following conclusions about the complaint concerning the location of the camp.

The camp lies within 3 kilometres of a major railroad choke point and marshalling yard, which the Senior Officers consider a first class military target, and incompatible with Part III. Sect. II Art. 9 of the Geneva Convention. Although this might be the case, the present camp had been established long before the air-war . . . which is experienced in Germany nowadays. The recent military development has forced the Germans to concentrate their Ps.O.W. into existing camps where they can give them at least some sort of accommodation and as pointed out by higher quarters it was not their intention to give this particular marshalling yard a protection in putting the Air-Force camp in its neighbourhood.[64]

The prisoners also complained about their diet, the crowded conditions, the lack of fuel, the rats, the mice, bedbugs, lice and fleas, the lack of disinfectant or antivermin powder.

Oh to be back at Sagan!

The prisoners' complaint ended with some proposals for the remedy of the situation. The first proposal asked that the prisoners sign paroles and be allowed to march to Switzerland where they would then be interned until the culmination of the war. The second proposal requested that the prisoners march to a different camp which would have better facilities and where Red Cross parcels could be obtained. The Germans considered the situation.

Meanwhile life at the camp had to continue. The report on the Red Cross delegate's visit of 13 March 1945 to the camp commented on the

---

[64] Public Record Office WO 224 63B

German and POW attitude to the situation.

> Materially speaking, the camp is not very satisfactory especially when comparing with the previous accommodation the officers had at Sagan. However, it is still better than with what other Ps.O.W. have to put up under the present circumstances. The German authorities show very much good will but on their side meet with insurmountable material difficulties. During the conference with the Germans the Delegate had very often the feeling of complete despair from the side of the Germans. In spite of all this, there are hopes that by and by this camp may grow into something which might be called a normal situation. The American and British Air-Force personnel still show a wonderful spirit and are, as stated by the Senior Officer, 'although slightly disfigured, still in the ring'.[65]

Arthur's POW logbook continued to record events at the camp which, not surprisingly revolved around the arrival of Red Cross parcels, the search for fuel and the spectacle of numerous Allied bombing attacks on Nuremberg.

> *Arthur's POW logbook:*
>
> *Mch 13th:* 3 Lorry loads (3600) parcels arrived in camp. $1/2$ parcel per man issue
>
> *Mch 16th:* 3 Lorry loads arrived from Geneva, making up full issue. 2 wagon loads arrived Nürnberg station, damaged by T.A.F [Tactical Air Force] 4000 parcels recovered 7.40 pm 'Newhaven' attack on city. V.G. marking. 4 a/c seen shot down. 1 definitely a fighter (Goon)

Bomber Command had dispatched 277 Lancasters and 16 Mosquitos on this raid to Nuremberg, losing 24 Lancasters. This was Bomber Command's last heavy raid to the city, which caused considerable damage. The size of this raid had quite a dramatic effect on the POWs at Nuremberg. The sound of distant sirens made them aware, quite early on in the evening, that there would be an air raid somewhere. However sirens closer to the camp soon started to go off, and it was not long before the recognisable hum of Merlin engines was heard. The flak guns opened up, the marker flares lit up the sky and the bombs started to go down. The POWs exited their huts quickly, many dived out of the windows, and rushed for the slit trenches. They had been warned that if they risked leaving their huts during

---

[65] Public Record Office WO 224 63B.

an air raid, they would be shot. However the guards had their own safety on their minds and were equally keen to find cover. From the relative safety of the trenches the POWs then witnessed the air battle, the weaving searchlights, the flak guns blazing, the explosions and the stricken aircraft, which for many would have brought back vivid memories of their own experiences. Indeed one burning Lancaster screamed over some of the camp huts and crashed to earth amongst some trees just outside the wire. Eventually the bombers left and the POWs returned to their huts as Nuremberg burned and black smoke filled the night sky.

The next night the raids continued but on a smaller scale. Arthur's logbook entries for March continued:

Mch 17th: 9.00 pm Mosquito 'spoof' attack on city.
Mch 18th: 'Spoof' attack on Nürnberg by Mosquitos.

Bomber Command had sent 39 Mosquitos to the city on the 17th, and 18 on the 18th. The raid of the 17th was not a spoof attack as Arthur had surmised, Bomber Command only taking part in minor operations on that night. The raid on the 18th was a spoof in support of two major attacks by heavies to Witten and Hanau.

Mch 19th: Issue of 1/2 R C parcel – ate 1/2 'D' Bar. 4 air raid
               alerts before 8.30 am.
Mch 21st: Germans have allowed a party of 30 Kriegies to
               go into the local woods to dig up tree trunks for
               camp fuel.
Mch 22nd: Issue of 1/2 parcels this morning. Store empty.
               Late evening 4 R C Lorries arrived with parcels,
               we hope. No air raids last night.

Despite the conditions, news of the general war situation filtered through to the camp, supporting morale, and food was getting through.

Mch 24th: 4 Red Cross lorries arrived and delivered 600
               french parcels, which were issued as 'gash' bulk.
               Had good feed tonight. 2 more R C lorries in with
               1400 parcels too. Things look much rosier.
Mch 25th: Dad's Birthday (God bless him)
               Terrific day. Allies crossed Rhine at Wesel and
               Oppenheim, and doing well. 12 train wagons of
               parcels in siding, should see us through to end of
               war. Parcel strength :-
               British   20000 approx
               Canadian   2000   ,,
               American   9000   ,,

Had biggest meal, so far, on the strength of it. Assured of full issue for 6 wks. Bashing 6 tins meat per day amongst 12 men. 'Lightnings' strafed N. part of city – no fighter opposition.

Mch 27th: Full issue of R C parcel – tins unpunctured. Expect to be moved from here, owing to allied advance. Bombing heard in distance most of day.

Mch 28th: Patton advancing very quickly. Everybody busy preparing 'hard rations' and marching packs.

Mch 30th: False alarm on the parcel issue, as over half the parcels which arrived on the 25th were not for us and have been forwarded on to another camp. Because of this and having to make hard rations, the mess will have to go easy on the food stakes.

Apl 1st: Patton and Patch still advancing quickly and spearheads (according to O.K.W) [a German source] are approx 58 mls away. Y 'Thunderbolts' seen strafing nearby district, no opposition seen. Had an Easter Sunday bash and had to 'stall out'myself. Wonder whether we shall move?

By this time, and with the Allied armies closing in, the Germans decided to accept the second offer made in the prisoners' complaint report of 13 March. On 4 April the prisoners at Nuremberg were, once more, on the road.

CHAPTER 20

FREEDOM

Arthur's POW logbook:

Apl 4th: Evacuated Nürnberg camp at 11.30 am and supposed to be marching to Moosburg, 145 km away. Today marched 25 km, feet blistered and pain in groin. Trading cigs and soap for bread and eggs. Slept in barn (or attempted to) with 150 odd men. Everybody worn out as all carrying food and personal belongings. No food issued by 'Goons'.

Apl 5th: Managed to cook eggs and meat roll on farm kitchen stove, and had good breakfast, with hot milk. Marched on to Newmark. Germans issued 1/9th loaf of bread per man as $1^{1}/_{2}$ days' ration. USAAF heavily bombed Nürnberg – concussion waves seen against clouds – marvellous sight. Gus Davies and I got in party of 22 sick and managed lift on lorry for 5 km, then waited till 10.40 pm and caught passenger train to Bergen. Fare 2 cigs per man. Slept in 'Guest House', had supper of 2 eggs and fried bread, coffee. Slept well and feel better for the rest.'

Another POW recorded, in his own log book, reports about the bombing of 5 April:

Later heard 147 American kriegies killed, 2,000 Russ-serbs, and 40 goons. Our camp was leveled – lucky so far.[66]

By this time the prisoners, along with their guards, had begun to straggle, and the march started toward complete disorder. Arthur was able to trade freely with civilians and hence bolster his food supply. It all seemed very carefree although there were some unsavoury incidents.

---

[66] G.W.Wenthe, Daily Log, April 4-June 4, 1945, quoted in Durand, A, *StalagLuft III – The Secret Story*, Louisiana State University Press, 1989.

Arthur's POW logbook:

Apl 6th: Breakfast – fried eggs and bread, coffee. Soap and cigs invaluable – wish I had more. 3 eggs for ¹/₂ bar soap. Rest of camp came in early this morning, all soaked through with rain, having marched since 8 pm in evening. Issue of ¹/₂ Red Cross parcel.

Apl 7th: Breakfast of eggs and spam this morning and in afternoon continued march at end of column, taking our time and quite enjoying situation. 'Postern' carried our kit for us on bicycle, as far as 'Belingries'. Stayed in restaurant long enough to cook some oatmeal and scrounge hot water for cocoa, some 'spuds' and bread. German guards turned us out, just as we finished meal. Carried on through village carrying packs and decided to hang back for day outside village. Picnicked by river from 1-5 pm, then went back to Belingries. Picked up by *Volkstorm* patrol and as we were cranked took us to *Lazarette* [German military hospital]. Put to bed, after a hot brew. Very snug room and comfortable bed.

Apl 8th: Breakfast of bread and honey, plus Goon tea, brought in by dutch nurse who speaks a little English. Feldwebel (Dr) Fritz came in and fired up to cook porridge in kitchen. Had best Goon dinner in Germany and made our own 'brew'. Had discussion on politics with Dr. Fritz in evening. 7 boys in room all told. Hope to stay here till Americans arrive.

Apl 9th: Only soup for dinner today, but bread pretty plentiful, 4 more lads arrived here today. Dr Fritz hopes we'll stay here. This evening left convent, entrained for French *Lazarette* at Neumark, arriving at 10.30 pm. Frenchman gave us jam, butter, bread and biscuits.

Apl 10th: Two soups a day, Goon issue and pretty poor. Saw French doctor this morning and he thinks we'll be moved. Taken to station this evening, waited in cold for 3 hours and made 'postern' take us back to *Lazarette*. Some of boys are pretty sick. Bread issue of a sixth of a loaf per man.

Apl 11th:	Neumark was bombed by small formation of 'Forts,' some French and Russian Kriegies were injured. Staying here another day at least. Soup a little better today.
Apl 12th:	Nothing much of importance happened today. Nazi Youth group moved into farm next door, just boys of 14 or 15.
Apl 13th:	A Friday too and what a day. Kicked out of hospital this morning by some square headed Goon. I mean kicked too. Marched along and picked up with army crowd. Put in barn, under Hungarian SS guards. 11.30 pm guard roused us out, he was drunk and wanted a good and a bad soldier to shoot. Knocked us around. Back in barn and called out a second time at 11.45 pm. Goon had pistol (*Kleinaltendorf*) out and placed it against 'Capt Goldberg's' head, but was pushed away. Wanted to shoot everybody, but German woman brought Wehrmacht *Oberfeldwebel* over and we managed to get back in the barn, with just a few knocks. No food at all issued from Goons.
Apl 14th:	Marched about 22 kms today, packs carried on waggon, but feet and groin still sore. British sorted out from Americans and Russians, put with party of Australians. Had good soup and managed to get some eggs. Village – Altmansberg.
Apl 15th:	Left Altmansberg about 7 am and travelled by foot to Oberdolling, a distance of 28 km. Met a woman who had lived in America for 8 years and traded a bar of soap for 6 eggs, 1lb bacon and piece of honey bread. Slept in barn as usual.
Apl 16th:	Stayed at Oberdolling, did some washing and had a bucket bath. 2 good soups today.
Apl 17th:	Marched only 5 kms today, to a village called Menning 15 kms from Ingolstadt, 1 km from Danube. Had 10 eggs given us by German civilian and can trade fairly easily.
Apl 18/19/20:	Stayed in farmyard, nothing of importance except bombing of aerodrome (3 km away) and a town (about 5 km away) by marauders. Terrific amount of air activity, no opposition whatsoever from Luftwaffe.

Apl 21st: Day started badly. Some of the boys had a binge on rum last night and this morning Gus's pack was missing. Found later in lavatory, most of his personal gear ruined. Cigarettes, bread and eggs taken. A very poor show. The lads bought a sheep this morning, which was served out this evening.

Apl 22nd: Stayed in farm all day, weather poor, little air activity.

Apl 23rd: Another day spent in village. Gus went to next village about Red Cross parcels but could not contact Moosburg. I had dinner with German people and am invited to breakfast.

Apl 24th: Left Menning this morning, supposedly on a 10 km march. Crossed the Danube approx 9.30 am and had 5 min rest after 2 hrs fast marching. Covered approx 28 km today arriving at Mainburg 2 pm, and going on 3 kms more to a small village called Steinbach. Now 26 kms from Moosburg. Food very scarce in this village.

Apl 25th: Contact made from Mainburg with Red Cross at Moosburg, expecting parcels tomorrow. Soup issue very poor and no bread. Complained to Oberleutnant in charge, but no satisfaction received. German guards went without.

Apl 26th: Parcels did not arrive, but French Command's Party gave us 130 French parcels (1 to 4 men). Had singsong in barn this evening. Have been hearing artillery fire all day. Fixed up POW signs.

Apl 27th: No further news from Moosburg. German SS troops retreating through town; mostly SS. Machine gun fire heard. Rained very hard most of day. Had a hot 'bucket' bath today. Parcel (French) arrived, 1½ per man.

Throughout March and April 1945 the Allies on the Western Front swept across Germany. On 25 April, US and Soviet forces linked up at the river Elbe, further north the Red Army encircled the capital of the Reich. General Patton's US Third Army had advanced through southern Germany and detachments approached Nuremberg.

Arthur's POW logbook:

Apl 28th:	Most marvellous day of krieg. This morning Munich radio announced '*Krieg fertig*' in Bavaria. Outbreaks amongst civilian population. Mid day American tanks entered village, and my kriegie life ended. Took over town, Capt Fisk USAAF in charge; and was put in charge of No 2 British Coy. (190 men). Several prisoners collected. Made Head-quarters and billets at *Schulhaus*. Had good food and bed; everything very rosy.
Apl 29th:	Up at 7.30 am this morning, and had good clean up. More American troops arriving. Contacted Am Hdqtrs in Mainburg and arrangements are under way to take us home. Can hardly believe that I'm a free man again. People in house are pro British and we're living like kings.
Apl 30th:	Contact officer did not return today, but all forms are made out and the men are ready for immediate removal. My total of company is 180 now, 10 men preferring to make it back under their own steam.
May 1st:	Transport arrived this morning and company embarked at 8 am. Arrived at Regensburg at 12.15 am, and had to go through a lengthy ritual of filling forms and being dusted down with DTT powder. Weather is bad over the Rhine and Channel, so will have to spend night here in a bombed out Messerschmitt factory. Went for a flip in a Stinson this evening, and did ½ hr of dogfighting – just like EFTS days.
May 2nd:	Worst weather in 30 yrs experienced in England, no hope of C.47s today. Went into Regensburg this afternoon, and scrounged some extra 'C' and 'K' rations for room. Am now in charge of No. 3 British Group (25 men). Managed to pick up a few articles to take home. Had my Goon pistol and bayonet pinched, plus most of my personal gear.
May 3rd:	Drew rations and handed blankets in at 8 am, and fell men in outside billet at 8.45 am to make 800 yds to airfield. Weather fair to poor

at moment. 27 C.47s arrived at 10.30 am, and I and 24 other men embarked at 11.25 am. Took off for Rheims at 11.35 am, did an hour at the controls myself (nice aircraft), arriving at Rheims about 2.15 pm. Taken by lorry, through city to receiving centre. Had a good hot meal and slept the night in a tent.

May 4th: Much hanging around this morning. Deloused and issued with American GI clothing, old stuff thrown away. Ate in officers' Mess. Our party of 400 British Army went home on Lancasters this afternoon, Van and I were left out, much to our disgust. In the evening went to 'C' Mess in town looked upon as Russians, I should think, by the way we were ignored. Later went to Red Cross Officers Club and were treated to coffee and doughnuts. French orchestra played and 4 Negroes sung some minstrel songs. Hitch hiked back to P.W. Camp.

May 5th: Weather too bad for flying today, so hung around camp. In the evening invited to Air Staff Mess SHAEF [Supreme Headquarters Allied Expeditionary Force] and got gloriously drunk. Talked with Air Marshal Sir Arthur Tedder and several other bigwigs, who were discussing the conditions of surrender with Admiral Doenitz's diplomats. Was violently sick on ride home. Sent off letter to Anne.

Since 26 April, Lancasters from Bomber Command's 1, 5, 6 and 8 Groups began Operation Exodus, flying to airfields in the liberated Low Countries to pick up the former POWs and return them home. A quick journey home, the POWs hoped.

Arthur's POW logbook:

May 6th: Up this morning at 7.30 am, and had good breakfast. Am feeling drunk from fumes of last night's 'binge'. Travelled to aerodrome this morning, in charge of 24 men. Waited for quite a time, but finally took off in Lancaster. Ropey crew, DR compass went u/s and pilot and navigator didn't notice it. Brought their attention to it and found ourselves 80 odd miles off Norfolk coast, en route for Norway. Turned onto 270 and crossed Norfolk coast, instead of at Dover. Arrived RAF Station, Wing, about 8 pm. De loused again, given meal, then waited till 1 am for train to Cosford. Arrived at 3 am, sent telegram, interrogated and re-equipped with battle dress etc. Had a bath (beautiful) and got to bed at 7 am. Up again at 8 am and finally caught train home at 2.25 pm. Arrive home at 9 pm and nearly got squeezed to death by Anne. <u>Boy oh boy, what a marvellous woman.</u> Cheerio to kriegie life, and now for 42 days leave.

CHAPTER 21

FRUSTRATION AT LUCKENWALDE

Meanwhile, during early April 1945 rumours persisted at the prisoner of war camp at Luckenwalde as to further Russian advances on the Eastern Front. Despite the imminent possibility of liberation, two British POWs attempted to make an unofficial escape. Unfortunately both men were shot whilst making the attempt, one died instantly the other died later from his wounds.

On Thursday 12 April the camp was evacuated and the prisoners marched to the nearby rail station, undoubtedly to take them south to Moosburg. The prisoners were concerned about the amount of air activity at the time, and managed to get the Germans to allow them to paint 'RAF – POW' in yellow on top of the carriages. The prisoners entrained for the night in expectation of moving out the next day. Again they were disappointed and on the Saturday the prisoners were marched back to camp. Russian and American advances had cut the rail lines between Berlin and the south of Germany.

On Saturday, 21 April, it became obvious to the occupants of the camp that the Germans were about to leave.

Gordon Puttick's POW logbook:

At morning Appell there were only a very few G's [Germans] around. At midday after a good deal of argument the two remaining G's in the compound were induced to give up the keys of the compound gates; a few minutes later the camp was in our hands.

The sentry boxes were now unmanned and the guards and sentries withdrawn. At noon the Germans paraded outside the main gate and the Commandant sent for General Otto Ruge, former Commander in Chief of the Norwegian Armed Forces, who was the Senior Officer of the camp. However the General could not be found quickly enough and with the Germans in a hurry, they handed over command of the camp to the nearest senior officer. They then left. Command was soon handed over to General Ruge and Wing Commander R.C.M. Collard DSO DFC took over the command of all the British POWs. The make up of POWs at the camp at this time was as follows (not including Russians who were kept separate).

	Officers	NCO's and other ranks	
British	1264	1476	RAF
		996	Army
Americans	548	4555	
Norwegians	1081	30	
Polish	685	79	
Yugoslav	29	692	
Czechs	–	97	
Italians	51	1815	
Roumanians	5	–	
French	520 (mainly Aspirants)	3566	
Total	**4183**	**13306**[67]	

These prisoners were far from free though. The camp was surrounded by German soldiers and the prisoners received warnings not to leave the environs of the camp.

Gordon Puttick's POW logbook:

There was some confusion but for the most part the change over went well. The Russians have not yet reached us but are quite close and we expect them here at any time. There was a small episode of a G [German] General and some rifles. SS men in the wood. Civilians are leaving the town. Rumours fly around in all directions. White flags flying. Red, white and blue emblems put up. POW signs. Weather very wet, low clouds.

The 'Kriegies' went to bed that night weighing up the possibilities of an American or Russian Liberation. Their hopeful slumber was rather shattered however when at one o'clock on the Sunday morning a German aircraft proceeded up the main street of the camp strafing. Nobody was hurt by the shells, but a few bruises undoubtedly resulted as higher tier bunks were evacuated to the pains of those on the lower bunks. The occupants of Luckenwalde later received the attentions of a group of Hitler Youth holed up in the nearby wood. They made their presence known by dropping a mortar shell into the camp, fortunately with no known injuries resulting.

At 0500 hours on the Sunday a light Russian armoured car drove into the camp, from which a small and dirty Russian emerged. He was surrounded by exalted prisoners and responded by hugging, and kissing anyone he

---

[67] Public Record Office AIR 40 1491.

could get to. Twenty minutes later he left for his headquarters with General
Ruge, the Senior American Officer and an interpreter. The latter two sat up
high on the armoured car and their journey ended rather quickly. As the
armoured car left the camp it was fired upon, whereupon they fell, unhurt,
into a ditch and the car sped away.

At 1000 hours several Russian tanks came into the camp.

Gordon Puttick's POW logbook:

After breakfast Russian tanks arrived, also lorry loads of
troops. The boys clamboured onto the wire and cheered
wildly.

Allan Burrell: [The Russians] had used their tanks to tear
down the barbed wire separating the various compounds . . .
The perimeter fence was left intact.

Derrick Bell: There were women on some of them. We
showered them with cigarettes cause we still had got
cigarettes. There seemed to be cigarettes everywhere but no
food.

One tank drove down the main street of the camp, knocking down posts as
it went along. Very little information was gleaned from these frontline
troops, except that the prisoners' position would be clarified once the
occupation troops arrived. There was some confusion as the tank
commanders wanted all the liberated POWs to take up arms and join in the
battle. Meanwhile the Russians quickly overran Luckenwalde town, with
very little resistance.

On the Sunday the Russian prisoners, who had been kept separate from
the Allied POWs, about 9,000, were released and those who were able were
given rifles and told to go out into the woods and shoot Germans. Some of
the Germans tried to surrender to the British or Americans in the camp and
they were taken in and handed over to the Russians. Eventually General
Ruge was taken from the camp, ending up at Marshal Koniev's headquarters near Sagan. Wing Commander Collard took over command of the
camp, and immediately issued standing orders to the camp personnel so as
to restore some order.

Over the next few days various Russian officers visited the camp but gave
no information to the expectant ex-prisoners as to how they were going to
get home. The Russians also filmed the camp and the prisoners. They filmed
the funeral of eight Russian soldiers who were found starved to death in one
of the camp's barracks. Collard continued to keep effective control of the
camp as the Russian staff's efforts proved inadequate. He had to implement
a number of measures to ensure the welfare of the camp personnel. One such

measure was the setting up of a supply organisation, which ran four large kitchens as well as carrying out foraging and issuing supplies. At one stage they had to obtain milk for the newly born babies of the civilian refugees now entering the camp. There was an interrogation centre to guard against entry into the camp of Germans and other undesirables. One of the main obstacles for food supply was a shortage of petrol needed for foraging. The supply organisation had to set up its own butchery.

Eventually a Major General Famin (a rather apt name considering the shortage of food) of the Repatriation Board on Koniev's staff visited the camp. The Major General informed Wing Commander Collard that with the two armies, Russian and Allied approaching, the prisoners were more than likely to make a westerly return home, and everything was being done to ensure this happened as quickly as possible. He also issued orders for organisation of the camp. By this time quarters were becoming overcrowded and dirty and the sanitation deplorable. General Famin ordered the British, American and Yugoslavs to be moved shortly to a former German camp where conditions were much better. However in the first few days of May there had been an outbreak of fighting around the camp as a large pocket of German troops had tried to break through to the west. This made foraging even more difficult. Also approximately 7,000 refugees were turned off the road, and were put in the German camp intended for the Stalag Luft IIIa [Luckenwalde] POWs. They proceeded to loot the camp, which rendered it uninhabitable. At the same time, and to make matters worse, 2,000 Italian refugees drifted into Stalag Luft IIIa.

Early in February 1945, Churchill, Roosevelt and Stalin met at Yalta to discuss a postwar Europe, for an agenda that included prisoners of war. Stalin insisted that all Russian prisoners liberated by the Allies must be returned to Russia, including any civilian labourer or POW who had been coerced into serving with the German forces. This last category included some Russians who had been on the western front and had willingly given themselves up to the Allies in the hope that they avoided repatriation. Churchill and Roosevelt agreed; conscious of the numbers of British and American POWs who would be liberated by Russian forces and could be used as hostages.

When the time came for Russian POWs to be repatriated they were extremely reluctant to return to their native land. Stalin had decided that there could be no circumstances in which a member of the Russian armed forces should surrender, and as any liberated Russian prisoners were considered to have done so, they could therefore expect a considerable time in a forced labour camp. The penalty for their 'surrender' was often more extreme.

When for example, the liner *Almanzora* docked at Odessa with a consignment of Russian prisoners from England, a

Soviet liaison officer told his British opposite number that
they would probably be sent to 'educational labour camps'. It
seems doubtful whether they got beyond the quay. Even as
they were being disembarked, the sound of machine gun fire
could be heard coming from behind a nearby shed.[68]

Allan Burrell commented on the liberation by the Russian forces at
Luckenwalde:

The first thing the Russians did was to remove their own
nationals. They were about 9,000 strong and rather
woebegone. They were not popular with their own troops
having committed the sin of being captured. We heard that
few, if any, ever reached home.

Some of the liberated Russian prisoners in Western Europe were fully
aware of the implications of their repatriation and a number committed
suicide whilst in Allied hands. As the fighting in Germany drew to a close
the Russian authorities had a considerable number of Allied POWs now in
their care. Without doubt their value as bargaining tools was not
overlooked.

The prisoners at the 'liberated' camp at Luckenwalde, who were at first
exalted at the quick prospect of returning home, soon began to realise that
this was not to be the case. Some prisoners took the opportunity of moving
in with German civilians, as the civilians hoped this would help them when
the American forces arrived. The Russians looked unfavourably on this and
warned the prisoners against this action, not before a few prisoners had lost
their lives.

Toward the end of April and beginning of May the camp's population
had grown to about 30,000 with the resultant problems of food distribution.
Large numbers of prisoners began to leave the camp to find their own way
home.

Gordon Puttick's POW logbook:

There has been a steady flow of bods out of the camp heading
SW. They are going in bunches ranging from two to eight
people. Nearly everyone is completely out of patience with the
constant waiting and nerves are getting more than a little
frayed.

Indeed this was happening all over Germany, prompting General
Eisenhower to broadcast orders telling the prisoners to stay put. Many still

---

[68] Richard Garnett, *POW*, David and Charles 1981.

decided to take matters into their own hands. Wing Commander Beaumont, at Luckenwalde, was one who if it wasn't for his responsibilities would have left the camp:

> All the boys want to push off west and are doing so in increasing numbers. I would be right with them if I hadn't this damned responsibility . . . Told officers and pickets to dissuade the men from going through the wire if possible but if told to 'b----- off', to 'b----- off' promptly and avoid incident.[69]

On 4 May Wing Commander Collard forwarded to the Supreme Headquarters Allied Expeditionary Force (SHAEF), via an American war correspondent, a report detailing his concerns on the conditions in the camp. But no doubt his fears were somewhat allayed as news came through that a Lieutenant Klietz of the American 83rd Division was to arrive the next day and start evacuating the American, British and Norwegian prisoners. Once again the feeling of expectation rose only to be checked. On 5 May the camp received news that the lorries to evacuate the prisoners had to travel that day from Hildesheim, 135 miles away. Later in the day however a further statement was issued saying that a convoy of trucks would arrive the next day in order to complete an evacuation. An American ambulance convoy did arrive, however, and took away all the American sick and six severe British sick cases.

On the evening of 6 May 19 American lorries arrived at the camp with Captain Sinkavitch, the American liaison officer. Again expectation was high. Captain Sinkavitch claimed he had orders to evacuate the prisoners but the Russians thought otherwise. The prisoners were informed that they would not be allowed to leave with the American trucks until permission had been received from the proper Russian authorities. However the prisoners decided they were going to go anyway. The next morning some prisoners began to leave in the lorries. The Russians opened fire over the lorries, which not surprisingly turned back and the prisoners once more entered the camp. The Russians searched the lorries and warned Captain Sinkavitch that his drivers and lorries would be interned should they remove any prisoners. The camp occupants then had to watch as the empty lorries drove past the camp and returned to the American lines. The morale of the camp plummeted, in particular that of those who had been POWs since very early in the war. However:

> *Allan Burrell:* A jeep arrived outside the main gate and an American climbed on to the back seat. He said, 'Listen you

---

[69] Wing Commander Beaumont quoted in *Prisoners of the Reich, Germany's Captives 1939-1945*, David Rolf, Leo Cooper Ltd.

guys, we will be placing trucks round this camp at a distance of 3 to 4 miles. The trucks will wait until 4.00 pm and we will be happy to take any of you who can reach them and we'll be able to give you a decent meal.

The Russians . . . had ordered a lot of Poles to position themselves round the camp to prevent anyone leaving. The Poles were not interested, however, and we proceeded to disappear. The trucks were there and needless to say Trevor and I were aboard.

Trevor Utton: The Americans had got word to us that they would leave a convoy of vehicles down in the village and anybody that could get down there would be on a lorry and taken away. I was in pyjamas. I got away round the back and with others into the village, to the convoy of trucks. They were driven by these big Negroes, who were tearing around. All you could see were the whites of their eyes. It was terrific.

Allan Burrell: That evening we had a very good meal of roast chicken, the first decent meal we had had for over a year. The Americans also supplied us with candy and cigarettes.

Trevor and Allan had got away but many men, including Gordon Puttick and Derrick Bell, still remained in the camp. Later on 7 May a Captain Grant, the American POW contact officer, arrived with another convoy of lorries. Wing Commander Collard persuaded him to go to Marshal Koniev's Headquarters to see General Famin. But on his way there, he met some Russian staff officers who said they were going to Luckenwalde with instructions for the repatriation. Captain Grant returned, but on the following morning it became obvious that the Russian officers had no such instructions. A decision was made to fill the lorries with British and Americans and make a final attempt.

Whilst a conference was being held with the Russian officers, due to a misunderstanding or ill discipline, some of the filled lorries left. A report came back to the conference that the lorries were driving off and the Russians demanded that the lorries should be stopped, but most had left. The Senior American Officer and Wing Commander Collard intervened in the 'unauthorised' evacuation and unloaded the last few lorries bringing the prisoners back to camp. Wing Commander Collard now took the view that any further evacuation attempts could have serious consequences and he decided to establish firm control over the British prisoners. He also pointed out to the Russians that whilst he would continue to help them they needed to establish effective control over the camp themselves.

By this time there were about 180 Americans and 2,000 British left in the camp, 1,700 having left in the last few days, mostly in the American lorries.

More and more prisoners had begun to leave on their own initiative, contrary to Wing Commander Collard's orders, but as he stated in his report made after the war:

> I did not take a very serious view of it at this period, in view of the extraordinary situation then obtaining. From then on, however, I took steps to enforce the order that all were confined to camp, and there was no further unauthorised departure by any British.[70]

Gordon Puttick's POW logbook:

So we are virtually prisoners in Russian hands. I am inclined to agree with the Russkis who I believe are trying to do their best for us. They want to get us out and they resent someone else trying to do the job for them. On the other hand it is damned hard for a Kriegie to sit around waiting to be sent home and having to curb his patience until correct authority is given when dozens of trucks are waiting to take him home by a non-recognised manner. The method of procedure does not in the least concern the Kriegie who is anxious to see his family, sweetheart and friends again, and I for one am exceedingly browned off with the whole affair. The question again arises – How much longer?

On 10 May General Famin came to the camp to meet Wing Commander Collard, who reported that he received a: 'somewhat insulting reproof on the subject of the 'unofficial' evacuation, this was done in front of his own and the camp Russian staff, who were standing round at attention and behaving with somewhat exaggerated deference.'[71] Collard was also warned that any further unauthorised evacuations would result in his being interned.

Meanwhile refugees still came into the camp, and Wing Commander Collard concluded that this constituted a menace to the health and discipline of the camp, as there could be no segregation. On 11 May he sent a letter to the Russians, and on the 13th all the British were moved into the quarters that had been originally occupied by German troops.

It was not until 19 May that proceedings started to move forward. Colonel Korofsky of the Red Army Repatriation Staff arrived saying that

---

70/71 Public record Office AIR 40 1491 Report by Wing Commander R.C.M Collard DSO DFC.

the British prisoners were to be taken to the river Elbe the next day where they would be handed over to the Americans. Sure enough, the next day a convoy of lorries arrived.

Gordon Puttick's POW logbook:

Sunday 20th May, Whitsunday and a memorable one at that. The sirens sounded again. Lorries (American-Russian) arrived early. We were put up into parties of 25 and numbered. I was in party 21. I ate 3 slices of bread and cheese and drank a cup of coffee before climbing into our lorry. The internee women's children were put into two lorries. We started, stopped, a hundred yds – stopped – another hundred yds, stopped – then away to a point on the Elbe via Treuenbrietzen. Many forest fires. Scenes of battles – scarred and broken tress, burned out cars, lorries and tanks, shell pierced houses, bombed houses, broken communication lines, twisted and fallen pylons, and to impede our progress most bridges over the autobahns and rivers had been blown up. The Russian drivers proved their skill, and the lorries, what they could stand up to when we made detours to avoid the crushing masses of concrete and steel. At one bridge the two ends adjoining the bank had been completely blown out leaving the rest of the bridge spanning the river, resting on the slender centre piece in the shape of a letter 'T'. Having started out at about 11.30 we arrived at our handing over point at 20.00 hrs. We stopped before a great bridge that had spanned the Elbe but whose two centre sections have now fallen into the swiftly flowing river. Somehow I thought the bridge looked rather majestic in the softening light, having been beaten but still endeavouring to maintain its dignity.

    We crossed the Elbe on foot across a pontoon bridge formed of 23 pontoons. I saw a party of Ruskees with tommy guns just before I crossed over. The Ruskees waved and grinned or saluted in a proper manner. The American lorries were waiting for us and we piled in, 40 to a truck. The handing over was a very simple affair. We merely climbed out of the Ruskee lorries, which were then lined up in a meadow on the east side of the river, we then walked across the bridge. Two speed boats were moored near the east bank. One was 'manned' by two Russian girls in uniform and a Helmsman, the other by a single Russian. On the opposite side of the river on the top of the bank German children clustered around to watch the event. There were also a number of young women looking on. To the left stood two high chimneys towering above a great oblong building upon the roof of which stood several people silhouetted against the blue sky. In less than an hour we were en route again. The surrounding countryside changed as we pushed farther West til instead of the continual sight of fir trees, I saw oaks, beeches, poplars and other dissiduous trees now clothed in the green of spring.

We sped on thro' little villages, some of them almost half demolished by bombs or shells. Just before midnight we approached the town of Halle. We went on into the town then stopped just outside in a big Luftwaffe camp. After waiting for an hour I registered my name, rank and No. etc, was put into a party as one of the 25 members and led to the sleeping quarters. I made up a bed on the top of a three tiered bunk (about 8 ft from the ground) then waited till the food call came. The beds are the standard metal type made to be adapted for one, two or more tiers. Boards are laid across and are covered by a stuffed palliasse. Food at last – and I was hungry. I followed the man ahead of me in the queue. Picking up my plate, mug and spoon I held them out to receive my portion of potatoes, mixed with fish and beans, and my first taste of white bread, bread whiter than snow, and coffee with bags of sugar. I enjoyed that meal and the sleep that followed it.

In Wing Commander Collard's report on the liberation of Stalag Luft IIIa he stated that despite the problems of relations and their extraordinary attitude toward repatriation, the Russians were consistently friendly. He also noted that it was easier to do business under the camouflage of a social occasion. He quoted one example, where during the official and final evacuation of the camp, in order to prevent the Russian commandant interfering and causing chaos it was better to get him mildly intoxicated, as a farewell gesture. He was then very friendly and there were no more difficulties.

We left Trevor and Allan with the Americans, just after their unofficial exit from the camp.

Trevor Utton: They drove us back, through some town that was absolutely gutted, it was just a pile of rubble. We finished up in Brussels. The British authorities took over then. When we were with the Americans we had stopped off at one or two American places, overnight, and they gave us chicken and white bread and god knows what. When we got to Brussels into the English camp, it was bangers and mash in a bloody old mess tin.

We were given an advance of pay and the night out. The girl at the YMCA desk got out a map and showed us where we were, the cinema's down that street, the pubs down that street and anything else you want is down that street. We all looked.

We were flown back in Dakotas after a day or two. You just took your turn, queued up and as an empty aircraft arrived, you would come back. That was one of the most embarrassing things in my life. When you landed in England, you stepped off the Dakota and there were two WAAFs either side of the steps. They had a flip spray, an old tin thing used to kill all the bugs and beetles. They would hold your trousers open and spray it down there and under your arms and chest. That was your delousing back into England. They always had a smile on their face. I don't know why.

Arthur, Allan and Trevor had returned home safely but their POW experiences would not leave them unaffected. Physically they had suffered losing a lot of weight; Trevor down to *five* stone on his return. Mentally too, they had been affected, the men having difficulties with some aspects of everyday civilian life, particularly going out, for example crossing the road now seemed a daunting prospect. The former POWs had returned approximately eight months after the evaders Alex, George and Pip. They had all 'done their bit', to defeat Nazi tyranny.

> *Alex Nethery:* The fact we survived, except Don, 30 operations, is a tribute to the spirit and ability of the entire crew: never forgetting the support of all the airmen and airwomen on the ground. I was a city boy, 20 years age and considered myself a man of the world. I came home a sadder and wiser man.

Debate and criticism of Bomber Command's role in the war flared up after the war, and continues today. The concept and application of 'area bombing' by the RAF remains a contentious issue. Fortunately groups such as the Bomber Command Association fight for the recognition of the young airmen who applied themselves through extreme conditions. Our seven young men, of a Bomber Command crew, had continually believed in their cause, put their lives on the line, come across extreme adversity, and one gave the ultimate sacrifice now resting in a Belgian cemetery. Those surviving could tell their story. Over 55,000 men were not able to do so.

EPILOGUE

Below are brief, post-war histories of some of the people involved in our story.

The people of the towns of Bon-Secours and Péruwelz: When the war ended the Resistance movement in the area had lost nineteen of its brave combatants, either killed in action, shot in prison by the Germans, or dead from their tortures and sufferings in concentration camps in Germany.

Many of the people featured in our story still live in the towns. Jean (holder of the Croix de Guerre) and Madeleine Henrard played host to Arthur's wife Anne and their children Eric and Annette in 1947. Almost fifty years later in 1996 Eric met up with them both again. Claire (who helped George Lorimer) Praet ran an electrical shop in Bon-Secours, but has recently become ill and is unable to maintain the business herself. Raymonde Rock unfortunately passed away in 1998. Jacques Nachez is now treasurer of 'L'Amicale des Associations Patriotiques de Péruwelz (the Patriotic Associations of Péruwelz Fellowship) of which the 'Amicale des Resistants de Péruwelz' (Resistance Members Fellowship of Péruwelz) is an associate member. Many of the members of this group recall the events in our story vividly. Jacques regularly comes to this country meeting up with the men themselves or the families of the veteran airmen, who were aided by the population of the two towns.

Alex Nethery: After the war, Alex trained as a mechanical draughtsman. He joined a steel fabricating company, helping to start up the processing and distributing division and becoming General Manager. After 20 years the division was sold and Alex along with 6 other employees started their own business. Alex retired in 1983 and living in Burlington, Ontario he uses up his spare time driving for the children's aid society of Halton County.

Allan Burrell: Allan returned to the large shipping company which he had joined in 1936, as an office boy, until he retired from the board having been appointed a Director some time beforehand. He married Muriel in 1950 and they had son and daughter and six grandchildren. They lived in Frinton on Sea and as Allan said, spent most of their time 'feeling like a non-paying hotel.' Unfortunately Allan passed away in March 2000.

Trevor Utton: After Trevor demobbed he returned to a career in the building trade. He married Glenis and they had two sons and seven grandchildren. Trevor retired when he was 66 and since then carried out some voluntary work for the NSPCC and meals on wheels. Trevor lived in Pinner, London, enjoying the company of his grandchildren. He remained a good friend of the Darlow family, maintaining his sense of humour and inflicting it upon them whenever they met up. Unfortunately Trevor passed away in 1999.

George Lorimer: George returned to Vancouver, British Columbia after the war and worked for a printing company as a book-binder until his retirement. He met Muriel, a registered nurse and they were married in 1952. They built their own home in Horseshoe Bay, just outside Vancouver and had two sons Graham and Derek, who are both married with families of their own. George passed away in May 1985 at the age of 68.

Philip Richards: Pip left the RAF after the war and opened a shop in Southampton repairing and grinding garden equipment. Prompted by his brother Dave they went into partnership in the car dismantling business, something their younger brother was already doing quite successfully. Pip and Dave returned to Belgium after the war and Dave ended up marrying Marie-Paule Tassart. Marie-Paule passed away a few years ago. Pip and Doreen had three sons and one daughter. Unfortunately Pip died in 1982, a heart attack whilst working on his roof at home. Doreen passed away in June 1997.

Derrick Bell: Derrick stayed in the RAF until 1947, flying Mosquitos at Leeming. His commission should have taken him to 1948 but when his new CO discovered he was due to leave, he felt he would be of no use to him and Derrick was released to civilian life. Derrick married a WAAF and they are both still alive and well, living in Nottingham, England, the parents of four boys and now nine grandchildren.

Gordon Puttick: Since the war Gordon developed a career in the planning departments of local authorities. He lives near Bristol, married to his wartime sweetheart Cynthia. He still sees his former comrades from the Photo Reconnaisance Unit, and is actively involved in their association. Gordon maintains a great enthusiasm for the subject, something that easily rubs off onto anyone speaking to him.

Arthur Darlow: Arthur remained in the RAF after the war. Anne and Arthur gave their son Eric a sister Annette. In December 1946 Arthur got posted overseas to the Far East as part of 110 Squadron. Below is a letter to Anne's parents, written in the officer's mess at RAF station Kai Tak, Kowloon, Hong Kong, highlighting Arthur's optimism for the future.

Sunday 26th Jan. 47

Dear Mum & Dad

Trust you . . . are keeping fit & well. As you can see by the address, I've finally arrived in China. Have quite a nice billet, in the town of Kowloon itself, & have just finished settling in. So far I haven't begun operating routes, but expect to start this Thursday. Our run is from Kai Tak to Rangoon via Saigon in French Indo-China; a round trip of four days. We have special rates of pay out here, so I shall be able to save quite a bit.

I've put in an application for Anne & the children to come out here, & am now hoping for the best. Its a grand climate & a very nice city. Food & clothes are plentiful, servants very cheap, & in fact everything would suit Anne. The officers married quarters have to be seen to be believed, very very modern, plenty of windows, flat roofed & beautifully furnished. It would be a marvellous holiday for Anne; goodness knows she deserves one. I could buy her all the things I've wanted too, & make her happy.

Well, my dears, look after yourselves . . . & to you I send my thanks & love for all you've done.

Cheerio, all the best

Your Loving Son

[Signed] *Arthur*

On 26 February 1947, Arthur boarded a 48 Squadron Dakota at RAF Changi to travel as a passenger to Saigon.

48 Squadron operations record book:

The schedule of the 26th ex Changi left for Saigon captained by F.L. H. de L. Watson. Normal contact was maintained with the aircraft over W/T channels from time of take off at 10.10 hours GH until the last message – a position report – was given at 10.44 hours GH, giving the aircraft's position as 02.28 N 104.18 E steering a course of 015 degrees T.

From this time on nothing was heard of the aircraft, which had an E.T.A. at Saigon of approximately 15.10 hours GH.

As soon as overdue procedure was instituted the Squadron called all aircrew to readiness and asked the Engineer Officer to attempt to make serviceable for the search such aircraft as were available. Ground crews worked throughout the night and by first light on 27 February 1947 all aircraft that were available had been readied and took off on the search. Almost continuous bad weather dogged the search aircraft which included the special York aircraft attached to the Squadron, but aircraft of the Squadron plus flying boats from Seletar and naval vessels in the area combined to maintain a continuous search over the probable area where KK120 was lost.

Despite this continuous effort no trace was found of the missing aircraft and search was officially abandoned on the 3rd March 1947.[72]

On the 29th March 1947 Anne wrote to Doreen Richards:

My Dear Doreen,

I must apologise for not writing before but I'm afraid I'm not feeling too well, I keep having violent headaches and feel very dizzy. Had a letter from Arthur's Nav. and he says that there doesn't seem much chance of them having survived and the weather at the time of the flight was very bad. After 3 days of constant searching it was given as hopeless. But somehow I'll never give up hope. I'll be leaving here in about 2 months time or maybe longer. Eric is going in a boarding school as I'm afraid I can't manage him. I hope to see you very soon Doreen dear. What was it you heard on the wireless about the plane?

Please forgive me for not writing but honestly Doreen my nerves are very bad. I'll send the stuff on next week. The Air Ministry have allowed me to have an allowance of £7 a week till the end of May and then I go on a widow's pension. Please try and come up to see me. You know I'd come down but I can't leave Eric or Annette with anyone. Give my love to Pip and Martin and please come to see me very soon.

Lots of Love
[signed] *Anne*

No trace of the missing Dakota or the passengers and aircrew has ever been found. Unfortunately Anne's headaches became more serious and she died later that year.

---

[72] Public Record Office AIR 27 2418.

APPENDIX

The table below details Bomber Command casualties on the raids involving our crew (so not including other raids on the same night). This includes aircraft crashing in England or damaged beyond repair or failing to return. In the main part of the book the losses mentioned for raids are only those for aircraft failing to return, taken from *The Bomber Command War Diaries* by Martin Middlebrook and Chris Everitt

Figures below do not include casualties in bombers that continued in service. The purpose of this table is to give some kind of indication of what odds the crew faced. The source for the figures are the books by W.R. Chorley *RAF Bomber Command Losses 1943* and *RAF Bomber Command Losses 1944*. Arthur Darlow, Philip Richards, Trevor Utton, Alex Nethery and Allan Burrell took part in all the raids listed below. Don Copeland became operational with the crew on the Bochum raid of 29/30 September 1943. George Lorimer became operational with the others on the Berlin raid of 29/30 December 1943.

Date	Target	A/c Lost	Killed	POWs	Evad's	Inj.	Interned
15/16 Sept 43	Montluçon	4	18	6	5	0	0
16/17 Sept 43	Modane	4	14	4	4	7 (1 later died)	0
29/30 Sept 43	Bochum	14	51	13	1	6	0
3/4 Oct 43	Kassel	28	119	52	1	10 (1 later died)	0
4/5 Oct 43	Frankfurt	13	59	15	3	6	0
22/23 Oct 43	Kassel	48	250	75	0	7	0
18/19 Nov 43	Mannheim	24	116	46	3	1 (later died)	0
19/20 Nov 43	Leverkusen	11	22	22	5	9	0
22/23 Nov 43	Berlin	32	169	26	0	5 (2 later died)	0
25/26 Nov 43	Frankfurt	13	48	36	4	0	0
3/4 Dec 43	Leipzig	26	120	44	0	1 (later died)	0
20/21 Dec 43	Frankfurt	44	192	96	7	1	0
29/30 Dec 43	Berlin	21	80	53	1	1	0
20/21 Jan 44	Berlin	42	181	63	10	7 (4 later died)	0
19/20 Feb 44	Leipzig	82	445	139	2	10 (1 later died)	0
20/21 Feb 44	Stuttgart	16	80	14	3	1	0
24/25 Feb 44	Schweinfurt	35	177	69	3	1 (later died)	0
25/26 Feb 44	Augsburg	23	101	43	9	4 (2 later died)	6
1/2 Mar 44	Stuttgart	6	28	7	0	2	0
15/16 Mar 44	Stuttgart	43	225	47	17	3	1
18/19 Mar 44	Frankfurt	25	111	58	0	5 (1 later died)	0
22/23 Mar 44	Frankfurt	35	181	56	2	3 (1 later died)	0
24/25 Mar 44	Berlin	74	391	134	7	0	0
26/27 Mar 44	Essen	12	58	2	3	3 (1 later died)	0

18/19 Apr 44	Tergnier	6	32	7	2	1 (later died)	0
20/21 Apr 44	Lens	2	5	3	1	4 (1 later died)	0
22/23 Apr 44	Laon	9	46	3	15	0	0
3/4 May 44	Montdidier	4	27	0	1	0	0
6/7 May 44	Mantes-La-Jolie	3	10	4	7	0	0
8/9 May 44	Haine St Pierre	9	37	15	13	0	0
Sub total			3393			98	
plus/less deaths from injuries			19			−19	
Totals		**708**	**3412**	**1152**	**129**	**79**	**7**

BIBLIOGRAPHY

Aders, G, *History of the German Night Fighter Force 1917-1945* (Jane's Publishing, 1979)

Bachy, P, *Vie et Mort du Val de Verne* (Amicale des Resistants de Péruwelz et environs, 1979)

Beeson, G, *Five Roads to Freedom* (Leo Cooper Ltd, 1977)

Bennett, DCT, *Pathfinder* (Frederick Muller, 1958)

Bekker, C, *The Luftwaffe War Diaries* (Macdonald, 1964)

Charlwood, D, *No Moon Tonight* (Goodall Publications Ltd, 1984)

Chorley, WR, *RAF Bomber Command Losses 1943* (Midland Publishing, 1996)

Chorley, WR, *RAF Bomber Command Losses 1944* (Midland Publishing, 1997)

Cooper, AW, *Free to Fight Again, RAF Escapes and Evasions 1940-45* (Kimber, 1988)

Squadron Leader Bryce Cousens (editor), *'The Log' Stalag Luft III Belaria newsletter* (published by Bryce Cousens. Printed by Burr's Press, Cheltenham, 1947)

Currie, J, *Lancaster Target* (Goodall Publications Ltd, 1977)

Durand, A, *Stalag Luft III – The Secret Story* (Louisiana State University Press, 1989)

Ehrman, J, *Official History of the Second World War, Grand Strategy Volume V* (London H.M.S.O., 1972)

Falconer, J, *RAF Bomber Airfields of World War 2* (Ian Allan Ltd, 1992)

Foot, MRD, and Langley, JM, *MI9 Escape and Evasion 1939-1945* (The Bodley Head, 1979)

Garbett, M, and Goulding, B, *Lancaster* (The Promotional Reprint Company Limited, 1992)

Garnett, R, *POW* (David and Charles, 1981)

Gibson, G, *Enemy Coast Ahead* (Goodall Publications Ltd, 1995)

Harris, Marshal of the RAF Sir Arthur, *Bomber Offensive* (Collins, 1947)

Hart, L, *History of the Second World War* (Cassell and Co. Ltd, 1970)

Hastings, M, *Bomber Command* (Book Club Associates by arrangement with Michael Joseph Ltd, 1980)

Hinchliffe, P, *The Other Battle* (Airlife Publishing Ltd, 1996)

Langley, JM, *To Fight Another* Day (Collins, 1974)

The Goebbels Diaries, translated by Louis P Lochner (Hamish Hamilton, 1948)

Maynard, J, *Bennett and the Pathfinders* (Arms and Armour Press, 1996)
Middlebrook, M, and Everitt, C, *The Bomber Command War Diaries* (Midland Publishing, 1996)
Middlebrook, M, *The Berlin Raids* (Penguin, 1990)
Murray, W, *The Luftwaffe 1933-45: Strategy for Defeat* (Air University Press, 1983)

Place, G, and Vanbellingen, P, *Les bombardments alliés de 1944 dans le Centre* (Cercle d'histoire et de folklore Henri Guillemin de Haine St Pierre et Haine St Paul, 1978)
Richards, D, *Royal Air Force 1939 – 45 Vol 1 – The Fight at Odds* (H.M.S.O., 1953)
Rolf, D, *Prisoners of the Reich, Germany's Captives 1939-1945* (Leo Cooper Ltd, 1988)
Saundby, Air Marshal Sir Robert, *Air Bombardment, The Story of its Development* (Chatto and Windus Ltd, 1961)
Shirer, W, *The Rise and Fall of the Third Reich* (Mandarin, 1991)
Speer, A, *Inside the Third Reich* (Phoenix, 1995)
Spick, M, *Luftwaffe Fighter Aces* (Greenhill Books, 1996)
Webster, Sir Charles and Frankland, Noble, *The Strategic Air Offensive against Germany 1939 – 1945* (London H.M.S.O., 1961)
Wyatt, B, *Two Wings and a Prayer* (The Boston Mills Press, 1984)
Wyatt, B, *Maximum Effort* (The Boston Mills Press, 1986)

INDEX

The index is arranged alphabetically on a word-by-word basis. Sub-headings are in approximate chronological order where appropriate.